THE
WHOLE PADDLER'S
CATALOG

The
WH
PAD

OLE DLER'S Catalog

Edited by Zip Kellogg

with drawings by Andrea Sulzer

Ragged Mountain Press
Camden, Maine

International Marine/ Ragged Mountain Press

A Division of The McGraw·Hill Companies

10   9   8   7   6   5   4   3   2   1
Copyright © 1997 Ragged Mountain Press
Essays © 1997 by the authors credited

Printed in the United States of America.

Library of Congress Cataloging-in-Publication Data
Kellogg, Zip
   The whole paddler's catalog / Zip Kellogg.
      p.   cm.
   Includes bibliographical references
   and index.
   ISBN 0-07-033901-5
      1. Canoes and canoeing—Catalogs.   2. Canoes and canoeing—
Directories.   3. Rafting (Sports)—Catalogs.   4. Rafting (Sports)—
Directories.   I. Title.
GV783.K45   1996
796. 1\22\0216—DC21   *96-37339*
                                                         CIP

Questions regarding
the content of this book should be addressed to:
Ragged Mountain Press
P.O. Box 220
Camden, ME 04843

Questions regarding
the ordering of this book should be addressed to:
The McGraw-Hill Companies
Customer Service Department
P.O. Box 547
Blacklick, OH 43004
Retail customers: 1-800-262-4729
Bookstores: 1-800-233-4726

A portion of the profits from the sale of each Ragged Mountain Press
book is donated to an environmental cause.

The Whole Paddler's Catalog is printed on 60-pound Renew Opaque Vellum,
an acid-free paper which contains 50 percent recycled waste paper (preconsumer)
and 10 percent postconsumer waste paper.

The Whole Paddler's Catalog has been set in 10-point Adobe Garamond

Printed by Quebecor Fairfield, Fairfield, Pennsylvania
Design and Production by Dan Kirchoff
Chapter-opener drawings by Andrea Sulzer
Edited by Jonathan Eaton, Jonathan Hanson, and Roseann Hanson

Contents

Acknowledgments

It's too bad that books don't simply appear from thin air. More time could be spent on the water if they did. What a pity.

When Jim Babb called me proposing a catalog like this one, I blithely said yes. If he were foolhardy enough to call again I'd surely tell him no. But it's also difficult for me to conceive of anyone being as understanding and supportive as he was over the course of this project. From the bottom of my heart, thanks Jim, for providing me with this opportunity.

And poor Jon Eaton. He has had the responsibility of turning about two wheelbarrow loads of debris and one little computer disk into a book. I believe Jon Eaton is an Olympic-caliber leger-demainist.

A very special thanks to Roseann and Jonathan Hanson for converting an unpublishable manuscript into—I hope—a useful book for paddlers. And I'm especially grateful to the writers who submitted articles for the book: Pope Barrow, Jeff Bennett, Tonya Bennett, John Connelly, John Dowd, Annie Getchell, Jonathan Hanson, Roseann Hanson, Verne Huser, Alan Kesselheim, Robert Kimber, Chris Kulczycki, Dorcas Miller, Roderick Frazier Nash, Harry Rock, Thomas Sebring, and Ken Wright. In my opinion they've added immeasurably to the book's quality and depth.

Jim's phone call way back when triggered a series of events that allowed me the luxury of taking time away from my everyday responsibilities to do some sleuthing for this catalog. What follows is almost certain to be an incomplete list of some of the people who housed me, fed me, provided answers to questions, or were generally understanding even though I couldn't explain very well what I was trying to do.

My entire (extended) family all had the opportunity to get sick of seeing me around. Ben Franklin said that fish and visitors stink after three days. Maybe another time my family will be lucky and only have to deal with fish. Thanks especially to my mother and father—always supportive, always loving and helpful, even after having raised six kids. That task alone ranks as the eighth wonder of the world. Thanks, too, to Bob, Judy and George, Greg and Ted, Betty and John, Sara and Jeff, Ben and Jacob, and Mary and Berndt.

Thanks to the entire staff of the University of Southern Maine Library. Every person on the staff assisted in some way—and there were some who weren't always aware of their parts in this. The staff often bent over backward to help me. I still don't understand why Casandra Fitzherbert, Barbara Stevens, and Marybeth Gendron don't double-bolt the interlibrary loan door when they see me coming. They in particular, as well as all others, receive my very warmest of thanks.

To the loads of others who assisted in all sorts of ways, from putting me up for a night or two or more to enjoying time on the water, I give my heartfelt thanks: Bill Evans; George and Nancy Wood and family; John, Laurie, and Nick Eddy; Aram Calhoun and Mac Hunter; Scott Finlayson; Leslie Hudson; the Bogarin family of Costa Rica; Annette, Dave, Sarah, and Chris Jaquette; and a thirty-year belated thanks to the Jalbert family of Fort Kent, Maine, for some fine times paddling on the Allagash.

And a special thank you to Andrea Sulzer for her wonderful drawings and companionship, as well as her highly cultivated appreciation for a good batch of pickled beets.

—Z.K., *Portland, Maine, July 1996.*

Zip Kellogg in his usual attire, a tuxedo and a top hat, for the Annual Kenduskeag Stream Race in Bangor, Maine. He is one of the more notorius fixtures in the yearly event.

Overview

OR

How to Get Into the Spirit of Paddling

*"If there is magic on this planet,
it is contained in water."*

—*Loren Eiseley*
(The Immense Journey, *1957*)

Brief Introductory Comments

Lost in the mists of prehistory is the identity of the person who first floated down a river on a log, to the cheers—or, who knows, perhaps jeers—of companions on the bank. Since then, though, water, and our ability to travel on it, has shaped our destiny as a species.

For most of the intervening millennia, water was simply a means to an end: a way to transport goods or people, a path for exploration, a dramatic theater for war. Not until the last couple of centuries, when we began to emerge as creatures of leisure, did we start to connect boats and water with the thought, "Wow, that looks like *fun*."

That turning point in our attitudes was also a turning point in the evolution of boats. Until then, they had been developed to carry more, to go farther, to be better armed. Suddenly, we could concentrate on making them *fun*. To some, that meant making them faster, a mania that has given us such aberrations as jet skis and 200-horsepower bassboats. But to others it meant returning to the essence of The Boat: a simple craft propelled by one person with a paddle (to fossil-fuel junkies who yawn at the thought, we suggest a run down Lava Falls or a kayak-surfing session off the Oregon coast as an opinion modifier).

At the dawn of the twenty-first

century, as our lives become ever more complex, we are experiencing a surge of interest in this return to the simplicity of the paddle. But simplicity in no way implies a lack of variety. From sea kayaks to whitewater squirt boats, from rafts to canoes, a paddler can explore any water on the planet. The flexibility is enormous, from short hops on the lake or around the harbor to multi-month expeditions along the Arctic coast or through the Boundary Waters.

A happy by-product of this rediscovery of our rivers, lakes, and coastlines is an appreciation of their beauty, and a desire to save them from destruction. No one who has paddled a wild river can ever look at a dam or effluent discharge the same way; no one who has camped on a pristine coast can trivialize an oil spill.

About This Book

The idea behind *The Whole Paddler's Catalog* can be found in the motto of the old *Whole Earth Catalog*: "Access to Tools." The tools in this case are books, magazines, newsletters, clubs, and organizations—and people. The reviews, interviews, and excerpts in *The Whole Paddler's Catalog* will give you a database from which to explore more extensively the world of paddlesports. Included here are essays written by leading paddlers; these articles will inform, inspire, and intrigue you. And sprinkled throughout are technical tips and bits of wisdom contributed by seasoned paddlers John and Roseann Hanson and Jeff and Tonya Bennett; graphic icons indicate whether a tip refers to whitewater kayaking, sea kayaking, or rafting. *The Whole Paddler's Catalog* won't tell you which boat to buy, nor will it recommend one brand of lifejacket over another. But it will give you the direction you need to make the right choice for yourself. Likewise, this book won't tell you where to paddle—but you'll find plenty of ideas to direct your own adventure. And lastly, you'll benefit from the inspiration of explorers, builders, instructors, and philosophers.

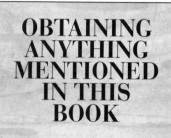

OBTAINING ANYTHING MENTIONED IN THIS BOOK

Most everything mentioned in *The Whole Paddler's Catalog* falls into three broad categories: (1) equipment; (2) books, magazines, videos, and other resource material; and (3) information and advice. All can be obtained readily and with a minimum of muss and fuss.

Regarding equipment: when products are mentioned, so are the locations and phone numbers of their sources—toll-free numbers are listed when available.

Regarding magazines: phone numbers to request a subscription or a sample copy are given.

Regarding books: some of these are in bookstores, some aren't. A very general rule of thumb is, if the date of publication is more than a decade ago, you will have better luck in a library or a used bookstore. But there are exceptions to this maxim. If the library doesn't have what you want, ask to talk with the "interlibrary loan" person. This person should be able to help you obtain a copy on loan from another library. *This is one of the single most important tips in accessing the books mentioned herein,* especially if buying the book isn't your goal or isn't possible. Each book citation should contain everything a bookstore clerk or librarian needs to obtain the item for you (title, publisher, etc.).

The Spirit of It All

✦

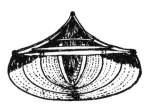

Simplicity. Even the techiest carbon fiber/Kevlar/Royalex/titanium boat and paddle combination is still just that—a boat and a paddle. Where it goes, how fast it moves, the distance it covers, are all up to you. At the end of the day, when you look back over your path, there is no trail of hydrocarbon waste to betray your passage. You have passed as cleanly over the water as a loon or an otter.

This brevity of equipment gives you time to think of other things besides the next oil change. It's not surprising, then, that many fine introspective works have been written by paddlers over the years. Some of these authors muse on history, others on nature, others on the human condition—or all three. Some mix humor with astounding adventure. Some even throw in paddling technique, as long as it doesn't get in the way of a good tale. What all have in common is a love of the paddle, and their ideas are their effort to share that love. They embrace both past and future, and the wisdom in them is likely to rub off on you. Any of these books and ideas may awaken in you the spirit of voyaging.

"I've known rivers:
I've known rivers ancient as the world and older than
the flow of human blood in human veins.
My soul has grown deep like the rivers."
—*from the poem* The Negro Speaks of Rivers *by Langston Hughes (1902–1967)*

Path of the Paddle

by Bill Mason
(Minocqua, WI: NorthWord Press, 1995)
and

Song of the Paddle: An Illustrated Guide to Wilderness Camping

by Bill Mason
(Minocqua, WI: NorthWord Press, 1988)

Bill Mason is a legend among paddlers, particularly canoeists. Despite his untimely death from cancer in the fall of 1988, his legacy of books, videos, art, and simple charm lives on. His sense of humor was dry enough to make the Sahara seem like a wetland.

Although these both are, in part, "how-to" books, they contain too much soul to be listed as mere works of instruction. Witness winter's watchman at work in Mason in *Path of the Paddle*:

"The canoeless season can be shortened somewhat by varnishing gunwales and sanding and painting canvas, unless you are the owner of a fiberglass or aluminum canoe . . . the canoeists I really bleed for are the paddlers who don't even own a wooden paddle to sand and varnish.

For those of you with aluminum or fiberglass canoes or paddles, you might try carrying your canoe around on the roof of your car anytime after New Year's Day. Anytime before that looks pretty ridiculous. But after New Year's Day, you just never know. Spring could be early."

Path of the Paddle and *Song of the Paddle* are well illustrated and full of practical pointers. There is a preservation ethic and a spirit that runs through Mason's works. He gives good solid advice in plain language. He is not one to use a lot of jargon, to invent technical terminology, or to submerge you in detail. He spent a significant amount of time paddling along Lake Superior's north shore trying to understand such varied things as (a) life on planet earth; (b) himself; (c) what art is. Certainly one answer he found was that the canoe is a master teacher.

When it comes to wiping out in rapids I can speak with authority. I have made every possible mistake at least once—as well as many variations of the same mistakes!

One of the problems associated with improved whitewater skills is the inevitable desire to run more and more difficult rapids. Getting better doesn't necessarily mean fewer wipeouts; what it often means is the wipeouts will be bigger, better and more spectacular.

The Happy Isles of Oceania

by Paul Theroux
(New York: Ballantine Books, 1993)

A consummate traveler, Theroux aims his sharp pen—and a folding kayak—at the islands of the South Pacific in this richly insightful work. Typically, he spares no one, not even himself, from his wickedly humorous cynicism, but the resulting bluntness peels back the facade of the "tropical paradise" and exposes the real land and people. Were there no resolution, Theroux's acidity could have swamped the tale, but his growth and healing throughout the book (his marriage had crumbled just before he left) weave a compelling story.

The Happy Isles is only peripherally about sea kayaking, but no matter. The paddling passages make clear the advantage of off-beat transportation for an amateur sociologist—no one stepping off a jet could ever insert themselves so quickly into the fabric of island life as a sunburned bum nosing into the village beach in a wood-and-canvas kayak.

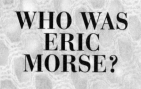

WHO WAS ERIC MORSE?

He was a paddler's friend. He paddled many Canadian rivers during the 1950s, '60s, and '70s, following the routes used by the Voyageurs and explorers of earlier centuries. Born in India in 1904, Morse moved to Canada in 1912. He studied history and international relations in college, and for several years he was the national secretary for the United Nations Association of Canada. He often paddled with diplomats and fellow conservationists such as Sigurd Olson. Morse wrote about the Voyageurs in *Fur Trade Canoe Routes of Canada/Then and Now* (reviewed in the "History of Paddling" section of this chapter), and he wrote his life story in *Freshwater Saga: Memoirs of a Lifetime of Wilderness Canoeing in Canada* (Toronto: University of Toronto Press, 1987).

By the time of his death in April of 1986 in Ottawa, Eric Morse had inspired a new generation of paddlers, a generation that not only loves to paddle but has a growing appreciation for river history and for wise use of those rivers.

Thank you Mr. Morse . . . .

"Who feels the confined work tell on his lungs, or his eyes, or shudders at that tremulousness of the shoulders and arms which precedes the breaking-down from over-work? All this can be cured by the sun and the wind and the delicious splash of the river on face and breast and arms. Those are they to whom a canoe is a godsend. They can get more health and strength and memorable joy out of a two-weeks' canoe trip than from a lazy, expensive and seasick voyage to Europe, or three months' dawdle at a fashionable watering-place."
—*John Boyle O'Reilly*, Ethics of Boxing and Manly Sport, *1888*

First Descents: In Search of Wild Rivers

edited by Cameron O'Connor and
John Lazenby

(Birmingham, AL: Menasha Ridge Press, 1989)

There is a mystique, a supposed prestige, about first river descents. Humans just love those moments of fame and glory.

Remember, though—except for a few streams built (rebuilt?) by the Army Corps of Engineers, most of our rivers and streams have been around for a long, long time. And people have been going up or down most of them for millennia, although not always in a squirt boat, an exquisitely outfitted raft, or a canoe jammed with float bags. . . .

Throughout human history, rivers often have been roads. Read a chapter or two in *To the Ends of the Earth: The Great Travel and Trade Routes of Human History* to get the idea. Nearly all of the major rivers of the world and some of the lesser ones have provided our ancestors with "road" networks.

Having said all that, *First Descents* is an entertaining book. It is a collection of essays about descents of all sorts of rivers and streams, some of them quite tongue-in-cheek. Take, for example, William G. Scheller's tale of urban canoeing down the Anacostia River on the outskirts of Washington, D.C. Scheller writes, "We like our rivers on the seedy side, running through cities and nondescript suburbs, and we go to great lengths to sabotage the squeaky-clean, Hiawatha-in-the-forest image of the canoe." Furthermore, he claims "you can paddle through Newark and see fewer people doing the same thing you are doing than you would if you were kayaking the Mackenzie Delta."

One essay (there are about twenty in all) tells of a hair-raising descent of the Colca River Canyon in Peru (the world's deepest canyon—about 10,000 feet). This trip was truly unknown to the paddlers—it took planning, a lot of teamwork, bravery, and a solid dose of lunacy to accomplish. There were drops that had to be run un-scouted because access to view-points was impeded by the sheer walls of the canyon. One refines one's decision-making skills at times like these.

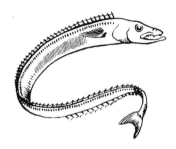

WHO TAKES PADDLING SERIOUSLY?

Verlen Kruger, for one. This man has made some very long voyages. One little jaunt took him over some of the old fur trade routes between Montreal and the mouth of the Yukon at the Bering Sea; see his book *One Incredible Journey* (Wilderness Adventure Books, 1988) for details. In another he and Steve Landick paddled some 28,000 miles here and there around the Western Hemisphere between 1980 and 1983. That trip was dubbed the Ultimate Canoe Challenge and, not surprisingly, it gave them the record for the longest canoe trip ever taken.

Kruger has been up and down the Mississippi and other rivers; he has also run the Finlandia Clean Water Challenge (racing about 1,000 miles between Chicago and New York).

Kruger currently is in his early seventies, and still won't give up. He and his wife, Valerie Fons-Kruger, may be completing a little circle trip as you read this. This one is called the Paddle to the Sea Expedition (only 14,000 miles—he seems to be slacking off a bit), named after the classic children's story *Paddle to the Sea*. Their itinerary includes all the Great Lakes, descending the Mississippi, rounding Florida, going north through the Intracoastal Waterway, ascending the Hudson River and the St. Lawrence, and finally coming full circle to home base in Michigan.

Kruger doesn't know what the interstate highway system is! He's got his own network of roads; they just happen to be wet ones. And the good news is *you have that same system*. Go use 'em. You don't have to become a maniac like Verlen Kruger, but you can consider him the definitive example of what's possible to accomplish with a boat and a paddle.

A NOTE ON TRIP ACCOUNTS

While it's beyond the scope of this book to list trip accounts for each of the areas you might want to paddle, a few tips on finding trip accounts, guidebooks, and other information on a particular river, lake, or coastal area might prove useful.

More than forty trip accounts (an entire book on a particular trip) for trips all over the world are listed in *Wilderness Waterways: The Whole Water Reference for Paddlers* by Ron Ziegler (see the "Sources for Resources" section in this chapter for more information on this book). Ziegler provides the reader with a short blurb on each book, so you can get an idea of whether or not the account listed will really be of interest. Another section of the same book provides a list of guidebooks for various states and provinces. Want a description of the Rio Grande? The Youghiogheny? The Stanislaus? The Suwannee? Find them listed in Ziegler's book.

Another source for guidebooks on particular rivers is Richard Penny's *The Whitewater Sourcebook* (also in the resources section). In addition to listing runnable sections of rivers, Penny gives you length-of-run, maps needed, best time to run, most useful guidebooks, and more. He covers dozens of rivers throughout the United States. Both Ziegler's and Penny's books list current guidebooks for the areas you need.

Another place you'll find quite a few accounts of trips is in old issues of *National Geographic* magazine. Most any library would have the *index* to the past one hundred years of articles and probably the articles themselves. Here, for example, are a few of possible interest to paddlers:

- "Kayaking the Amazon," April 1987
- "White-water Adventure on Wild Rivers of Idaho," February 1970

- "Kayak Odyssey: From the Inland Sea to Tokyo," September 1967
- "Kayaks Down the Nile," May 1955
- "Winter Brings Carnival Time to Quebec" (canoe race), January 1958
- "Raft Life on the Hwang Ho" (Yellow River in northern China), June 1932
- "Hurdle Racing in Canoes: A Thrilling and Spectacular Sport Among the Maoris of New Zealand," May 1920
- "Hokule'a Follows the Stars to Tahiti," October 1976
- "A Canoe Helps Hawaii Recapture Her Past," April 1976
- "Autumn Flames Along the Allagash," February 1974
- "Down the Danube by Canoe," July 1965
- "Labrador Canoe Adventure," July 1951
- "Down the Susquehanna by Canoe," July 1950
- "Down the Potomac by Canoe," August 1948
- "Through the Heart of England in a Canadian Canoe," May 1922
- "An Expedition to Mount St. Elias, Alaska," May 1891
- "Rafting Down the Yukon," December 1975
- "Down Mark Twain's River on a Raft," April 1948
- "The Great Falls of the Potomac," March 1928
- "Niagaras of Five Continents," September 1920
- "The Falls of Iguazu," August 1906
- "Canada's Rivers in Conflict," February 1994
- "Water: The Power, Promise, and Turmoil of North America's Fresh Water," November 1993

If you are going on a trip and you would like to see who else has done it or what has been written about the place, the safest assumption is that someone *has* been there and that write-ups exist. It's only a matter of ferreting them out.

Seekers of the Horizon

edited by Will Nordby
(Old Saybrook, CT:
The Globe Pequot Press, 1989)

This collection of sea kayaking stories spans a world of possibilities. The selections vary in length from day trip to 8,000-mile solo paddle, in locations from the tropics to Iceland, in intent from sightseeing to ocean-crossing. The net effect is sheer inspiration, no matter what your own intent or ability.

Whether you join Paul Kaufmann for an outing on San Francisco Bay, or Greg Blanchette on his circumnavigation of the Hawaiian Islands, these stories offer fascinating insight into the world of the sea kayaker.

The Hidden Coast

by Joel W. Rogers

(Rothell, WA: Alaska Northwest Books, 1991)

The lovely photographs in this book sweep down the coast of North America from Alaska to Mexico. The essays that accompany the pictures raise the work above coffee table status, but the overall impression is of visual richness first, literature second. And that's just fine, for Joel Rogers has documented some of the finest sea kayak voyages possible for either armchair adventurers or those in the romantic but serious planning stage.

A Boat in Our Baggage: Around the World with a Kayak

by Maria Coffey

(Camden, ME: Ragged Mountain Press, 1995)

This is not a glorious account of a massive expedition funded by a cigarette or oil company. Maria and her husband set off with a folding double kayak and a tight budget with the intent of hopping around the world, paddling in as many out-of-the-way spots as they could find and afford. The result was a journey rich in human rather than geographical discovery.

Coffey's book hops from Fiji to the Ganges River to Africa's Lake Malawi to the Danube to Ireland. Along the way, she delves with great compassion into the lives of the inhabitants, while relating with modest understatement the adventures that inevitably follow any trip in a small boat. A most humble yet deeply rewarding book.

The Exploration of the Colorado River and Its Canyons

by John Wesley Powell
(New York: Dover, 1961)

John Wesley Powell's account of his astonishing journey down the Colorado River is perhaps the most famous river-running chronicle in history. Powell (1834–1902) was the son of a well-educated couple. He was an excellent public speaker, had an insatiable appetite for natural history, and was an independent thinker. He lost his right arm below the elbow at the Civil War battle of Shiloh, an event that slowed him not a bit. As a kid growing up he had taken off on long trips alone down portions of the Mississippi and Ohio Rivers, and in 1869 those experiences culminated in his pioneering exploration of the Colorado River.

This book is the story of that trip and its staggering difficulties, catastrophes, and successes. Powell speaks of the land surrounding the river (including the Grand Canyon) as "so strange, so wonderful, and so vast in its features . . . "

For those traveling on the Colorado today, this book makes for great reading, but it also speaks to the colossal tragedy of the modern river. Numerous places described by Powell are submerged by the impounded waters of dams. Nary a drop of rain that falls into the Colorado watershed isn't managed, directed, rerouted, or earmarked for some form of human use. So the free-flowing Colorado described so beautifully by Powell is, sadly, a relic, a fragment of what it once was. Even so, portions of it are still extraordinarily scenic, geologically unbelievable, and, for the paddler, among the most worthy places on earth to visit.

Voyage of the Paper Canoe: A Geographical Journey of 2,500 Miles, from Quebec to the Gulf of Mexico, during the Years 1874–5

by Nathaniel H. Bishop
(Boston: Lee and Shepard, 1878)

This is one of the early classics. Between 1850 and 1875 the idea of paddling for pleasure began to take hold, and this is one of those early accounts of a long trip. How about doing it today—and see just what has changed in eastern North America since 1875 . . .

The canoe traveller can ascend the St. Lawrence River to Lake Ontario, avoiding the rapids and shoals by making use of seven canals of a total length of forty-seven miles. He may then skirt the shores of Lake Ontario, and enter Lake Erie by the canal which passes around the celebrated falls of Niagara. From the last great inland sea he can visit lakes Huron, Michigan, and, with the assistance of a short canal, the grandest of all, Superior. When he has reached the town of Duluth, at the southwestern end of Superior, which is the terminus of the Northern Pacific Railroad, our traveller will have paddled (following the contours of the land) over two thousand miles from salt water into the American continent without having been compelled to make a portage with his little craft. Let him now make his first portage westward, over the railroad one hundred and fifteen miles from Duluth, to the crossing of the Mississippi River at Brainerd, and launch his boat on the Father of Waters, which he may descend with but few interruptions to below the Falls of St. Anthony, at Minneapolis; or, if he will take his boat by rail from Duluth, one hundred and fifty-five miles, to St. Paul, he can launch his canoe, and follow the steamboat to the Gulf of Mexico. This is the longest, and may be called the canoeist's western route to the great Southern Sea.

Alone at Sea

by Dr. Hannes Lindemann
(Germany: Polner Verlag, 1992)

Forget those piddling little Class V rapids. In 1956, Hannes Lindemann crossed the Atlantic Ocean alone in a

17-foot folding kayak. His diet on the seventy-two day journey consisted mostly of evaporated milk, beer, and raw fish. Actually, the trip was something of an anticlimax for Lindemann—he had already crossed the same ocean in a 23-foot dugout canoe the previous year.

Alone at Sea is surely one of the most understated trip accounts you'll ever read. But the story is all the more astonishing for its lack of overt drama. Lindemann's cool, detached descriptions of the hardships imposed on a human body exposed to the sea for over two months will make you hesitate before you embellish that savage, week-long canoe trek through the Boundary Waters.

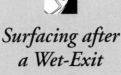

Surfacing after a Wet-Exit

If you capsize your sea kayak in wind and have to wet-exit, be sure to surface on the downwind side of the hull and hang on. Even a moderate breeze can blow the boat away faster than you can swim.

—JH & RH

The History of Paddling
⌘

The pioneering Neanderthal who rode that log down the river soon found that changing direction was difficult without a tool (we hope he wasn't headed for a large waterfall when he realized it). From this experience came the paddle, a device that has survived to the present with astonishingly little change. The log/boat gained sophistication when it was reasoned that having a dry cockpit in which to sit beat clinging to the outside. Considerably greater hull speed was attained by early hydrodynamicists who rounded the ends and hacked off protruding branches.

From those beginnings new designs proliferated. An unknown innovator found that many logs lashed together, while not as fast as a single log, were more stable and could hold large Coleman ice chests with ease. One group of explorers, traveling farther north than their kind ever had, found a new ocean with no nearby trees, and learned to construct seaworthy boats from nothing but animal bones and skin. To keep the frigid water from dousing them, as well as to avoid being forcibly boarded by large marine mammals, they decked over their boats and constructed skirts to seal the gap around their torso. Since swimming in this water meant swift hypothermic death, they developed techniques to roll back upright if capsized.

The individual exploits of these early paddlers are lost. Fortunately, later writers have recorded the history of their efforts, and later travelers have given us evocative accounts to inspire and amaze us.

Water Transport: Origins and Early Evolution

by James Hornell
(Newton Abbot, UK: David & Charles, 1970)
This book puts rafts, bark canoes, kayaks, coracles, dugouts, and other small craft in a world historical context. The author traces the history of each craft and shows where in the world each was (and is) used. He includes a map of the world "showing the distribution, present and recent, of certain kinds of primitive watercraft." His use of the term "primitive" might well be arguable, but, that aside, he has done a very fine job. He has included some marvelous photos showing scenes such as:

- a ferryman carrying his inflated ox-hide boat (in Kashmir)
- a person gathering lotus leaves, supported on a tandem float of two inverted pots (in southern India)
- a ferry raft buoyed by earthen pots (in Egypt)
- a panel from the tomb of Ptah-hotep, 5th Dynasty, Egypt, showing papyrus-bundle canoes under construction
- a banana-stem raft from the Marquesas Islands, Pacific Ocean
- a dugout canoe from Sierra Leone

WHY I SEEK THE BIG DROPS

by Roderick Frazier Nash

"Put-ins" are where river trips begin. They are exciting places, hopeful places, nervous places. Put your boat on moving water and it's all down-hill—except some of the hills are steeper than others. These are Big Drops: rapids, whitewater, places where rivers go wild.

Big Drops have been around as long as precipitation has fallen on land higher than the sea. You find them where the irresistible force of flowing water meets immovable objects: rocks. In the long run, of course, the river always wins. The moving water reduces the continents to sand and carries them to the ocean floor in preparation for the next continental uplift and the next generation of rapids. But for a time

the hard rock resists, turning rivers into writhing white snakes. Put a boat on that stream of energy and motion and you are in for a big ride.

Moving water expends energy in the form of waves, but there are differences. In oceans and lakes the water remains stationary; the waves move. The opposite occurs on rivers. The waves stand still and the water moves through them. So, instead of being carried along on the face of a wave like a surfer, the river runner goes up and down as on a roller-coaster. To get an idea of the scale involved, think of yourself as sitting in a boat on the floor of your living room. The waves in Big Drops can be as high as the ceiling—of a room on the second story! Now think of being on the roof of that two-floor house and looking down twenty feet

to the bottom of a dark, churning hole. Of course, it's only water!

If river waves were smooth and regular, whitewater boating would be like an amusement park attraction—fun, a little scary, yet essentially predictable and safe. But the tons of water moving down a rapid every second have a nasty way of rising up and exploding unexpectedly in your face. There are reversals and whirlpools and surging eddy lines that can trap and hold boats and bodies for anxious seconds or minutes. Boatmen talk about "the May-tag treatment" and "washing machines without walls." One thinks that running a big rapid is an experience comparable to that which a mouse has when it is flushed down a toilet! Now consider a generous assortment of exposed rocks randomly

The Ship: Rafts, Boats and Ships from Prehistoric Times to the Medieval Era

by Sean McGrail

(London: Her Majesty's Stationery Office, 1981) This book is a summary (about 80 pages) of the *very* early history of rafting, bark-covered craft, dugouts, etc. You will find out a bit about the bark boats of Tierra del Fuego (southern South America), reed boats from the marshes of southern Iraq, rafts crossing the Rhine in Caesar's time, Thor Heyerdahl's boats *Kon-Tiki* and *Ra,* and early travels on the Nile, Tigris, and Euphrates Rivers, among others.

You will see that it's much more

the materials than the boats themselves that have changed. At the turn of the last millennium they didn't have Hypalon and other such rugged fabrics. But they managed to travel rivers, lakes, and oceans just the same.

This little book will get you thinking, remembering those days of your youth when you made a simple, crude raft of boards, scrap lumber, or who knows what. That process has had a long, long history and some of its outcomes have had significant impacts on commerce, trade, and development all over the world.

Canoes the World Over

by Terence T. Quirke

(Urbana, IL: University of Illinois Press, 1952) The general design of the canoe—a craft with symmetrical or nearly symmetrical ends—is copied over and over all over the earth. Terence

sprinkled down the rapid, add a border of logs and brush, include at times water so cold that it drains a swimmer's energy in seconds, and the full dimensions of the whitewater challenge become clearer.

So why do it? Why fool around with Big Drops? The answer is invariably subjective, but perhaps it is possible to do a little better than the mountain climbers' "because it is there." One starting point is the pleasure of riding a magic carpet of moving water into some of the wildest country that remains in the contiguous United States. There is indescribable beauty here and a chance to reduce life to its essentials, to be truly self-reliant. Another factor is the satisfaction of being part of the most basic natural process: the washing of the earth back into the sea. Rivers are

the blood of the rocks. Everything eventually ends up there—including river runners. People also float whitewater to find the challenge, indeed the fear, that our normally overcivilized lives occasionally crave. But if you are the kind of person who is paralyzed rather than energized by fear, stay home and look at someone's slides. Boatmen seek to find in themselves that grace under pressure that Ernest Hemingway defined as courage. For many it is a religious experience absolutely necessary to their psychological welfare. Then there is the importance of being humbled by forces far stronger than themselves. Only the foolish, or the very novice, talk about "conquering" rapids; what you really conquer, if only for a moment, is your own insecurity. But that can be exhilarating, a

peak experience. And so the boatmen come back, time and time again, to stand beside a wild river scouting a Big Drop.

—Adapted from *The Big Drops, Ten Legendary Rapids of the American West* by Roderick Frazier Nash (Boulder, CO: Johnson Books, 1989)

—Rod Nash is a giant among river people. He is now retired but taught for many years at the University of California at Santa Barbara. He wrote *The Grand Canyon of the Living Colorado; The Big Drops: Ten Legendary Rapids of the American West;* and many other books of interest to conservationists and lovers of wilderness. He loves moving water.

Quirke gives us an overview of the types: simple dugouts, reed canoes, skin- and bark-covered craft, and those with outriggers, sails, and other appurtenances. A few sketches clearly show the variations in this extraordinarily versatile craft.

If the canoe is your craft of choice, and you want to observe just how broadly this type of boat has been used and for what purposes, you'll enjoy this slim but informative book.

˅

Early in the Christian Era, great outrigger ships were built by the highly cultured and skillful Javanese. The double outrigger gave room on the booms, straddling the single narrow hull, for cabin space for crew,

passengers, and cargo. At the same time the superstructure, erected on booms or poles above a single dugout hull, was much cheaper and less laborious than the construction of equal room in a hulled ship. Today double outriggers have spread west to the east coast of Africa, south to northern Australia, east to New Guinea, and north to the Philippines. In spite of the evident advantages of the double outrigger or sailing canoes, the single outrigger persists for river and inshore service in many places where double outrigger canoes are used for sea voyages.

˄

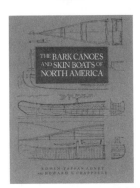

The Bark Canoes and Skin Boats of North America

by Edwin Tappan Adney and Howard I. Chapelle (Washington, D.C.: The Smithsonian Institution, 1993)
We are lucky to have had the likes of Adney and Chapelle look closely

at the background of the little vessels we zoom around in on weekends. Adney, the collector and observer of countless aspects of these small craft, and Chapelle, the undisputed dean of American small boat design and author, editor, and compiler of this book, collaborated on researching the history, the materials of early construction, the designs, the regional variations in kayaks and canoes, and more. Both the photographs and the drawings are excellent. This book is easily among the ten most significant books ever published on the history of paddlecraft.

Pleasure Boating in the Victorian Era

by P.A.L. Vine
(Chichester, UK: Phillimore & Co., 1983)

This book bills itself as "an anthology of some of the more enterprising voyages made in pleasure boats on inland waterways during the nineteenth century." While this book deals with European—mostly British—trips, it makes entertaining reading. Among the selections is that of John MacGregor in his *Rob Roy* canoe. From the 1860s on, when MacGregor caused interest to flare in canoeing, the sport was a middle-class phenomenon. Hordes were attracted to the boats, clubhouses, and riverbanks to try canoeing or to watch. But there were many others besides MacGregor who took to the waters and

then wrote about their experiences. Jerome K. Jerome took a trip on the Thames and wrote the eternally popular *Three Men in a Boat* (1888); Edmund Harvey took an expedition across Europe in the *Undine* (1853); Robert Louis Stevenson took a voyage through Belgium and France (1876). Summaries of these trips and many more paddling and rowing trips are included in *Pleasure Boating in the Victorian Era.* It's good winter reading, not too long and with plenty of handsome old engravings and sketches.

A Thousand Miles in the Rob Roy Canoe on Rivers and Lakes of Europe

by John MacGregor
(London: British Canoe Union, 1963)

This book, originally published in 1866, is one of the undisputed classic books in all of paddling history. It's the book that really got the masses to look at small craft like canoes and kayaks. MacGregor had a wonderful time traveling the rivers and streams of Europe, seeing the sights and meeting people as he went.

Unfortunately, this book is currently out of print. The British Canoe Union (Adbolton Lane, West Bridgford, Nottingham, England NG2 5AS; 0602-821100) has reprinted it in the past and we can hope they will again, making it more widely available.

John MacGregor ("Rob Roy")

by Edwin Hodder
(London: Hodder Brothers, 1894)

This is a full-length biography of the man who popularized canoeing back in the mid-nineteenth century. Hodder wrote that he wanted "to draw a true portrait of a man who exercised a wide and still-spreading influence by his courage, perseverance, reverence, and buoyant hopefulness; whose character may be summed up in one word—manliness, in the fullest, freest sense—physical, moral, and spiritual."

Times have changed. Maybe manliness has, too. But for anyone who would like all the details—450 pages' worth—on MacGregor's childhood, career, travels and adventures, philanthropy, family life, love of children, and more, here it is. *John MacGregor ("Rob Roy")* is based on interviews with his wife, as well as on MacGregor's own diaries and correspondence.

WHO WAS JOHN MACGREGOR?

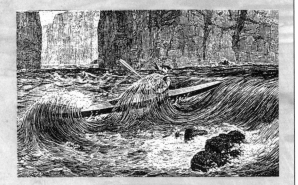

He was a British slowpoke—he took up canoeing fifteen years after Henry David Thoreau.

In truth, John MacGregor (1825–1892) was responsible for an astounding increase in the popularity of paddling, first in the United Kingdom, and later in North America. It was the 1866 publication of his book *A Thousand Miles in the Rob Roy Canoe* that brought him fame and focused public attention on paddling.

He was born at Gravesend, England (near London), and as a boy was an avid reader, had good mechanical aptitude, and was absolutely nuts about boating. The Thames River traffic surely gave him plenty of food for thought.

He got himself a respectable education at Trinity College in Dublin and found after a while that traveling and philanthropy were his thing. So he traveled around Europe, the Middle East, Russia, North Africa, and eventually Canada and the United States.

But that wasn't enough.

He launched the canoe he called the *Rob Roy* in the summer of 1865 and plied the waters of numerous European rivers, among them the Rhine, the Danube, the Main, and the Seine. He simply went on a good, long camping trip around Europe and then wrote a book about

it. The book was an instant hit. Following this, numerous canoeing clubs were formed and the sport really caught on. But MacGregor still wouldn't quit.

Probably to get away from all the folderol that his book created, he took off again for Norway and Sweden and eventually the Suez Canal, the Red Sea, and the Jordan River. The man enjoyed his paddling.

Eventually his speaking engagements and royalties allowed him to become a philanthropist, helping underprivileged and destitute children.

13

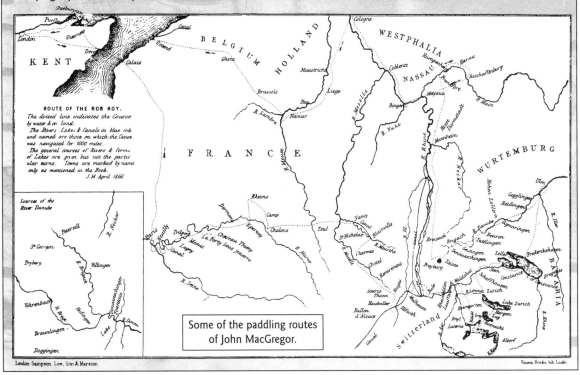

Some of the paddling routes of John MacGregor.

THE SPIRIT OF PADDLING

Rushton and His Times in American Canoeing

by Atwood Manley
(Syracuse, NY: Adirondack
Museum/Syracuse University Press, 1968)

The name Rushton quickly becomes part of the vocabulary of anyone who develops a love of the paddle. J. Henry Rushton (1843–1906) built canoes in the little village of Canton in upstate New York during the late nineteenth century. Because his workmanship approached flawlessness, his reputation spread far and wide. These days a number of his craft are in museums and those that aren't are closely guarded by their owners. Those of us who aren't lucky Rushton canoe owners have a very difficult time not breaking the commandment "Thou shall not covet" when we see them.

Atwood Manley does a marvelous job of telling Rushton's story. In his youth, Manley watched

> *"There is scarcely a river, stream, or lake in the civilized world that has not been explored by canoeists, some of the cruises extending over thousands of miles, and taking several months' time."*
> —*from* Canoe Cruising and Camping *(1897)*

Rushton in his shop in Canton. As an adult, he pulled the whole story together. *Rushton and His Times in American Canoeing* is one of the classic books that any paddler is likely to find enjoyable reading.

Rushton's Rowboats and Canoes: The 1903 Catalog in Perspective

by William Crowley
(Camden, ME: International Marine
Publishing Company, 1983)

This book, a reprint of Rushton's 1903 catalog, is a fascinating companion to *Rushton and His Times in American Canoeing*. In addition to the catalog, Crowley has added a "backgrounder" on Rushton, including information about his upbringing, his significance to the boating community, and the company he created. There is also a "Rushton Album" of photos, line drawings, and offsets for would-be builders.

The Big Drops: Ten Legendary Rapids of the American West

by Roderick Frazier Nash
(Boulder, CO: Johnson Books, 1989)

This book is a wonderful idea. Nash has selected ten classic rapids of the American West and, for each, outlined some of the geologi-

cal, ecological, and historical background. Moreover, he's run every one of them, interviewed and surveyed people, rummaged through libraries, and come up with great little vignettes on each of the following rapids: Clavey Falls (Tuolumne River, California), Rainie Falls (Rogue River, Oregon), Hell's Half Mile (Green River, Colorado/Utah), Warm Springs (Yampa River, Colorado), Satan's Gut (Colorado River, Utah), Redside (Middle Fork of the Salmon River, Idaho), Big Mallard (Salmon River, Idaho), Granite Creek (Snake River, Oregon/Idaho), Crystal (Colorado River, Arizona), Lava Falls (Colorado River, Arizona).

The author bemoans the attractiveness of such drops to hydropower developers. At the end of the book he appends an "honor roll" of drops that "have given their lives in the service of a civilization that, some feel, has yet to prove fully worthy of their sacrifice." The honor roll drops have been cast in concrete or swallowed whole by the "modernization" of that great but surely voracious country called the United States.

Fur Trade Canoe Routes of Canada/Then and Now

by Eric W. Morse
(Toronto: University of Toronto Press, 1979)

Pick up a copy of Morse's book and plan a trip to nearly any part of Canada. Nothing smaller than a world will open up to you.

It was essentially the pursuit of beaver pelts that opened up a 4,000-mile network of rivers and lakes to trading in that commodity. The story is an absolutely fascinating

ROD NASH

River historian and conservationist Rod Nash is widely respected as a waterman, a professor, a writer, and an authority on environmental history. His enthusiasm for rivers is the stuff of legends; moreover, he shares his passion. Here's a brief history of his involvement with rivers:

⅄

"I suppose that rivers are in my blood since my distant ancestor Simon Fraser had considerable involvement with western whitewater. A spelling change makes my middle name 'Frazier,' but Simon's son was named Roderick and so it went down the flow of genealogical time. I learned to paddle as a boy on the lakes of southern Ontario where my family vacationed. Later, during summer breaks from Harvard, I worked in Grand Teton National Park at the new Rockefeller Lodge near Jackson Lake. Part of my duties involved floating the Snake River in war-surplus pontoons. This was 1957, about the time Georgie White started running commercially in the Grand Canyon. Parenthetically, it was in the Tetons that I met one of my oldest river pals, Verne Huser. A decade later we boated the Grand Canyon. After that 1967 trip I started running the Grand regularly. Eventually my total of private and commercial trips has reached fifty-plus. There is just nowhere I'd rather be when it comes to floating on moving water. I also boated widely throughout the west; when I wrote The Big Drops (first edition, 1978) I don't think many people had run all the ten rapids I described. Presently I have followed rivers down to the sea and in a tugboat, Forevergreen, have been explor-

ing the coastal wilderness from the Sea of Cortez (Baja California) to Glacier Bay, Alaska. But the river music still calls and my 18' Grand Canyon style dory, Canyon Dancer, is ready to rock and roll."

⋏

On wilderness and access, Nash says:

⅄

"I have been a champion of the 1968 Wild and Scenic Rivers Act—along with national parks and designated wilderness areas, one of the best ideas our country ever had. Indeed, I'd like to see all free-flowing water placed in a kind of environmental safe deposit box and extracted for development. In other words, this is a reversal of policy. Preserve everything and put the onus on developers.

"The river corridor is wilderness (park policy to the contrary notwithstanding) and should be managed as such. I think a Grand Canyon river trip should be one of the premier wilderness experiences on this planet.

"I suggest that the core of any definition of wilderness is the idea of the uncontrolled. This implies a degree of uncertainty, risk and self-reliance. Wilderness should be as unlike civilization as possible . . . a commercial guide detracts from the wilderness aspect of the experience. Sure, people on commercial trips have a great time, but the guides provide an element of security and control that works against wilderness. Guides (like myself!) decrease risk, limit opportunities for self-sufficiency, reduce pride in achievement and, in a sense, eliminate discovery. A safari experience is not a wilderness experience.

"So, if society determines to manage the river corridor as wilderness and for the realization of wilderness

values, then noncommercial trips should be favored over guided and outfitted ones. Don't, of course, admit every yahoo who shows up on the creek (preparation, even licensing, is an important part of any wilderness experience), but definitely get rid of the nine year—actually 9.7 years if you do the math—wait. And make the commercial ticket more difficult than one phone call and a credit card.

"I say maximize the wilderness values of one of the world's great wildernesses: ban motors, lower total user numbers and at least bring noncommercial use up to fifty percent of visitor allocation.

"The allocation/permit issue is a biggie. It has the potential to blow the river community apart at the seams. The problem of getting permits detracts from the freedom we'd like to associate with wild rivers. But of course it's a necessary evil or we would love the places to death."

one, well told by Morse. He is quite convincing when he says that, both historically and even now, the rivers and lakes were and are Canada's roads.

Oh, the lucky ones to have paddled with Morse, who died in 1986; he was said to have been a terrific companion and a veteran lover of the paddle and the waters.

- It is no mere accident that the present Dominion [of Canada] coincides roughly with the fur trading areas of northern North America.
- Thirty years before Americans had a foothold even west of the Mississippi, there was in Canada the steady pulse of east-west commerce between Montreal and the Athabasca Country [northern Alberta].
- The beaver by its defenselessness, no less than by its value, was responsible for unrolling the map of Canada.

The Romance of the Canadian Canoe

by John Murray Gibbon
(Toronto: The Ryerson Press, 1951)
Gibbon looks at the history of the canoe broadly and not in great

depth, but for the person who would like an overview of who used canoes and why (the American Indians, Cartier, Champlain, the Voyageurs, La Salle, Alexander Mackenzie, and scores of others) it makes fun reading.

In the very first chapter Gibbon poses the question "What did most to pave the way for the development of the Dominion of Canada?" He answers his own question by saying "The Canoe." He builds his case for its significance throughout Canadian history.

Portage Paths: the Keys of the Continent

by Archer Butler Hulbert
(New York: AMS Press, 1971)
Portage Paths, originally published in 1902, takes us back a century or two to a time when, to get from one watery path to another, people portaged or carried their canoe and dunnage (personal gear). There were hundreds if not thousands of these portages linking one watershed to another. Names like Grand Portage (northern Minnesota), the Onion Portage (northwestern

Alaska), the Rat Portage (Ontario), and Grand Pass (from the Hudson River Valley to Lake Champlain) all have a story. Hulbert tells us that "portages are found wherever lakes or rivers lie, and our subject is therefore as broad as the continent." Hulbert addresses specifically those portages of eastern North America—the St. Lawrence River and New England region as well as connections between the Great Lakes and the Mississippi River basin. He provides a discussion of the nature, use, and evolution of portages, as well as a catalog of some of the most significant portages in these areas.

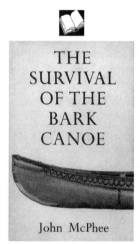

THE SURVIVAL OF THE BARK CANOE

John McPhee

The Survival of the Bark Canoe

by John McPhee
(New York: Farrar, Straus and Giroux, 1982)
John McPhee, known for the incredible breadth of his interests as well as the clarity of his writing, sought out Henri Vaillancourt, the master bark canoe builder, and wrote of the man and his craft (or, more appropriately, his art). McPhee summarizes the history of bark canoe building and laments that its builders are a dying breed.

McPhee and Vaillancourt paddled the Allagash River in northern Maine but didn't get along well, as it turns out. They survived their trip together but must have realized that they're made of very different stock. McPhee's book is a short literary essay, just over one hundred pages long. It makes a light, quick read but if you are really interested in the history and construction details of bark canoes, a better book is E.T. Adney's *The Bark Canoes and Skin Boats of North America.*

The Canoe: A History of the Craft from Panama to the Arctic

by Kenneth G. Roberts and Philip Shackleton
(Camden, ME: International Marine Publishing Company, 1983)

This handsome coffee table–style book, loaded with color photos, provides a basic overview of the canoe through the years. For the paddler who would like the big picture without a lot of detail in which to get mired, this is the book.

Roberts and Shackleton first survey the linguistic origins of the word "canoe"—what it meant to Columbus and what it means to us today. Then they divide their book into five parts: (1) rafts and floats; (2) the dugout; (3) the skin boat; (4) the bark canoe; and (5) the modern canoe. If you haven't seen this book you're in for a treat. Set aside yet another winter evening and forget about that silly old television. This book will take you all over the hemisphere. And because it's so loaded with great pictures, sketches, illustrations, etc., it might even entertain a video-glazed child for a while.

The World Is Three-Quarters Water:
Paddler's Paradises

Now the fun begins. You might be familiar with the waters of your backyard. You might even be familiar with those of the next county, state, or province. But if you thirst for paddling on the other side of the country, or even in another country, you'll need help. The books listed in this section will allow you to think regionally, nationally, and internationally. Warning: the resultant thinking can be hard on personal bank accounts.

Great Rivers of the World

edited by Alexander Frater
(Boston: Little, Brown and Company, 1984)

What'll it be—the Yangtze, Volga, Irrawaddy, Mississippi, Loire, Zaire, Danube, Amazon, Nile, Zambezi, or the Ganges? Why not start planning that trip in an armchair with this attractively illustrated book on your lap?

The editors sent several writers to various parts of the world to get fresh insights into "their" rivers. There were frequent encounters with the unexpected, and with the kindness of strangers: "A man called January allowed them to sleep in his small, rat-infested house." Ah, yes, the pleasures of a river lover.

Great Rivers of the World

edited by Margaret Sedeen
(Washington, D.C.:
National Geographic Society, 1984)

Like Frater's book of the same title (and year), this is a coffee table book. It features the incredible photos we expect from *National Geographic* and excellent background on fifteen of the world's major rivers. Good maps accompany the text.

You'll find a bit on the Ganges, the Mississippi–Missouri, the Nile, the Volga, the Yangtze, the Amazon, the Yukon, and others.

Be forewarned. Books like this one unhinge the human mind, releasing grandiose plans and unrealistic goals to run amok through our workaday lives.

17

SOME THINGS JUST MAKE YOU CRY

You will probably never see the Yangtze River Gorges of Hubei Province in east central China. The world's largest hydroelectric project is under way now, and will be until 2009 A.D. A body of water roughly four hundred miles long will be created behind the mammoth dam being built, submerging one of the world's greatest riverscapes.

This is the sort of press coverage we're seeing about the project these days:

"Travelers who are thinking about taking a riverboat trip down the Yangtze River to see the soaring cliffs and mist-shrouded peaks of Central China would be well advised to make the journey before the winter of 1997–98."

By then, if all goes according to plan, construction crews, working round the clock at Yichang, will succeed in killing China's mightiest river with a gargantuan dam.

And if that weren't bad enough, odds are that people near you are backing it. A number of North American businesses are seeing dollar signs these days in east central China; it doesn't take much imagination to ponder what they're up to.

tuous, from the sublime to the overwhelming. Think of these rivers as restoratives; visit them when your piggy bank begins to feel heavy. If it's not heavy enough, then dream. It's cheaper and you can get started today.

Jenkinson is author of another book, *Wild Rivers of North America,* (New York: Abrams, 1981) that gives details the paddler would find useful for planning a trip. Its scope is all of North America, but coverage of rivers is selective. Nevertheless, if you're wondering where might be a nice place to go, either book could start you salivating.

Whitewater Adventure: Running America's Great Scenic Rivers

by Richard Bangs
(San Diego: Thunder Bay Press, 1990)

This is a big coffee table book with a collection of large, handsome color photos heavy on action shots. Although this is primarily a picture book, river vignettist Richard Bangs shares with us tales of the following rivers: the Kennebec (Maine), the Chattooga (Georgia/ South Carolina), the Rio Grande (Texas/Mexico), the Colorado (Ari-

Wilderness Rivers of America

by Michael Jenkinson
(New York: Abrams, 1981)

Put this book on your table if you want to get your next cocktail party conversation off on the right track—no more idle chatter about work, television, or the new donut shop—talk about wilderness rivers!

There are about twenty pages devoted to each river, four or five

of which are text, the rest dandy photographs taken by professionals. The rivers covered are: the Noatak (Alaska), Fraser (B.C.), Salmon (Idaho), Colorado (several western states), Rio Grande (New Mexico and Texas), Boundary Waters region (Minnesota and Ontario), Buffalo (Arkansas), Atchafalaya (Louisiana), Allagash (Maine), Hudson (New York), and the Suwannee (Georgia and Florida). These rivers cover the gamut from renowned to tumul-

TRAILS OF THE PADDLE

If you like the idea of paddling more than five or ten miles on some local river, think trail! There is a growing movement afoot to paddle any number of trails around the Western Hemisphere. There is, for example, a Chesapeake Bay Trail, a Vancouver to Alaska Trail, a Florida Sea Kayaking Trail, a Lake Superior Water Trail, a Maine Islands Trail, and plenty more. Others are in the planning stages or being worked on by small organizations,

bureaucrats, and others. These trails often trace the route of an explorer or perhaps connect one watershed to another via a portage.

There are at least two ways to find out more about water trails. The first is to read "Nation's Top Water Trails" in the December 1994 issue of *Paddler* magazine, pp. 51–58. The second is to contact one of the paddlers' associations listed in Chapter Two.

zona and Utah), the American (California), the Rogue (Oregon), the Salmon (Idaho), the Snake (Wyoming and Idaho), and the Tatshenshini (Yukon Territory and British Columbia).

The American is literally a river of gold. On its banks in 1848, James Marshall discovered gold in the tailrace of Sutter's mill. His find launched the great Gold Rush of 1849 and poured fortunes into San Francisco, Sacramento, and the entire state. Today fortune hunters still pan the cobbled river bed, and passing river runners can still hear cries of 'Eureka' as the occasional nugget is gleaned.

America's Wild and Scenic Rivers

edited by Donald J. Crump
(Washington, D.C.:
National Geographic Society, 1983)

The books put out by the National Geographic Society enjoy the same reputation as the well-known magazine—they are well written, well edited, and the photos are often stunning.

In the front of the book is a map showing the network of rivers that comprise the Wild and Scenic "system." Although the map and the book are more than ten years old, they both give the general sense of

that system. The book is divided into four sections: the East, the Heartland, the Southwest, and the Northwest, each of which is handled by a different writer. The text weaves the history of an area and an appreciation of each river's surroundings with some local color and good, basic background on the rivers. This book gives one a much more comprehensive idea of what a river is about than can be had by simply zooming from point A to point B in a boat. The poet Langston Hughes wrote, "My soul has grown deep like the rivers." Time on the rivers mentioned in this book may make yours grow deep too.

American Rivers: A Natural History

by Bill Thomas
(New York: W.W. Norton, 1978)

Can you guess which U.S. state boasts the longest river within a single state's boundaries? It's probably among the last you'd think of—Nevada; the Humboldt River according to the author Bill Thomas. Have you ever heard of the Humboldt? It never even reaches the ocean! It's swallowed by sand and sun out in America's Great Basin.

If you believe that dreaming can be dangerous, approach this book with caution. It's one of those coffee table specials, loaded with attractive photos of U.S. rivers and their surroundings from coast to coast. It's divided into fourteen chapters, covering prairie rivers, desert rivers, those of the Rocky Mountains, the deep south, the north woods, New England, and more. The final chapter is titled "To Kill a River" and is

19

THE *RIVERS OF AMERICA* SERIES OF BOOKS

Back in the thirties Constance Lindsay Skinner conceived the idea for producing a series of books about rivers of North America. Skinner was raised in the Peace River region of British Columbia; the frontier, the trading posts, and exposure to the Indians and their way of life all left their marks on her. Her father was an agent for the Hudson's Bay Company, whose tentacles reached even the remotest backwaters of Canada. All of these things, plus her own literary interests, culminated in her series of books on rivers.

Skinner corresponded with Frederick Jackson Turner, who had written an important essay on the theme of frontier in American history. He persuaded her to limit the scope of her series to American rather than world rivers. She took his advice.

Originally the series (by various authors) was to include twenty-four rivers, but it was so popular and such a commercial success for its publisher, Farrar and Rinehart, that it eventually covered more than forty, from the Allagash to the Yukon. The books are considered more literary than historical in tone.

Although Constance Skinner died in 1939, she had laid the groundwork for many of these books. Most of them appeared in the '40s and '50s and some are still available in bookstores today. While they won't be the most up-to-date thing you could read on any of the respective rivers, they provide interesting and colorful background.

"We began to be Americans on the rivers."
—from the introductory essay of the Rivers of America *series*

an appropriate ending, citing the many problems that face these vibrant yet threatened, wonderful but abused ecosystems. For each region there is a map and a short essay highlighting the rivers of that area. The quality of the photos is generally excellent.

Wild Waters: Canoeing Canada's Wilderness Rivers

edited by James Raffan
(Toronto: Key Porter Books, 1986)

Get this book during the winter and prepare to daydream for many months. The photographs of the eight expedition-length rivers profiled—the Moisie, Missinaibi, Clearwater, Kazan, Hood, Bonnet Plume, Nahanni, and Liard—will surely send you looking to see just how full your piggy bank is. Maybe it's a dream today, but what about tomorrow?

Danger: leaving this book open on a table could bring on unpredictable behavior such as reclusive trip planning, extraordinary penny pinching, and lengthy disappearances.

Sources for Resources

Often you don't need a whole book about one spot—just a quick reference or a statistic or two with which to impress your friends. The following sources are just the ticket—they condense a vast amount of information into a short space.

Standard Encyclopedia of the World's Rivers and Lakes

edited by Dr. R. Kay Gresswell
and Anthony Huxley
(New York: G.P. Putnam's Sons, 1965)

This book is some thirty years old, and it would be great to have an updated version, but it's still useful because it gives a quick overview of a river's or lake's significance. For each of the five hundred short blurbs on this or that river or lake, it lists such vital statistics as length, location in the world, history, etc. The blurbs are usually only two or three para-

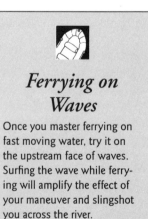

Ferrying on Waves

Once you master ferrying on fast moving water, try it on the upstream face of waves. Surfing the wave while ferrying will amplify the effect of your maneuver and slingshot you across the river.

—JB & TB

graphs apiece, but handy and to the point. Pray for someone to compile a new edition soon, but in the meantime use it when someone mentions a place you've never heard of.

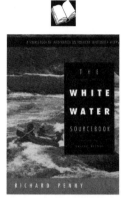

The Whitewater Sourcebook: A Directory of Information on American Whitewater Rivers

by Richard Penny
(Birmingham, AL: Menasha Ridge Press, 1991)

Richard Penny has done paddlers a *big* favor in gathering together information on guidebooks, gauge readings, phone numbers, river descriptions, etc. If you plan to do any paddling in an unfamiliar area, this book could well be a godsend. A quick check for the vitals on a river or state will quickly turn up all sorts of useful material for planning and preparing for a trip. This book is a gold mine for paddlers.

In addition to compiling a useful directory for paddlers, Penny has been honest in doing so. He admits he hasn't run all the rivers listed in the book. Moreover, his state-by-state listing of information sources for popular whitewater rivers covers about thirty-five states. He apologizes for having left out the other states and poses an amusing question to people living in those states: "Have you ever thought of moving to a state that has *mountains*?"

Penny asks for corrections and suggestions for updated editions (which we all should hope there will be). Here's one: include the same information for provinces of Canada in the next edition.

The Water Encyclopedia

edited by Frits van der Leeden and others
(Chelsea, MI: Lewis Publishers, 1990)

Holy cow! This book is a tour de force for those who need any statistic imaginable that has to do with water. It may not make entertaining bedtime reading, because it's composed of table after chart after table after chart—roughly six hundred tables and one hundred illustrations—but if you need any number, any statistic, any data, on any aspect of water use or abuse, find this book. There are chapters on climate, hydrology, surface water, ground water, water quality, water problems, resource management, water law, treaties, and one whale of a lot more.

> ***"A river is more than an amenity; it is a treasure."***
> *—Oliver Wendell Holmes (1841–1935), U.S. Supreme Court Justice, in* New Jersey v. New York *(1931)*

This book is probably more often consulted by hydrologists, engineers, planners, and that lower life form known as dam builders, but paddlers will also find plenty of interest here. One caution: some of the tables are dated and, because environmental regulations change frequently, this book should not be relied on for the most accurate and

THIS LAND IS YOUR LAND . . .

Well, sort of. Certainly many people have treated it as if it were their own. Unfortunately, though their tenancy on the land is always short-lived (on the grand scale of things, humans don't live long), their legacy looms large. About fifty years ago Aldo Leopold was calling for a land ethic. We never got one and nothing points to this more than the "malling" (mauling?) of America—the use of thousands upon thousands of acres of land for shopping mall construction, that is. Or, if that isn't discouraging enough for you, ponder the precious few miles of free-flowing rivers that remain. Our society has not left our rivers alone.

As you paddle anywhere—Canada, the United States, Europe, Nepal, Mexico, wherever, reflect on these comments attributed to Chief Seattle (probably about 1855) as he and his tribe ceded roughly two million acres of land to the U.S. government:

How can you buy or sell the sky, the warmth of the land? The idea is strange to us.

If we do not own the freshness of the air and the sparkle of the water, how can you buy them? . . .

So we will consider your offer to buy our land. But it will not be easy. For this land is sacred to us. The shining water that moves in the streams and rivers is not just water but the blood of our ancestors. If we sell you land, you must remember that it is sacred, and you must teach your children that it is sacred and that each ghostly reflection in the clear water of the lakes tells of events and memories in the life of my people. The water's murmur is the voice of my father's father.

The rivers are our brothers, they quench our thirst. The rivers carry our canoes and feed our children. If we sell you our land, you must remember, and teach your children, that the rivers are our brothers and yours, and you must henceforth give the rivers the kindness you would give any brother.

If Chief Seattle could issue a report card today, it could be nothing but a failing grade. But at least there is the beginning of an awareness that we must change the ways we treat our land and waters. And we paddlers can be part of that positive change, rallying to the support of Chief Seattle's lands and waters. As you paddle along, think about what this or that trip would have been like in Chief Seattle's day.

up-to-date statistics. But for most paddlers' purposes it's fine.

Added note: in a strong wind a solo paddler could use it as a bow weight, but if you drop it on a toe you'll require immediate medical attention.

Wilderness Waterways: The Whole Water Reference for Paddlers

by Ronald Ziegler
(Kirkland, WA:
Canoe America Associates, 1992)

In *Wilderness Waterways,* Ziegler has pulled together a very useful list of books, maps, videos, and other information for the paddler. If, for example, you are planning a trip and need to know what paddling guidebooks exist for your destination, just check *Wilderness Waterways,* because Ziegler lists them all. If you want to speak with someone in a paddling club in Minnesota or New Hampshire and would like the phone

number or address of that group, again, check *Wilderness Waterways.*

That's the good news. The bad news is that this sort of information goes out of date fairly quickly, so let's hope a new edition of this book appears about every five years or so.

Another glitch with the book is that when it was printed, two parts were accidentally left out, and are supplied as loose inserts. With any luck this will be remedied with a new printing or a new edition in the future. In spite of these shortcomings, Ziegler's book could easily expand your paddling horizons.

Paddle America: A Guide to Trips and Outfitters in all 50 States

by Nick Shears
(Washington, D.C.: Starfish Press, 1994)

If you want to hire an outfitter or guide, this book is a great resource. It is a state-by-state directory of paddling companies; it lists their company names, addresses, phone numbers, and offers a blurb on their specialty. *Paddle America* also gives a short overview of paddling conditions in each state.

For the person who wants a guided trip *Paddle America* may be helpful, but since the addresses and phone numbers in this sort of directory change so frequently it will need to be updated every year or so to prove really useful.

Tennessee boasts some of the most challenging whitewater and spectacular scenery in the East. But the hazardous rapids on many mountain streams are runnable only in winter and early spring. For example, there are two awesome gorges in the state's northeast corner along the border with Virginia and North Carolina. . . . Tennessee's star year-round attraction for thrill seeking paddlers is the dam-controlled Ocoee River. . . . For family canoe trips, the Elk River in south central Tennessee is a good bet, with its gentle current and profusion of trout, bass, and blue herons, and basking turtles.

The Ultimate Adventure Sourcebook: The Complete Resource for Adventure Sports and Travel

by Paul McMenamin, et al.
(Atlanta: Turner Publishing, 1992)

This book is a directory of outfitters and their contact information; it also summarizes some of "the best" (by one person's standards) adventure trips. By adventure trips the author means everything from rafting, kayaking, and canoeing to high performance auto racing, downhill skiing, snowmobiling, windsurfing, bicycle touring, ballooning, and lots more.

Types of Paddling

OR

How to Launch Yourself

"Perhaps we relate to the kayak on an even deeper level—it represents a means of man becoming at one with the rhythms of the sea; and as a means of transportation, it represents a singular image of freedom."

—*David W. Zimmerly in* Qajaq: Kayaks of Siberia and Alaska *(Alaska Division of State Museums, 1986)*

Pondering Your Paddling Options

You can float down a lazy river, or subject yourself to a rinse-and-spin cycle on a Class IV rapid. Glide along the shore of a quicksilver lake, or duel with a dumping surf off a rocky ocean coast. You might be piloting a wood-and-canvas canoe, a self-bailing raft, a sturdy sea kayak, or a tiny squirt boat that barely floats when it's empty, much less with your lower half stuffed into it. You can dangle your fingers in the water and doze to the sound of laughing loons, or shoot so much adrenaline through your system that you won't need sleep for a week.

The only thing all these activities have in common is the means of control: just you and a paddle.

It's the simplest of combinations, yet one of the most elegant—the means by which you master your course and speed and, in some cases, your fate.

Perhaps you've not experienced any of these worlds yet. Perhaps you've savored one or two, and found your appetite, well, whetted for more. You might be surprised at how quickly skill in one paddlesport translates to another. In any case, you will want to learn more—to embrace the wisdom of the masters, ponder the zen of your chosen endeavor, become one with the world of water—before you whip out that Visa Gold and flog it within an inch of its limit.

Launching on a
Sea of Information

✈

Go ahead, dive in—there's no worry you'll hit your head on the bottom here. But where to start? Below are some ideas to help get you launched on the sometimes confusing sea of paddling information out there. See the end of this section for sources. Whether you pick up a used magazine or sign up for a two-week outfitted trip, with each step you will gain insight about the sport: what it's like, what you will need, where to go, and how to do it.

- Magazines offer the most up-to-date information on equipment and technique. Most paddling magazines put out annual buyer's guide issues that are full of invaluable information for the paddling consumer. Regular monthly issues provide trip accounts that give you a feel for the experience, and product reviews—if they're not afraid to criticize potential advertisers—that will help when the time comes to buy. There is a list of paddling magazines at the end of this section, but also look around locally for regional publications, which are almost always excellent sources of good information.
- Symposia are wonderful events at which to build your excitement, surrounded by people with the same interests. Talks, seminars, and on-the-water demos allow you to ask ques-

tions of the right people and get hands-on experience with equipment. Paddlesports symposia are held all over the country, usually in spring, summer, and early fall. Check with paddlesports organizations—Trade Association of Sea Kayaking, American Whitewater Affiliation, American Canoe Association, or other groups, as well as clubs to find out who is putting on what.

- Seek out stores that offer demo days or have a regular demo fleet so you can get a feel for different craft. Many paddling stores are on the water and have special try-out rental rates or even free try-outs, so you can easily try before you buy—a very important step for the new boater. Folks who are landlocked may

need to plan a mini-vacation to one of the coasts.
- If you've never tried a canoe or kayak or raft, you should get some substantial on-water time under your belt before you just jump in, in case you find out you'd really rather watch it on ESPN than sit on a cold, hard seat for days on end, dirty, wet, covered with bug bites. . . .

To immerse yourself, consider an outfitted tour. It's a good way to try out a new craft, and it's nice to have someone else do the cooking. To find a reputable outfitter, check with paddlers' associations, clubs, or outfitters' associations such as the National Association of Canoe Liveries & Outfitters (refer to the list of associations at end of this section). There is also a great book (reviewed in Chapter One) called *Paddle America: A Guide to Trips and Outfitters in all 50 States* by Nick Shears (Starfish Press, 1994), and *Adventures in Good Company* by Thalia Zepatos (Eighth Mountain Press, 1994), a resource

The author, Zip Kellogg, on the information highway

24

The Stern Draw

Kayakers are notorious for veering off course, both in flat water and whitewater. One of the best strokes for adjusting your course is the stern draw. By pulling your paddle inward near your stern you can dramatically change your boat's direction, even put it back on the course you originally intended to go on.

—JB & TB

book for trips for women only.

- Before you ever hit the real wet stuff, surf the Internet. There are hundreds of sites with information for paddlers; some good places to start, called hubs, are listed at the end of this section. For example, a quick check on the GORP (Great Outdoor Recreation Pages) hub listed dozens of links for paddling outfitters, gear, newsletters, clubs, publications, book dealers, conservation, and more. Other options are electronic newsletters and mailing lists, which you can sign up for via your e-mail. Periodically (usually daily) and automatically, postings from other mailing list members are zapped right to your computer. You can follow and take part in debates, get equipment reviews, or if you have a question about a place or piece of gear or technique, you can post the question and be deluged with amazingly useful advice from fellow list members and paddlemaniacs. It's also a great way to meet other paddlers.

- Check out some of the many book resources listed in this book—nothing beats the benefits of others' experiences, and no matter how much we may be enamored of the Internet, there's nothing that will ever beat the value of a good book, a roaring fire, and cup of hot chocolate.

Paddlers' Associations

American Canoe Association, Springfield, VA, (703) 451-0141; acadirect@aol.com (http://world.std.com/~reichert/aca.html)

American Whitewater Affiliation, Phoenicia, NY, (914) 688-5569; awa@rahul.net (http://www.awa.org/ or via CompuServe at 72732,401)

Canadian Recreational Canoe Association, Hyde Park, Ontario, (519) 473-2109; staff@crca.ca (http:www.crca.ca/)

National Association of Canoe Liveries & Outfitters, Butler, KY, (606) 472-2205

National Organization for River Sports, Colorado Springs, CO, (719) 579-8759

North American Paddlesports Association, Mequon, WI, (414) 242-5228; (http://www.halcyon.com/wtr/tn/n/napsa.html)

Trade Association of Sea Kayaking, Mequon, WI, (414) 242-5228; (http:www.halcyon.com/wtr/TASK.html)

Wooden Canoe Heritage Association, Blue Mountain Lake, NY

12812, FAX (518) 327-3632; secretary@wcha.org (http://www.wcha.org)

General Outdoor Organizations

America Outdoors, Knoxville, TN, (423) 524-4814

American Recreation Coalition, Washington, DC, (202) 662-7420

American Recreation Unlimited, Eden Prairie, MN, (612) 943-2002

Association of Outdoor Recreation & Education, Boulder, CO, (303) 444-3353

Events and Symposia

March: San Francisco Chronicle Great Outdoors Adventure Fair, (415) 777-7120

April: Trade Association of Sea Kayaking East Coast Canoe and Kayak Symposium, Mequon, WI, (414) 242-5228; (http:www.halcyon.com/wtr/TASK.html)

May: Trade Association of Sea Kayaking Chesapeake PaddleFest and

Trade Association of Sea Kayaking Alaska Sea Kayak Symposium, see contact information above.

America Outdoors/National River Cleanup Week, Knoxville, TN, (423) 524-4814

June: The Great Midwest Regatta, sponsored by the Wisconsin Chapter of the Wooden Canoe Heritage Association, Blue Mountain Lake, NY 12812, FAX (518) 327-3632; secretary@wcha.org (http://www.wcha.org)

July: Wooden Canoe Heritage Association Annual Assembly, see contact information above.

Cape Breton Seakayak Symposium, sponsored by Island Seafari Seakayaking, Louisbourg, Nova Scotia, (902) 733-2309

September: Trade Association of Sea Kayaking West Coast Sea Kayak Symposium, see contact information above.

Wooden Canoe Meet at Lake Samish, Bellingham, Washington, sponsored by the Northwest Chapter of the Wooden Canoe Heritage Association, see contact information above.

Events calendars appear frequently in all the paddling magazines. It's best to consult them (see list below), and then call for current information.

Magazines and Journals

American Canoeist (published by the American Canoe Association), Springfield, VA, (703) 451-0141

American Rivers (published by American Rivers), Washington, D.C., (202) 547-6900

American Whitewater (published by the American Whitewater Affiliation), Phoenicia, NY, (914) 688-5569

Canoe & Kayak, Kirkland, WA, (206) 827-6363

Kanawa Magazine (published by the Canadian Recreational Canoeing Association, Ontario, (519) 473-2109

Paddler Magazine, Oceanside, CA, (619) 630-2293

Paddle Sports Magazine, Box 1388, Soquel, CA 95073

River Voices (published by the River Network), Portland, OR, (503) 241-3506

Sea Kayaker Magazine, Seattle, WA, (206) 789-9536

Wooden Canoe (published by the Wooden Canoe Heritage Association), Blue Mountain Lake, NY 12812

A Few Noteworthy Regional Publications and Newsletters

Atlantic Coastal Kayaker, Ipswich, MA; (http://www.qed.com/ack/)

Confluence, 1343 North Portage, Palatine, IL 60067

Folding Kayaker, New York, NY, (212) 724-5069; rdiaz@ix.netcom.com

Hurley's Journal (Traditional Canoeing); (http://members.gnn.com/mchurley/index.htm)

Wave~Length, Gabriola Island, BC, (604) 247-9789; (http://www.wie.com/~wavenet/)

World Rivers Review (published by the International Rivers Network), Berkeley, CA, (510) 848-1155

Paddling Publishers

There are many presses that publish paddling material, but some specialize in paddling. Try:

ICS Books Inc., (800) 541-7323

Menasha Ridge Press, (800) 247-9437

Ragged Mountain Press, (800) 262-4729

Westwater Books, (800) 628-1326

Wilderness Press, (800) 443-7227

Internet Resources

The obvious place to begin looking for information on the Internet is with the World Wide Web page of a paddling organization such as the American Canoe Association or the American Whitewater Affiliation—see the listings above for many of the associations that run web pages. All good web pages will have dozens of links to other sources.

You can also start with a well-known "hub" that will provide you with links to other resources. A recent look at the paddling section in GORP (Great Outdoor Recreation Pages) netted book reviews, more than a dozen trip accounts with pictures, commercial ads for gear and outfitters, and lots of magazine and club listings—all to do with some kind of paddling.

When surfing the Internet, don't overlook mentions of mailing lists, FAQs (documents called Frequently Asked Questions that are very informative), and newsgroups. Mailing lists are administered through electronic mail. Via your e-mail software, you "subscribe" (it's free) to a mailing list such as the one for paddler's competitions (Paddle-Comp). Periodically, e-mail messages about upcoming races or clinics are automatically sent to you. (The address for Paddle-Comp is request@rsbs-admin.anu.edu.au; to subscribe, send the message "subscribe paddle-comp"). Newsgroups are similar but are administered on an Internet site; you read a newsgroup via your own news-reading software. Messages from anyone can be posted on the newsgroup "page" and read at any time by anyone. For example, on the "rec.boats.building" newsgroup, you could post a question about how to deal with fiberglass resin in hot weather. You will be amazed how many people will answer!

GORP (Great Outdoor Recreation Pages) (http://www.gorp.com)
Outdoor & More Online (http://www.outdoornet.com)
Yahoo (http://www.yahoo.com)
Outdoor Action Guide (http://www.princeton.edu./~rcurtis/outother.html)
Newsgroups: rec.boats.paddle; rec. boats.building
Mailing lists: see Paddle-Comp above, and for sea kayakers there is Wave_Length (Wave_Length-Request@bbs.sd68.nanaimo.bc.ca)
And these FAQs are worth looking at: Sea Kayak FAQ

OTHER ELECTRONIC RESOURCES

The RiverWave bulletin board is an independent, commercial on-line service providing all sorts of stuff for paddlers, including classifieds, demo information, a file library, chat-room, e-mail with other paddlers, and more. You can access RiverWave at (303) 259-3185; log on at 14,400 bps any time of day or night for a glimpse. The glimpse is free, but if you get the bug, you will be charged about $10 per month for five hours of log-on time, payable with a credit card.

The first canoe club to form in the United States was the New York Canoe Club, of Staten Island, NY, in 1870.

(http://siolibrary.ucsd.edu/preston/kayak/sfaq/toc.html); and Surf Paddling FAQ (http://ssnet.com/~bef/SurfFAQ.shtml)

A software program that understands "gopher" or "telnetting" protocols is very useful as well. Most major universities have converted their old card catalogs to on-line versions available via Gopher, Telnet, or World Wide Web that anyone with a computer and modem can search. Sometimes you can even arrange an interlibrary loan from your home computer!

If you are really new to computers and the Internet and all the possibilities of electronic communication, try *The Whole Internet: User's*

SOMETHING OLD, SOMETHING NEW

When you are starting out in a sport like kayaking, canoeing, or rafting, you will need up-to-date *information* about that sport. You will need to know about current equipment, including costs, strengths, and weaknesses. For this sort of thing be sure to use (a) current advice of knowledgeable people such as outfitters and guides, (b) new or nearly new books (last five years), and (c) equipment reviews in magazines generally no more than a year old.

At the same time, don't neglect speaking with old-timers. They can share perspectives on water, technique, and equipment that will add other dimensions to your understanding of the sport.

Guide and Catalog by Ed Krol (Sebastopol, CA: O'Reilly & Associates, 1996, and updated frequently).

Clubs

Because there are over 100 paddling clubs in North America, with more coming and some going every day, the best places to look for cur-

If you had been a passenger on a vessel of a sixteenth-century New World explorer, you would have seen canoes that looked very much like those of today. The canoe is undoubtedly one of the most extraordinary, yet simple, gifts of the Native Americans to humanity.

Contrary to popular perception, canoes are not difficult to paddle or maneuver. Moreover, canoes are as versatile a craft as one can imagine, equally comfortable on small brooks, large rivers, and, at times, the open ocean.

Canoeing Made Easy: A Manual for Beginners with Tips for the Experienced

by I. Herbert Gordon
(Old Saybrook, CT:
The Globe Pequot Press, 1992)

If you are looking for a book that treats canoeing broadly—one that

rent club information is in the back of paddling magazines, via an Internet search, and on bulletin boards at your local paddling supply stores. There is a newsletter called *Confluence* (see page 26) that is a compilation of information and stories from dozens of paddling clubs across the country.

Canoeing

❈

touches on safety, taking the family, liveries, short trips, longer trips, using maps, cooking, reading the water, conservation, and more— then *Canoeing Made Easy* is for you. It's well organized and well written and has plenty of good illustrations.

The book's photos are often a bit underexposed, but this doesn't detract much from the overall value of the book. It has some good appendices that list useful sources of supplies, canoe and kayak schools, etc. For people just getting into canoeing, this would make an excellent first book.

⌄

Obvious routes—if you are not certain of the portage, remember several considerations. First: A portage almost inevitably will take the shortest route possible from take-out to put-in. Thus, if the rapids occur on a bend, the portage will cut across the curve. Second: If there is one steep bank and one low bank, look for the portage on

the easiest slope. Third: If there is an island in the middle of a river with heavy rapids on either side, the portage may well be on the island itself. This is especially true if the downriver end of the island is level with the water, and both banks are rough cliffs gouged out by the river over the millennia.

The Canoe Handbook: Techniques for Mastering the Sport of Canoeing

by Slim Ray

(Mechanicsburg, PA: Stackpole Books, 1992)

This is among the very best of the new breed of books for recreational canoeists. Many books on paddling seem to be a rehash of the same old stuff, but this one is fresh and original, and even is well written. Ray's chapter on boats and equipment provides the paddler with an excellent, concise intro-

> *"Indefinitely ancient, eternally youthful, a tangible reminder of freedom and unclouded rivers, the canoe lasts into our time from days when man lived closer to nature and it retains the aura."*
>
> —*Walter Teller, from* On the River *(Sheridan House, 1988)*

duction to the staggering array of equipment and accessories available these days. He gives definitions for technical terms that have crept into the vocabulary of the active paddler, but ideally, he would have included a glossary because there are many of them and because he clearly has a grasp on the "dialect" of river rats.

One of the most distinctive elements of any canoe's design is rocker, loosely defined as the amount of curve in a boat's hull from bow to stern, just as in a rocking chair. A boat with a straight keel from stem to stern has no rocker. Put it on a level surface and it sits flat from front to back. It resists turning, since the entire hull sits in the water with equal depth. But it is very easy to move in a straight line, since it resists the turning force of those unbalanced power strokes. The more rocker in the hull, the easier the boat is to turn, because the ends sit higher in the water and offer less resistance to sideways movement.

Learn How to Canoe in One Day: Quickest Way to Start Paddling, Turning, Portaging, and Maintaining

by Robert Birkby

(Mechanicsburg, PA: Stackpole Books, 1990)

This book's catchy title suggests that you will be on your way after a single eight-hour day and to some extent that's true, but it probably wouldn't come from reading this book alone. Birkby's book and a good teacher for a few hours might make a better combination for the eight-hour approach to learning to paddle. Birkby's eight-hour approach includes: selecting a canoe, one hour; moving onto the water, two hours; paddling, two hours; solo canoeing, one hour; landing and portaging, one hour; care and maintenance, one hour . . . for a total of eight hours.

One does have to start someplace, and this book may be the right one for you. But we humans have all sorts of learning styles. Some people can read a book about anything and just go do it. Others would forget the book approach and find a teacher or a clinic. Still others would simply wing it and get the hang of paddling on their own. Others might try the "winging it" approach and get into trouble. There are better and certainly more comprehensive books out there on learning paddling, but if you just want a quick read, this book is okay.

Solo Canoeing : A Guide to the Fundamentals, Equipment, and Techniques for Running Rivers Solo in an Open Canoe

by John H. Foshee
(Mechanicsburg, PA: Stackpole Books, 1988)

Many people learn to paddle tandem—that is, with two people in the canoe. Sometimes those two people move together with grace and ease, and sometimes their every move strikes a sour note. Such is life.

No matter whether you are a beginner or a veteran tandem paddler, there's something to be said for paddling alone at some point. Foshee's book does a good job of

"For many years the motorcar and outboard motor have rather eclipsed the paddling canoe in popularity. But we believe that someday canoeing, especially the old sport of running quick water, will come into its own again."
—*John C. Phillips and Thomas D. Cabot in* Quick-Water and Smooth *(1935)*

outlining the pleasures and the hazards of paddling alone (by the way, he does advocate being alone in a canoe, but does not advocate going off alone to paddle). Although quite a lot of this book's information can also be found in other canoeing books (about PFDs, rescue bags, canoe terminology, draws, pries, braces, etc.), a fair amount is directed specifically at the solo canoeist (equipping a canoe with pads, straps, flotation, etc.). Some of these tips about modifying a canoe are very helpful. If you're a tinkerer, Foshee has plenty of suggestions to help you set up your boat for solo travel.

Sports Illustrated Canoeing: Skills for the Serious Paddler

by Dave Harrison
(New York: Winner's Circle Books, 1988)

It's hard to imagine that a magazine that specializes in sports like football, basketball, and hockey and is world-famous for its bathing suit issues could turn out anything respectable on canoeing, but by teaming with writer Dave Harrison they've done it.

Harrison, who is co-publisher of *Canoe & Kayak* magazine, has written a solid, general overview of the sport. He includes chapters on all the basics—quiet-water paddling,

fast-water paddling, canoe tripping, going on expeditions, safety, competition, PFDs, and plenty more. The book is well done and includes plenty of illustrations and photos to clarify this or that point.

In one of the most memorable lines in any of the basic books on canoeing, Harrison writes, "Perhaps the canoe's greatest virtue is that it makes larger a world which in most other ways is becoming ever smaller."

The Open Canoe

by Bill Riviere
(Boston: Little, Brown and Company, 1985)

There are few finer, more comprehensive, more thoroughly researched books out there on the subject of canoeing. Period. The author, Bill Riviere, has been at this for decades—so many that he might be reluctant to say just how many. And we are his beneficiaries.

In *The Open Canoe*, Riviere covers a great range of topics and often shares with the reader some topics' historical background. This alone is worth the price of the book. For example, he devotes individual chapters to these construction materials: birchbark, wood and canvas, strippers, lapstrake, aluminum, fiberglass and Kevlar, Royalex, and polyethylene. For each, he mentions prominent builders, shops, and key points in the history and development of the use of the material. He also summarizes the most important points to consider when buying a canoe, gives an overview of competition in canoes, includes a section on reading whitewater, a chapter on safety, and even a chapter titled "Canoeist's Library" (on collecting guidebooks, catalogs, etc.)

The Open Canoe is an excellent, thorough, well-researched, and worthwhile book to own. Among paddlers, Riviere deserves elder statesman status. In addition to this book, Riviere has written these titles that may be of interest to paddlers:

- *The Camper's Bible* (Doubleday, 1984)
- *Family Camper's Cookbook* (Holt, Rinehart and Winston, 1965)
- *Pole, Paddle & Portage* (Little, Brown, 1969)

- *Backcountry Camping* (Doubleday, 1971)
- *Family Camper's Bible* (Doubleday, 1975)
- *L.L. Bean Guide to the Outdoors* (Random House, 1981)

The Canoe and White Water

by C.E.S. Franks

(Toronto: University of Toronto Press, 1977)

For those paddlers who are beyond the basics and would like to: (a) get a bit more background on the history of paddling (particularly in Canada); (b) learn more about river turbulence and how to deal with it successfully; and (c) ponder even an entire chapter titled "Canoeing Judgment," this book is for you. It is well illustrated and is sprinkled with artists' works showing canoes in frothing foam, some realistic, some highly stylized and romanticized. Fun to look at in either case!

Judgment in paddling, by the

Playing the Kick

Almost every hole and broken hydraulic on the river (with the exception of perfectly horizontal holes) kick left or right. If you know how to use this kick to your advantage you'll be able to make some dramatic lateral maneuvers. If a hole is kicking right and you're on the left side of the river, you can enter the hole left and exit it on the right. You must, however, choose which holes you attempt these moves in wisely.

—JB & TB

way, is one of those things that simply comes with experience, and Franks discusses that. One could even say that paddling consists, in part, of a process of rapid-fire decisions. Watch out for this rock here, that ledge there, those standing waves, that hole, this overhanging tree, that falls, etc. Paddling is good practice for life-skills development.

The Canoe and White Water would make good pre-voyage reading, especially if that trip is anyplace in Canada, because the book focuses largely on canoes, paddling, and waters of the north country.

Canoeing

by Laurie Gullion

(Champaign, IL: Human Kinetics Publishers, 1994)

Laurie Gullion has written a concise, attractive book on canoeing for the beginner. In about 140 pages, she surveys the sport, hitting on equipment needs, safety issues, basic strokes, good places to go, etc. The color photos are excellent and the sketches clarify her points. The book is both attractive and a good length—most beginners don't want or need laborious detail; they need time on the water, an effective teacher, and the lessons that come with mistakes. *Canoeing* should help put a cap on the latter.

Gullion includes loads of simple tips and presents her ideas in ways that will get the beginner *thinking* about equipment, technique, and safety. Prefacing an excellent list of soul-searching questions, she writes, "Assess your personal needs, and be honest with any potential partners about your preferences. Your paddling comfort and long-term enjoyment of canoeing are at stake here." A great book for beginners and cross-over paddlers.

Beyond the Paddle— A Canoeists' Guide to Expedition Skills: Poling, Lining, Portaging and Maneuvering Through Ice

by Garrett Conover
(Gardiner, ME: Tilbury House, 1991)
Books on technique are, in some senses, a dime a dozen these days. What makes *Beyond the Paddle* so welcome an addition to this plethora of books is that Conover really does go well beyond the paddle and into several of the auxiliary paddling skills that one invariably needs. For example, if you are out on the water in the early spring,

you just might encounter a pack of ice blocking your way. Very messy . . . and potentially very dangerous. Conover's voice reflects plenty of experience: "Test all ice encountered. Then retest it. Apply your ever-expanding body of knowledge but refrain from thinking that you know ice. Never completely trust the rules or yourself."

The illustrations by both Conover and his friend Jerry Stelmok are marvelous, and combined with the photos, add a great deal to the book.

If you've been paddling for many years you still could learn a thing or two from *Beyond the Paddle*. Conover has done us all a great favor in writing about what he knows—and he does know his paddling.

Canoeing and Kayaking: Technique, Tactics, Training

by Marcus Bailie
(Ramsbury, UK: Crowood, 1991)
One of the most interesting things about this 125-page paperback is that the author recognizes that people have different learning styles. Some simply get on the water and do it (paddle, that is), some need a strong teacher, some do better through the written word, and so on. In the preface, the author writes, "I didn't want to write a book about canoeing and kayaking; I wanted to write a book about how we learn, and how this should influence how we teach."

Bailie covers the basics of paddling with plenty of color photos and clearly drawn illustrations. It has a decidedly British slant (places mentioned, word spellings, etc.) but in no way does this diminish

from its value as an introduction to the basics. There is plenty of good, practical advice here.

More Good Books on Canoeing

Whitewater Handbook, 3rd Edition by Bruce Lessels (Boston: Appalachian Mountain Club Books, 1994)

Hearst Marine Books Canoeing Basics by Melinda Allan (New York: Hearst Marine Books, 1994)

Freestyle Canoeing: Contemporary Paddling Technique by Lou Glaros (Birmingham, AL: Menasha Ridge Press, 1994)

Basic River Canoeing by Robert E. McNair, Matty L. McNair, and Paul A. Landry (Martinsville, IN: American Camping Association, 1987)

The Boy's Book of Canoeing: All About Canoe Handling, Paddling, Poling, Sailing, and Camping by Elon Jessup (New York: E.P. Dutton, 1926)

Canoe Handling. The Canoe, History, Uses, Limitations and Varieties, Practical Management and Care and Relative Facts by C. Bowyer Vaux (New York: Forest and Stream Publishing Co., 1888) For a little historical perspective and a surprising amount of still-valid information, this little book can't be beat.

Sea Kayaking

Like canoeing, sea kayaking has a long North American history and has become a popular modern sport. But sea kayaking has become a nationally known recreation option only in the last decade—and its popularity has risen as fast as a high tide in Baja. Sleek and sporty surf kayaks take bold (or just crazy) thrill-seekers into the frothy surf zones—there's even a "club" in the San Francisco area called the Tsunami Rangers who think it's fun to go out in stuff even the Coast Guard shuns. Rugged and seaworthy touring boats, both singles and doubles, take adventurers on voyages all over the world, across the major oceans, lakes, and slow-moving rivers. And small day-trippers take thousands of folks seeking solitude out for a relaxing day on the water. Whether touring for long distances, tooling around quiet bays and lakes, or toying with the surf off the local beach, sea kayaking offers many options for all ages.

The Complete Book of Sea Kayaking

by Derek C. Hutchinson
(Old Saybrook, CT:
The Globe Pequot Press, 1995)

Hutchinson has been at this game for some thirty years, so he speaks with a voice of authority and experience. The scope of his book is broad, hitting on everything from equipment design to hazards of some species of wildlife. The points he makes are often clearly illustrated.

Kayak Touring

by William Sanders
(Mechanicsburg, PA: Stackpole Books, 1984)

The subtitle of this book is "The First Complete Guide to Using a Kayak to Get Where You Want to Go." That may have sold a few extra copies of the book, but it's really a general guide to kayaking, including all you'd expect—a section on reading whitewater, a chapter on kayaking in the ocean, one on camping gear, one on equipment maintenance, a checklist, etc. It's liberally illustrated. This book will provide a beginner with an adequate introduction to the sport.

Sea Kayaking Basics

by David Harrison
(New York: Hearst Marine Books, 1993)

When sea kayaks are sold, the dealer should include with the sale a book like this one. It gives beginners a good, solid introduction to what the sport is all about.

Harrison has been associated with *Canoe & Kayak* magazine for a long time (he is co-publisher) and, although he admits "my own paddling resume is longer on canoe tripping than on sea kayaking," he is no greenhorn. The book hits on all the basic information a person could want. He is brief and to the point; the book is well organized and includes many simple, clear illustrations. He hasn't belabored any topic, yet has given the reader sufficient information to get on the water safe and soon. After all, isn't that the object?

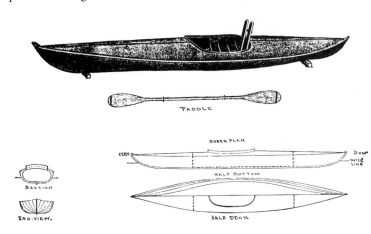

PADDLE

SHEER PLAN

STERN BOW WATER LINE

HALF BOTTOM

HALF DECK

SECTION

END-VIEW.

33

The Coastal Kayaker's Manual: A Complete Guide to Skills, Gear, and Sea Sense

by Randel Washburne
(Old Saybrook, CT:
The Globe Pequot Press, 1993)

If you are about to buy or have just bought a sea kayak, this would make a good companion to it. One might say that it covers the water-front. Washburne touches on all the basic information someone new to the sport would probably want. He also includes tips on entering and exiting rough water (invaluable when the time comes), emergency signaling, flares, use of radios and the appropriate frequencies, prob-lems of hypothermia, etc. Addi-tionally, he gives plenty of back-ground on navigation, tides, and planning a trip.

If you are looking for a solid 100-level course in sea kayaking, then add this book to your shelves.

The Essential Sea Kayaker: A Complete Course for the Open Water Paddler

by David Seidman
(Camden, ME: Ragged Mountain Press, 1992)
Seidman's approach is a pretty good one. He runs through what he calls sea kayaking 101 and then 102, giving, as might be ex-pected, the basics and then a few items beyond the basics. He touches all the fundamentals—getting a boat, transporting it, get-ting in and out, Eskimo rolls, weather, etc. The photos are help-ful and the illustrations very good and informative. One of the best

things about the book is that it has fewer than 150 pages. No extra baggage here.

Sea Kayaking: A Manual for Long Distance Touring

by John Dowd
(Seattle: University of Washington Press, 1988)
Dowd's 300-page manual gets high marks for giving the serious sea kayaker a comprehensive overview of the sport. An appen-

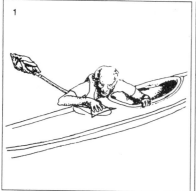

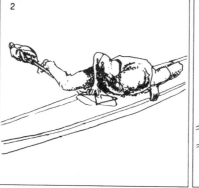

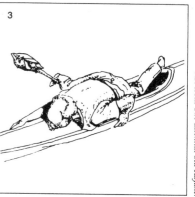

Art from The Essential Sea Kayaker

dix on transoceanic solos should tell one that this book isn't for the paddler looking for a day outing. There is plenty to digest—like the use of a drogue (a device to help one wait out a serious storm), emergency procedures, survival situations, rescues, dealing with sharks and other potential hazards, and plenty more.

One could safely say that Dowd knows his stuff. If you are planning any major sea kayaking trip, reading this book should be very high on your priority list.

Eskimo Rolling, Second Edition

by Derek Hutchinson
(Camden, ME: Ragged Mountain Press, 1992)
These days rolling a sea kayak is considered fundamental, and it sure

---

Improvising a Cargo Hatch Cover

If you lose a cargo hatch cover on your sea kayak, an emergency replacement can be made from a dry bag and bungie cord. Cut the dry bag open to lie flat, then trim it to a shape a few inches larger than the hatch opening. Tie a bungie cord into a circle that will fit tightly around the hatch rim to hold the makeshift cover in place (you can cannibalize a deck bungie if you don't have spare lengths).

—JH & RH

---

says something about how far kayaking has come that an entire book has been written on techniques of rolling. What used to be a chapter in most anything written about kayaking has been admirably and quite thoroughly expanded by Hutchinson.

The roll was originally developed by the Inuit and other peoples of circumpolar regions to save their hides from the frigid waters. If you had been hunting for walrus a thousand years ago off the west

coast of Greenland and suddenly a nearby iceberg flipped over, and the huge waves caused by its flip flipped you, you would have needed to roll.

There are numerous variations on a roll. There is the Pawlata Roll, the Screw Roll, the Steyr Roll, the Greenland Roll, the Kotzebue Roll, and others. Hutchinson takes readers through sufficient detail to master each of them. He encourages you to build up a repertoire of techniques of rolling so that, as the circumstances change, so can your choice of techniques to right yourself. The book includes basic sketches that clarify points made in the text. Also, there are many wonderful stories of rolling successes and some positively abysmal failures—most told by seasoned veterans.

Hutchinson even includes a chapter titled "party tricks," in which he tells how to amuse your friends by keeping a lighted cigar dry as you demonstrate an Eskimo roll.

If you learn to sea kayak, you should learn to roll. Rolling is not just a convenient means to right oneself after a capsize, but a way to save equipment, time, or even a life.

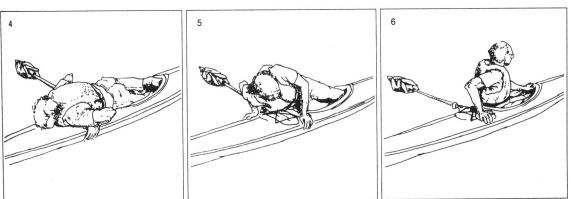

Art from *The Essential Sea Kayaker*

More Good Books on Sea Kayaking

The Complete Folding Kayaker by Ralph Diaz (Camden, ME: Ragged Mountain Press, 1994). An excellent guide to everything you need to know about buying and using a folding sea kayak. *Kayaking: Whitewater and Touring Basics* by Steven M. Krauzer (New York: W.W. Norton and Company, 1995)

Whitewater Kayaking

◆

There is probably no craft on earth that allows you to get as intimate with water as the whitewater kayak. Because you "wear" a whitewater kayak, you are both on the water and in it at the same time. And perhaps there is also no craft that has covered so much of the world's most wild places: rivers. From the Colorado of the Grand Canyon to the Bío Bío in Chile, from Africa's Congo to the Mackenzie in the Arctic, kayakers have been there. Whatever your chosen form of kayaking, expect adrenaline to be your constant companion.

Wildwater

by Lito Tejada-Flores
(San Francisco: Sierra Club, 1978)
An excellent overview of whitewater kayaking. Although somewhat dated, this book still contains lots that any kayaking enthusiast just ought to know—such as rolling technique, river rescue, tips for long trips, nomenclature of rivers

and rapids, and more. The Sierra Club has published many good books over the years for lovers of the wilds, of the rivers, of the mountains. In this case, they and Tejada-Flores produced a book on kayaking (and to a more limited extent, rafting) that will endure.

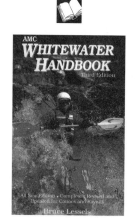

Whitewater Handbook, Third Edition

by Bruce Lessels
(Boston: Appalachian Mountain Club Books, 1994)
The first edition of this book came out in 1965, and since then it has been updated periodically. For

"Rapids have a relentlessness about them that is unusual in the spectrum of outdoor recreation activities. There is no turning back, no reconsideration, no second chance. Commit a boat to the power of a Big Drop and you must make the run—in the boat or in the water, in one piece or several. By way of contrast, the mountain does not pull the climber upward at twenty-five miles per hour, demanding instant and irrevocable decisions. You can rappel off the cliff. You can also brake a sports car, fall down on the ice or off a surfboard, and luff a sailboat into the wind. But rapids do not grant incompletes. Only pilots, skydivers, and hang gliders, who also deal with gravity in a fluid medium, face a comparable everything-on-the-line finality. They know with the boatmen what Winston Churchill meant when he observed that if you "play for more than you can afford to lose, . . . you will learn the game."
—From The Big Drops, Ten Legendary Rapids of the American West by Roderick Frazier Nash (Boulder, CO: Johnson Books, 1989)

many modern-day paddlers, this has been *the* book on technique; many would call it a classic, and for good reason. It covers all the basics for both canoeists and kayakers as well as advanced techniques for both. And while many things about paddling have changed since we entered the age

36

REMINDER

Just about all of the books mentioned in this catalog can be obtained by:
(a) patronizing a local bookstore;
(b) contacting one of the many paddling suppliers listed in Chapter 3 (most have toll-free phone numbers); or
(c) inquiring at a library. See also the section in Chapter 1 called "About This Book" for good sources of hard-to-find books.

of plastic, Lessels tells us "the soul of the sport is still the same." Kayakers and canoeists who like books and who want to have an excellent overall book of technique on hand would do well to add this to their library of paddling books.

It is broad in scope, hitting on strokes, river terminology, equipment, safety and first aid, Eskimo rolling, river hazards, knots, racing, river politics and policy, and more. Moreover, its publisher, the Appalachian Mountain Club, has long been a friend of paddlers, having produced numerous books over the years on safety and technique as well as paddling guides to various regions. They are also an active conservation organization.

The book's strong point is its clear, concise instruction. Read it cover to cover and you'll have a superb general background on what paddling is all about.

Unlike a wetsuit, a drysuit keeps water out. Aside from your own perspiration, you should have virtually no water inside a well-fitting drysuit after paddling. Drysuits are made of coated nylon with latex seals at the neck, wrists, and ankles and usually have a waterproof entry zipper on the front or the back of the chest or a seal between the top and bottom. While more expensive than a wetsuit, a drysuit is the ultimate in cold-weather wear, since it creates a total barrier between you and the water. . . . Drysuits must be custom fitted to each individual by stretching or cutting the latex seals at the wrists, ankles, and neck. These seals are somewhat delicate and can tear if treated roughly, or exposed to sunscreen, bug repellent, cosmetics, or too much ultraviolet light. Maintain them regularly by treating them with a silicone vinyl treatment such as Armor-All or Seal Saver. They can be replaced when they wear out.

The Backward Glance

After coming through any rapid, whether difficult or a cinch, it pays to stop and look back upstream at it. By doing this you can see a perspective entirely different from the one you saw looking downstream at the rapid. This new perspective can help you understand where the rocks were, why the channel was where it was, etc. Call it reading backwards if you like, but try it. It's likely to pay off when you run the next rapid.

The Complete Guide to Kayaking

by Raymond Bridge
(New York: Scribners, 1978)

This provides a good and thorough introduction to the sport, but it is somewhat dated. That is, kayaks, the stuff they're made of, and the kayakers, and maybe even the stuff *they're* made of, have all changed a lot lately. For example, materials like Kevlar and a whole host of plastics used in building boats have all come on the scene since publication of this book. So this book's value lies in its breadth, not its currency. It includes chapters on wilderness travel, racing, the Eskimo roll, and a lot more, exposing the reader to the range of experiences and skills one might encounter or need in the seat of a kayak. If, however, you're looking for something more up to date, it would make sense to get this book out of your library and then sink a few bucks into a subscription to *Paddler* magazine, *American Whitewater*, or a similar publication. That way you'd get your introduction from *The Complete Guide to Kayaking* and get up to speed by reading a magazine regularly.

37

CONFESSIONS OF A WHITEWATER CHICKEN

by Pope Barrow

"Even the bravest of warriors yet knows the dark clutch of fright upon his stalwart heart."
—Lim-Du, *in* The Necromancers

I hate those "No Fear!" bumper stickers. What I need is a bumper sticker that says "TOTAL FEAR!"

"No Fear" is silly. Everyone fears something: snakes, spiders, the I.R.S. Some people fear vampires. Baptists fear God. Newt Gingrich and Rush Limbaugh are afraid of tax-and-spend liberals.

I can always find something to fear. When I was 13, I was afraid of asking out girls. These days I am scared of whitewater. Fear of whitewater is intense, physical, and immediate. Fear strikes suddenly whenever I am about to run big, heavy, steep, out-of-control whitewater.

Fear is taboo in whitewater literature. I must be the only person in whitewater sports who experiences the full impact of whitewater fear (or at least the only one who admits it). In whitewater stories no one is ever afraid of anything, except maybe giardia.

But fear of whitewater might not be entirely bad. One could certainly get paralyzed by too much of it, and even a little is uncomfortable. But without fear, there is no adrenaline. Without adrenaline, how can you enjoy the hardest whitewater?

Fear goes way back deep in the genes. Our prehistoric ancestors knew more fear than we will ever know. Every time they stepped out of the cave a saber-toothed tiger or some other horrible mammal or reptile tried to have them for dinner. Talk about fear!

Now we are genetically programmed to go out and experience fear. We need it. We need to experience a dose of the same powerful brain chemicals that our ancestors experienced every day when they left the cave on their daily commute down to the jungle to kill dinner. This is the only explanation I can come up with for why I go kayaking in frightening Class V whitewater.

Standing on the bank above a fearsome whitewater descent, fear ambushes me. First I notice the dryness in my mouth. I get a drink of water. Seconds later my mouth is dry again. Another drink. Mouth still dry. Another. This is not *working* . . . Gradually a discomforting alien force takes over my entire being. I focus on the two most ancient human options: *fight* or *flight*.

In my case, I go first to the *flight* option. I begin to scan the shoreline. Where is the damn portage? How do I get out of this? The litany of excuses begins. My boat leaks. My spray skirt keeps blowing off. My shoulder is sore. What the hell is my excuse anyway?

As often the case in Class V whitewater, there is no damn portage and no way out. I am stuck in a situation where the canyon walls are almost vertical for about 800 feet

---

White Water Kayaking

by Ray Rowe
(Mechanicsburg, PA: Stackpole Books, 1989)
Ray Rowe, a veteran kayak racer who has experience paddling the world over, has pulled together a good, brief overview of whitewater kayaking. He emphasizes such topics as instruction, respect for the rivers, and one's ability to relax.

The book is easy to read and the significant points are highlighted, making it easy to head for the river with a few key things to concentrate on. There are plenty of excellent photos and graphics to help you understand the principles. Several of the photos are spectacular.

The Kayaking Book

by Jay Evans and Eric Evans
(New York: NAL/Dutton, 1993)
This is one of the very best of books about whitewater kayaking. Jay (father) and Eric (son) Evans are household names to many avid kayakers. Jay has been an Olympic coach and Eric an Olympic kayaker. But the book is good not only

up. There is a mile and a half of virtually continuous unknown Class V whitewater ahead, and no way to get back upstream.

Another drink of water. Then a trip behind the boulders to flush out all that water. Heart beating pretty fast.

Maybe I'll just puke and get it over with. Better check the equipment. That might calm me down. . . . Yeah, get back to basics. *Where the hell is my paddle??* Oh Jesus, did it float away? Oh, there it is underneath the boat.

As my brain gradually detaches from my body, it splits into two parts, each vying for control. A dialogue begins.

Left brain says to right brain: "Don't panic, you idiot. You'll definitely get wasted if you panic here."

Right brain says back: "Okay, okay. Just scout this monster one more time. Got to get a line through this figured out somehow. There *must be* a way to sneak down the side of this."

"No sneak anywhere."

"That sucks."

"Well, I guess that's why it's rated Class V."

"Why did God make Class V whitewater anyway?"

"No time for theology now. Looks like you could start left, miss the small hole at the top in the center left, then the big one just below in the center. But don't get caught in the rock sieve on the left. Then charge hard right through the huge curlers to reach the canyon wall. Maybe a short pause next to the wall below the log to get your bearings and figure out what happens next—especially down below with all those huge exploding waves and boils. What a mess!"

"Well, maybe there *is* a way to get through this first part if everything goes right. So what's the problem? Only about three people have died here recently and the water level was probably different when that happened. Definitely. Must have been higher. Or maybe lower."

"Get going you idiot!"

My body, by now totally detached from the mental turmoil, slowly, reluctantly, slips into the kayak.

I plunge in, paddle cautiously, weakly, but picking up speed—to

the point of no return and then, suddenly, I am into it.

Holy smokes . . . This stuff is huge beyond belief! I am suddenly swallowed up by massive chaotic waves, the most gigantic slabs of confused whitewater I have ever seen. I flip, roll up, backender and flip again. Roll up.

This is horrendous. It's wild! But—where the did fear go?

Too much else going on here. No time for fear now.

—Pope Barrow is a frequent contributor to the journal American Whitewater *and co-author of* Rivers at Risk, *the leading handbook for citizen dam fighters. He is Vice President of the American Whitewater Affiliation and in 1987 was named River Conservationist of the Year by the Perception Company. He is married and has three children, and earns a living writing environmental legislation for the U.S. House of Representatives. When not scaring himself silly boating blindly down Andean rivers, Pope lives in Washington, D.C., and gets his adrenaline at Great Falls on the Potomac.*

because the authors have good credentials; it is also good because it is comprehensive (including even comments on the history of lifejackets), well written, and to the point. This is the sort of book any kayaker would do well to own as a reference book. The book is longer than many of the other books on kayaking you'll see, but surprisingly not any more expensive. And the authors cover about everything you would

want to know but were afraid to ask. It's generally a book of sound, solid advice. If you bought one book to go with your kayak, this one wouldn't make a bad choice.

▼

If you're new to kayaking, you must shed the notion that you sit in a kayak: what you really do is wear it, because the kayak feels almost like an extension of your body. Then, ideally, it will respond to a command from your brain.

There are a few things though, that you'll need to check out before you wear your kayak in the water, because if the fittings are too tight, your legs will soon fall asleep, and if the fittings are too loose, you'll rattle around inside the boat like a loose tie-rod.

If you are tall, you may wish to move the footbraces forward toward the bow to be sure there'll be enough room for your legs to stretch out . . .

▲

Kayak: The Animated Manual of Intermediate and Advanced Whitewater Technique

by William Nealy

(Birmingham, AL: Menasha Ridge Press, 1986)

William "Not Bill" Nealy is a silly boy. He is both a cartoonist and a paddler and he applies one skill to the other. But which? In addition to tackling intermediate and advanced whitewater technique humorously, "Not Bill" clearly knows what he is talking about. The artistic license he takes with techniques, river scenes, etc., demonstrates things that no photo could. For example, he shows a kayaker progressing downstream on a huge moving belt (the river) that travels under and over cylinders (souse holes, keepers, etc.). What kind of brain conjures up such a scene?

Nealy stresses safety, but he doesn't belabor it, which is nice. In his chapter "Joy of Flood," for example, he tells the reader not to paddle rivers on the rampage, but if you do . . .

The book even has one of those moving cartoons that you see if you flip the pages of the book quickly. If Nealy doesn't make you laugh, then quit paddling and take up lawn bowling.

Performance Kayaking

by Stephen B. U'Ren

(Mechanicsburg, PA: Stackpole Books, 1990)

Don't be confused by the title. This is not so much a racer's book (although there is a chapter on slalom racing) as it is one to help you improve your technique, style, and understanding of just what is going on between you, your paddle, and the water. U'Ren likens the kayak paddler to a river otter, seemingly frolicking over and under the water. He writes, "Kayaking makes you feel vibrant; it both nourishes the body and stimulates the mind."

There is plenty in this book for beginner and expert alike—beginners, because U'Ren explains things clearly and has had them illustrated or photographed well; experts, because any expert would do well to assume he or she doesn't really know it all and can learn a thing or two from someone else's vantage point.

The Squirt Book: The Illustrated Manual of Squirt Kayaking Technique

by James E. Snyder

(Birmingham, AL: Menasha Ridge Press, 1987)

Hot dogging has come to kayaking in a big way—and the epitome is "squirt boating." Some of the things the squirt boaters do will not only stretch but also *warp* your imagination if you've never seen their antics. Who would have dreamed of intentionally doing cartwheels in a small boat just a few years ago?

A squirt boat (from the handy glossary in *The Squirt Book*) is "a low volume kayak designed to have little volume above the water in order to facilitate its submersion in the act of squirting." Squirting

involves using currents and paddle strokes to sink a portion or all of the boat temporarily. If all goes well, it then pops up or "squirts" as a bar of wet soap will do when squeezed. Snyder tells the reader that "a well-cut [designed] squirt boat is only a glorified life jacket." That is, it gives the human body a bit more flotation than it has naturally.

Because squirt boaters do different things in their boats than most other paddlers, they have developed a dialect for their sport. Speaking with a squirt boater may remind you of the last conversation you had with a teenager. You might hear about charcs ("angle of approach to a current"), or boofing ("a technique for flat landing from vertical drops"), or moonstroking ("moving backwards on a current while it looks like you're paddling forward").

Although this book is one of few that deal with this growing "subspecialty" of kayaking, the writing style is convoluted and hard to follow, partly because of all the invented language. Try this: "Keep carving your hip into oncoming currents with orchestrated peak points." Or ". . . the evolutionary acceleration on the rock has been estimated to be around five thousand years. The karmic whiplash on yourself can literally tear abdominal muscles and tendons."

The book does have "focus points" or key things to ponder when learning squirt boating. They are scattered here and there to help one to identify and deal with the usual beginners' problems. Unfortunately they, too, are jargon-encrusted—"focus your peak points on the heart of the squeeze" or "try mystery moves in the seams in the current."

More Good Books on Whitewater Kayaking

The Bombproof Roll and Beyond by Paul Dutky (Birmingham, AL: Menasha Ridge Press, 1994)

The White-Water River Book: A Guide to Techniques, Equipment, Camping, and Safety by Ron Watters (Seattle: Pacific Search Press, 1982)

The Complete Inflatable Kayaker by Jeff Bennett (Camden, ME: Ragged Mountain Press, 1996). Includes equipment as well as technique. (Reviewed on pages 45–46.)

Oxygen Consumption During Kayak Paddling by Georgina Louise Gray (University of British Columbia, 1992). This was Gray's masters thesis in physical education. It's informative, but always proceed with caution when reading theses and dissertations; they tend to lack humor.

Rafting

↓

Once a fringe activity for a few crazy people with Army surplus rafts, river rafting is now a hugely popular recreational endeavor. More than 20,000 people float and flail their way down the Colorado River in the Grand Canyon each year—and that's just a fraction of the numbers that float other rivers in North America, from the American to the Nantahala, as well as around the world. Though it's big business for thousands of outfitters, there is still a handful of adventuresome people who buy their own rafts and outfit their own trips. The work is substantial, but so are the payoffs. An inflatable raft can carry hundreds and hundreds of pounds of provisions and gear, allowing a group to enjoy a fully supported trip for weeks at a time through some of the most outstanding wilderness in the world. People strap amazing things onto the frames of their rafts:

lawn chairs, 150-quart ice chests, cabin-sized tents, even a child's playpen . . .

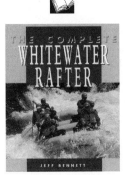

The Complete Whitewater Rafter

by Jeff Bennet (Camden, ME: Ragged Mountain Press, 1996) It has been a long time since a good, comprehensive book on rafting has come out. And given the recent growth in the popularity of the sport, this book is a welcome arrival. This is the sort of book that outfitters should make required reading for their guide trainees, and in fact many do. Bennett touches on about everything from John Wesley Powell of Grand Canyon fame to running steep creeks, from raft "anatomy" to camping and cooking, from racing rafts to oar maintenance and repair. Along the way he peppers the book with illustrations, photographs, and helpful hints. He includes appendixes that deal with safety, equipment suppliers, conservation groups, knots, map sources, and more. There is even a glossary those new to the sport would find helpful; paddlers speak a language all their own and Bennett will help pry and draw newcomers through it. Thinking of outfitting your own rafting trip? Working for an outfitter? Don't miss this book. Are you an outfitter? Buy a copy for each of your guides.

In some boulder- or hole-riddled rapids there simply isn't enough time to execute a turn or to ferry around an obstacle. In fact, some rapids will wrap or flip any raft that lets itself turn broadside. In these types of situations, a quick horizontal maneuver may be the only way to find safe passage.

The fastest and most efficient sideslipping strokes for paddle rafters are the draw, cross-bow draw, and pry stroke. Done correctly, each of these paddle strokes move rafts laterally across the river in a hurry . . .

The White-Water River Book: A Guide to Techniques, Equipment, Camping, and Safety

by Ron Watters
(Seattle: Pacific Search Press, 1982)

It's a funny thing that people with names like Watters and Riviere write books on paddling and rivers. But then, people who own boxer dogs sometimes have pug faces, and then there was a dentist by the name of Doctor Payne . . .

Ron Watters has pulled together a fine collection of material for rafters (both paddle and oar) as well as kayakers. It would be nice to have it updated, but it has aged fairly well. That is, the materials have changed, but how one approaches a rapid or a river in spate has not. Watters includes chapters on reading water, on raft technique, on day and overnight equipment, on kayak technique, on river cuisine, on safety, environmental impact, and more.

For the person thinking of getting into rafting or thinking about going to work next summer for a rafting outfitter, *The White-Water River Book* would make a good preliminary read.

Lowsiding

Highsiding is the name for throwing your crew's body weight toward an obstacle to prevent a flip or wrap. Lowsiding—throwing your crew's body weight away from an obstacle—can come in handy when entering slots slightly narrower than your raft. By centering your crew's weight on the lowside of the raft, the opposite tube will rise, narrowing your raft's profile, and helping you slide through the slot unscathed.
—JB & TB

Class V Briefing

by William McGinnis
(El Sobrante, CA: Whitewater
Voyages/River Exploration Ltd., 1985)

This booklet was written for rafting guides who are headed for *big* water. It is intended as a crash course or review of the key points to remember prior to entering that big water. At fewer than thirty pages long, it won't cover everything, but McGinnis' other book, *Whitewater Rafting*, will.

McGinnis includes pointers on

packing, rigging, preparation, a "put-in talk," techniques, portaging, flips, wraps, evacuation, and more. Each of the comments or suggestions is just a sentence or a few sentences long. For example, following the wrapping of a raft on a rock, he suggests, "During a wrap or flip one guide should remain with the trip members not involved in the incident and keep them informed." And regarding gear (specifically helmets), he writes, "All Class V paddle crews wear helmets. No exceptions. Helmets not only protect paddlers should they go overboard, they also diminish the chance of injury from clanging heads or waps to the noggin by paddle handles."

This booklet provides the guide or trip leader with a quick review of relevant safety issues. It also includes plenty of common sense pointers. But it is not a comprehensive overview of the sport of rafting.

More Good Books on Rafting

Whitewater Rafting in North America: The 200 Best Rafting Adventures in the United States, Canada, Mexico, and Costa Rica by Lloyd Dean Armstead (Old Saybrook, CT: The Globe Pequot Press, 1994)

Whitewater Rafting Manual: Tactics and Techniques for Great River Adventures by Jimmie Johnson (Mechanicsburg, PA: Stackpole Books, 1994)

Whitewater Rafting: An Introductory Guide by Cecil Kuhne (New York: Lyons & Burford, 1995)

The Basic Essentials of Rafting by Jib Ellison (Merrillville, IN: ICS Books, 1991)

White Water Waftin' is Whight On Eh! by George Bennett (Renfrew, Ontario: George Bennett Enterprises, 1986). An amusing, if silly, collection of cartoons about the love of rafting.

The Rivermen (New York: Time-Life Books, 1975). This picture book makes interesting reading and is peppered with old photos and sketches of what river life was like during the eighteenth and nineteenth centuries.

Whitewater Rafting by William McGinnis (New York: New York Times Books, 1978)

43

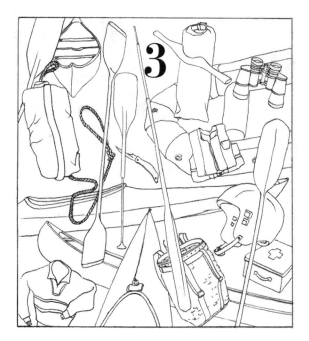

3

Boats and Gear

OR

How to Choose Your Craft

*"We do not go to the green woods and crystal
waters to rough it, we go to smooth it.
We get it rough enough at home."*

—*George Washington Sears,
who wrote under the pen name "Nessmuk,"
in* Woodcraft *(Dover, 1963)*

Boats
Is Boats

This is where you can drown in a sea of choices. There are so many products out there, and so many terms, that if you're not careful you could get *really* confused and find yourself frantically ruddering a 19-foot sea kayak down Lava Falls in the Grand Canyon, or launching a handmade wood and canvas canoe on a solo attempt to round Cape Horn. Okay, maybe it's not that bad, but you get the point.

Fortunately, the hundreds of boats and thousands of accessories available to today's paddler are only matched by the number of books, magazine tests, buyer's guides—and unsolicited opinions—also within easy reach.

First, highly recommended reading is *Stuart Little* by E.B. White. It's a kid's book and it's short, but mighty sweet. It will help you determine the seriousness of your disease.

Next, especially if this is your first boat, consider a four-part approach to your purchase:

1. Talk with two or three people who have experience with the type of boat you are interested in. Try to avoid people who sell boats, since their answers could be biased by the products they sell.
2. To realize the full extent of your options, get a copy of *Canoe & Kayak* or *Paddler* magazine's annual buyer's guide. Each lists thousands of products for paddlers, as well as the address and telephone number for each manufacturer represented.
3. If it is at all possible, try before you buy. The only sure way to see how a boat performs on the water is to try it *on the water*. This has the added benefit of getting you away from the sales hype for a while—unless you're trying a double kayak or canoe and have

brought the salesperson with you. . . . Many dealers have demo days on the water, or are located on a waterfront and rent the boats they sell.
4. One of the best ways to accomplish (3) is to attend one of the numerous symposia held each year all over the country. These almost always include opportunities to paddle and compare different products side by side, and a chance to talk with the builders and other paddlers. The many demonstrations and workshops can be very helpful as well. And if you get lucky with door prizes, you might not have to buy any gear at all. (See Chapter 2 for lists of symposia and paddling organizations.)

No matter what type of boat you are interested in, you can eliminate a lot of choices by defining in advance what you want to do with it (see Chapter 2). There is no sense trying out 12-foot whitewater canoes if you plan on doing month-long tours in the Boundary Waters. And you don't need an expedition-equipped sea kayak if all you want to do is putter about the harbor. At the same time, don't buy yourself short if your goals are still vague. The harbor might be enough for now, but the horizon could beckon later.

Use Your Body

Body English is very effective when paddling a sea kayak in rough conditions. If punching through waves bow-first, lean back to help the bow ride over the wave rather than dive through it. When waves are coming from the side, lean sideways into each one to keep the boat upright. In quartering seas you often must combine the two leans to maintain stability.

—JH & RH

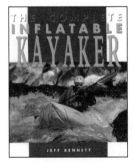

The Complete Inflatable Kayaker

by Jeff Bennett
(Camden, ME: Ragged Mountain Press, 1996)
The popularity of inflatable kayaks, or "rubber duckies," has grown substantially in the last few years

45

HAVE BOAT, WILL TRAVEL

Part of the romance of boats involves the places we paddle them. Sometimes these places can be right by home, and some of them can be in exotic locales, thousands of miles away. Since that means getting there by plane, you may want to consider folding or inflatable boats. Check out the books below for more information on these wonderful craft.

and there are several reasons for this. One is that they are a more forgiving craft than most rigid-shelled boats. Another reason is that synthetic materials have become much, much more durable. While inflatables still need to be treated with at least *some* care they are not like those miserable air mattresses (always leaky and flat) from days of yore. Plastics technology has changed that. And finally, they can be very cheap!

If you are thinking of trying an inflatable kayak, take a look at this book. It's comprehensive. Besides having chapters on safety, paddling techniques, and everything else you could imagine, there is even a section on river camping.

Also, take a look at *The Inflatable Kayak Handbook* by Melinda Allan (Boulder, CO: Johnson Books, 1991). Though it's a little older, it also contains useful information.

Complete Folding Kayaker

by Ralph Díaz

(Camden, ME: Ragged Mountain Press, 1994)
This is an excellent, thorough book—absolutely required reading if you want to go the folding route with your kayak. A small warning: to Diaz, who edits the newsletter *Folding Kayaker* (see Chapter 2 for contact information), the use of folding boats borders on religion. His passion is not just kayaking, it is kayaking in boats that fold up into small packages.

Complete Folding Kayaker includes three parts: "What You Should Know" (why folding boats, choosing a folding boat, and acces-

sories); "Handling Skills for Foldables" (paddle strokes, tips on paddling a double, sea savvy, etc.); and "Using and Enjoying" (traveling with a folding kayak, sailing,

modifications, etc.). The text is straightforward and to the point, with lots of useful information. The photos are so-so, but the useful text makes up for it.

Boatmakers— A Sampler

Sea Kayaks

Aquaterra, Easley, SC,
  (803) 859-7518
Easy Rider, Seattle, WA,
  (206) 228-3633
Eddyline Kayaks, Burlington, WA,
  (360) 757-2300
Feathercraft, Vancouver, BC,
  (604) 681-8437
Klepper Folding Kayaks, Sacramento, CA, (800) 323-3525
Necky Kayaks Ltd., Abbotsford,
  BC, (604) 850-1206
Northwest Kayaks, Redmond, WA,
  (800) 648-8908

Ocean Kayak, Ferndale, WA,
  (800) 8-KAYAKS
Pacific Canoe Base, Victoria, BC,
  (604) 382-1243
Superior Kayaks, Whitelaw, WI,
  (414) 732-3784
Wilderness Systems, High Point,
  NC, (910) 883-7410

Whitewater Kayaks

Dagger Canoe Co., Harriman, TN,
  (615) 882-0404
Kiwi Kayak Company, Windsor,
  CA, (800) K-4-KAYAK
Mega Performance Kayaks,
  Placerville, CA, (916) 642-9755

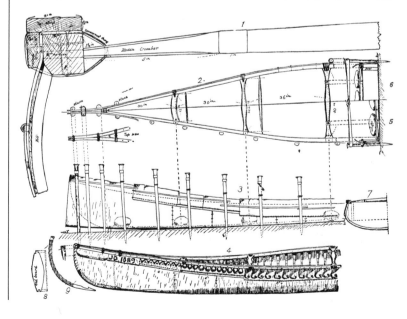

New Wave Kayak Products, Middle-
town, PA, (717) 944-6320

Perception/Aquaterra, Easley, SC,
(803) 859-7518

Pyranha/Impex International,
Bellport, NY, (516) 286-1988

Prijon, Boulder, CO,
(303) 444-2336

Savage Designs, Asheville, NC,
(704) 251-9875

Walden Paddlers, Inc.,
Concord MA, (508) 266-1300

Wave Sports, Inc., Steamboat
Springs, CO, (970) 736-0078

Inflatables

Achilles Inflatable Craft,
Everett, WA, (206) 353-7000

AIRE, Boise, ID, (208) 344-7506

Avon Inflatables, Irvine, CA,
(714) 250-0880

Hyside Inflatables, Kernville, CA,
(619) 376-3723

Jack's Plastic Welding Inc.,
Aztec, NM, (505) 334-8748

Maravia Corporation, Boise, ID,
(800) TOP-RAFT

Northwest River Supplies,
Moscow, ID, (800) 635-5202

Sevylor, Los Angeles, CA,
(213) 727-6013

Soar Inflatables, St. Louis, MO,
(314) 436-0016

Wing Inflatables, Arcata, CA,
(707) 826-2887

Canoes

American Traders Classic Canoes,
Greenfield, MA,
(800) 782-7816

Bear Creek Canoe Inc.,
Limerick, ME, (207) 793-2005

Bell Canoe Works, Zimmerman,
NM, (612) 856-2231

Blue Hole Canoe Company, Gor-
donsville, VA, (540) 832-7855

Canoes by Whitesell Ltd.,
Atlanta, GA, (404) 325-5330

Dagger Canoe Company, Harriman, TN, (615) 882-0404

Grumman Canoes, Marathon, NY,
(607) 849-3211

Mad River Canoe, Waitsfield, VT,
(802) 496-3127

Mohawk Canoes, Longwood, FL,
(407) 834-3233

Nova Craft Canoes, Ltd.,
London, ON, (519) 652-3649

Old Town Canoe Company,
Old Town, ME, (207) 827-5513

Sawyer Canoe Company,
Oscada, MI, (517) 739-9181

We-no-nah Canoe, Inc.,
Winona, MN, (507) 454-5430

Paddler's Paraphernalia

✢

Once you've got your paddlecraft,
it will be mighty tempting to rush
out and buy the first paddle, PFD,
and dry bags you see—just so you
can get out on the water. But beware: accessories can be just as important as a boat for safety as well
as comfort. So take as much care
buying gear as you do with a boat.

Many paddling accessories can
do double or even triple duty. Most
dry bags, for example, work equally
well in sea kayaks or canoes or rafts.
Other products that you might
think would be just as versatile,
though, can be pretty sport-specific.

The high-flotation life jackets that
whitewater kayakers and rafters use
are too bulky for sea kayaking,
where trim models with flip-up bottoms serve better. And another ac-
cessory dear to oar-frame rafters just
doesn't work strapped on the deck of
a skinny Greenland-style sea kayak.
We're talking, of course, about those
150-quart Coleman ice chests.

On page 48 is a list of paddling
suppliers that offer mail order, in
case you don't have a local outfitter
or can't find an item easily. This list
is not exhaustive, so check with
friends, clubs, associations, or

47

A PROPER OUTFIT

In Thoreau's day, natural fibers were used to repel rain and insulate against cold—among them waxed cottons, "rubberized" canvas, and wool. Here are some of his comments on equipping for a two-week trip in the mid-nineteenth century:

"*Wear*—*a check shirt, stout old shoes, thick socks, a neck ribbon, thick waistcoat, thick pants, old Kossuth hat, a linen sack.*

"Tent—six by seven feet, and four feet high in middle, will do; veil and gloves and insect wash, or, better, mosquito-bars to cover all night; best pocket-map, and perhaps description of the route; compass; plant-book and red blotting-paper; paper and stamps, botany, small pocket spy-glass for birds,

pocket microscope, tape measure, insect-boxes.

"Provisions—Soft hardbread, twenty-eight pounds; pork, sixteen pounds; sugar, twelve pounds; one pound black tea or three pounds coffee, one box of a pint of salt, one quart Indian meal, to fry fish in; six lemons, good to correct the pork and warm water; perhaps two or three pounds of rice, for variety. You will probably get some berries, fish, etc., beside.

"A gun is not worth the carriage, unless you go as hunters. The pork should be in an open keg, sawed to fit; the sugar, tea or coffee, meal, salt, etc., should be put in separate water-tight India-rubber bags, which have been proved to be water-tight and durable. Expense of preceding outfit is twenty-four dollars."

Internet resources for more options (see Chapter 2).

Paddling Suppliers

Cascade Outfitters, Springfield, OR, (800) 223-7238. Everything from replacement raft valves to Perception kayaks, riverboards to dry bags.

Colorado Kayak, Buena Vista, CO, (800) 535-3565. All kinds of equipment, primarily relating to kayaking.

Down River Equipment Company, Wheat Ridge, CO, (303) 467-9489. Whitewater inflatables (rafts, catarafts, inflatable kayaks, etc.) and associated gear.

Ecomarine Ocean Kayak Center, Vancouver, BC,

(604) 689-7575. Boats and accessories for sea kayaking.

Four Corners River Sports, Durango, CO, (800) 426-7637. Variety of kayak, rafting, and canoeing equipment and accessories.

Headwaters, Inc., Harriman, TN, (615) 882-8757. Canoe and kayak accessories.

Igas Island, Waldoboro, ME, (207) 832-5255. Custom-made canoe packs, cargo bags, fanny packs, anoraks and other rain gear, and lots more. Will also do some custom work to *your* specifications.

L.L. Bean, Freeport, ME, (800) 221-4221. A wide variety of paddling equipment, clothing and accessories.

Nantahala Outdoor Center Outfitters Store, Bryson City, NC, (800) 367-3521. Wide range of supplies and equipment for paddlers.

Northwest Outdoor Center, Seattle, WA, (800) 683-0637. Sea kayaks and accessories.

Northwest River Supplies, Moscow, ID, (800) 635-5202. Everything for river runners.

Northwoods Canoe Company, Atkinson, ME, (207) 564-3667. Hard-to-find items for the traditionalist (such as brass canoe tacks, clinching irons, canvas filler, and bronze carriage bolts).

Old Town Canoe Company, Old Town, ME, (207) 827-5513. Canoes of their own make and a variety of accessories.

48

Pacific Water Sports, Seattle, WA, (206) 246-9385. Sea kayaks and accessories.

Paddle & Pack Outfitters, Nashville, TN, (800) 786-5565. A broad range of equipment (sandals, videos, roof racks, boats).

Seda Products, Chula Vista, CA, (800) 322-7332. Their own line of PFDs plus a broad range of paddlers' supplies, especially for kayaking.

Spring River Corp., Annapolis, MD, (800) 882-5649. Sea kayaks and accessories.

Voyageur, Waitsfield, VT, (800) 843-8985. Supplies of all sorts for the whitewater enthusiast (repair kits, cane seats, saddles, paddles, throw bags, etc.).

Wildwater Designs, Blue Bell, PA, (800) 426-2027. Run by Charlie Walbridge, the whitewater safety guru; offering about anything a paddler could want.

Wyoming River Raiders, Casper, WY, (800) 247-6068. River supplies galore.

Paddle Captaining

One of the hardest things to do as a paddle captain is to stop an excited crew from paddling once they've started digging in. One of the easiest ways to cure overstroking is to limit the number of strokes in your paddle command by saying something like "Forward two strokes" rather than just saying "Forward."

—JB & TB

Other Ideas

As a rule you're more likely to find paddling equipment through dealers of paddler's wares. However, no one has everything, so

here are the names of a few more suppliers of general boating equipment and supplies.

E & B Discount Marine, Edison, NJ, (800) 262-8464. Electronic gear, rainwear, marine paints, and lots more marine gear and gadgetry.

Hamilton Marine, Searsport, ME, (800) 639-2715. All sorts of marine supplies.

Jamestown Distributors, Jamestown, RI, and Beaufort, SC, (800) 423-0030. Fasteners, boatbuilding and woodworking supplies.

West Marine, Watsonville, CA, (800) 538-0775. General recreational boating supplies.

If absolutely all attempts at locating something fail, make it yourself. You won't be the first to try this strategy.

Suppliers for Do-It-Yourselfers

Seattle Fabrics, Seattle, WA, (206) 632-6022. Gore-Tex to fleece, mosquito netting to sailcloth—everything you could need.

PADDLER'S SYMPOSIA

For a paddler who is in the market for nearly any piece of new equipment, a symposium can be an excellent place to see and try out products. Symposia provide paddlers with opportunities to talk to experts, listen to lectures, try out products on the water (usually), and generally gab with other demented paddling addicts.

Symposia are held all over North America, from Madison to Muskegon, Chesapeake Bay to Charleston, and Seattle to Houston. The dates and details of these generally appear in magazines such as *Paddler, Canoe & Kayak, Sea Kayaker* and *American Whitewater.* You can also find listings on some of the on-line services for paddlers (see

Chapter 2 for information on Internet resources).

If you plan to attend a symposium, you may want to find out which experts will be speaking, how much on-water time is available for testing, etc. You wouldn't want to fork over good money to attend something that is not much more than a trade show.

Some sources for information about symposia include the April 1994 issue of *Paddler* magazine ("North America's Top Paddling Symposiums," pp. 40–50), paddlers' associations and electronic resources (see Chapter 2 for information on associations and the Internet).

THE NAMING OF CANOES

by Robert Kimber

If Gertrude Stein was right and a rose is indeed a rose is a rose, why is a canoe not a canoe not a canoe?

Don't get funny on me, you may say. Don't start muddying the waters of my favorite sport with the verbal meanderings of a rather eccentric lady who ate too many brownies laced with Mary Jane.

Besides, you may say, a canoe *is* a canoe is a canoe. What else could it be?

Well, just for starters, take a look at what the people who make canoes choose to call them: canoes are Trippers, Trappers, and Wanderers; Explorers, Packers, and Guides. Canoes are Scouts, Adventurers, Voyageurs, and Prospectors, not to mention Blazers, Pioneers, Rangers, and Nomads. The logic of those names is inescapable. Once French settlers in North America had apprenticed long enough to the canoemen of the Cree and the Montagnais, the canoe in fact became a scout and explorer, a trapper and prospector. As we canoe folk are fond of pointing out to our landlubbing friends, it was the canoe, not the Conestoga wagon, that carried Marquette and Jolliet across Wisconsin and then down the Mississippi to Arkansas; it was the canoe that scouted, explored, and pioneered the first routes across the continent. It was the canoe that carried commerce and civilization, along with all their concomitant blessings and curses, from Atlantic to Pacific.

What we choose to emphasize now, of course, is the more benign aspect of our Trappers and Rangers, their capacity to take us out into the wild world, away from the distur-

bances and discontents that have followed in the wake of the Voyageurs' canoes. And so you will find, among the eight-hundred-plus canoe models you can choose from on today's market, an Escape and a Hidden Pond. Take a Departure and go in search of Independence, Liberty, Freedom, and Solitude. Give yourself up to Fantasy and Reverie. Even larger, however, than the liberation or exploration group is the critter category. Who would not want a canoe as water-wise and playful as an Otter, as sleek and streamlined as a Loon, as buoyant as a Brant? In our canoes we are no longer alien, no longer Lear's poor, bare-forked animal, but creatures among fellow creatures, chattering and swooping along the riverbank with the Kingfisher, soaring and diving with the Osprey and the Eagle, quorking and cavorting with the Raven. The more aggressive among us are Piranhas, feeding, I suppose, on any of our comrades foolish enough to capsize. Or if it should be a forging of bonds with the human rather than the animal world we desire, we can take to the water with a Pal, Chum, or Companion; a Sweetheart or, indeed, a whole Family.

On the other hand, if this buddy-buddy stuff and the company of a mere Fisherman or Duck Hunter or plain old Sportspal sounds just too ho-hum, you can forge a chancy liaison with a Fanatic, a Maverick, or an Acrobat, go on a Rampage or flip out in an Outrage. You can go nuclear with a Fusion, heliocentric with a Sunburst, intergalactic with a Rocket, a Probe, or a Starship; blow yourself into Infinity, pick up the

pieces with Synergy, and fry a flap-jack over a Flashfire.

What's in a name? Our yearnings, of course, our hopes of becoming the hottest of the whitewater rodeo riders, of cruising along on the six-foot swells of the Nahanni or following the 1,600 miles of the Yukon from Lake Tagish to the Bering Sea. We name our canoes for the rivers we want to travel, for places we'd like to be, for creatures and people whose powers, spirit, and grace we wish we possessed: the Falcon, the Peregrine, the Penobscot, the Micmac, the Ojibway.

Canoes inspire, however, not just the advertising consultants whose job it is to think up zingy names for their clients' products. Just about any devotee of the canoe will, given half a chance, wallow in simile and metaphor, too. Wallace Nutting, writing in *Maine Beautiful* (1924) about the virtues of the guide canoe, could hardly contain himself. "The shape is the embodiment of an Indian dream. We may think that the horns of the moon and the curves of the graceful birch, and the crescent beach of the Maine lakes gave the suggestion. The result at least is perfection. The canoe combines more than any other human creation the practical and the ideal, reminding us of `the perfect woman, nobly planned.'" If Nutting had but one canoe to name, what would he choose to call it? Indian Dream, Horns of the Moon, Crescent Beach? Or would Wordsworth prevail with "Perfect Woman"?

As for me, I have my eye on a boat that would, I suspect, even surpass Nutting's Indian dream. Not many years back, Rollin Thurlow of

Atkinson, Maine, designed a wood-and-canvas canoe he called the Atkinson Traveler. Based on the classic 18-foot, 6-inch E.M. White guide canoe, it has all the beauty and handling qualities of its venerable ancestor, but coming in a foot shorter and fifteen pounds lighter, it's easier for runtier types like me to handle solo and on the portage trail. And when I go up to Atkinson to build my Traveler under Rollins tutelage, I'll make it not twelve but fourteen inches deep, so I will have a canoe that in name and in the flesh will inspire me to work at becoming what I still yearn to be—a Deep Traveler, a thinking and thoughtful traveler, a profound and playful and goofball traveler, an otter and thistle and loon of a traveler, plying the waters of this sweet earth in a canoe that is a canoe that is all canoe and then some.

—Author of A Canoeist's Sketchbook, *Robert Kimber is a freelance writer whose articles on outdoor and environmental subjects appear in regional and national magazines. He lives in Temple, Maine.*

The Wooden Boat Shop, Seattle, WA, (800) 933-3600. Supplies, plans and assistance for do-it-yourself kayak builders.

Vermont Canoe Products Company, Newport, VT, (802) 754-2307

On Overconsumption

Let's be morbid for a moment. It is a week after your death and those close to you are getting together to "dispose" of your belongings. None of them, it so happens, is interested in paddling—the loves of their lives are computers, video games, and hanging out at malls. What are they going to do with six canoes, fourteen kayaks, four rafts, enough PFDs to demonstrate the entire history of the product development of the PFD, and God-only-knows what other flotsam and jetsam. So,

as is the custom in our society, someone makes a run to the dump with all that stuff no one can even identify, much less use.

Hey, save them a dump run! Curb those nasty collecting habits. Trim your belongings. Simplify your life. If you do get something new, give away something you don't use. You will be happier if you ever have to move (as in moving van) and you won't be contributing to excessive abuse of our world's resources—hey, where do you think all that plastic and wood comes from? Not from thin air!

Better yet, before you even head out to the paddler's supply store, consider repairing that ripped PFD or chipped fiberglass kayak. You say you're clueless? That's all right— Maine outdoorswoman extraordinaire Annie Getchell is not, and her

book, *The Essential Outdoor Gear Manual* (Camden, ME: Ragged Mountain Press, 1995) can walk you through most common repairs from stitching up a PFD to laying fiberglass patches. This is a very readable, very useful, very delightfully illustrated book.

Nylon web seat is a good alternative to cane for those who store canoes outside.

Writing about maintenance and repair brings guilty moments—every glance at the fading hulls racked outside my office window is a reminder that our boats sure could use some TLC. So I felt a lot better after spotting Zip Kellogg's (a local canoe

RUMINATIONS ON ROOF RACKS

In 1935, John C. Phillips and Thomas D. Cabot wrote on carrying a boat on a car in *Quick-Water and Smooth*: "In the absence of beams or frame, the best method is to put two pillows, an old quilt, a mattress or an old tire at each end of the car roof, and if these will not raise the canoe high enough for the gunwales to clear and to give full vision for the driver, place a wooden crosspiece in front between the canoe and the pillows."

Times change. Today we head out to the store to buy a fancy roof rack, or roof "system," as they sometimes call them. The difference between a roof "rack" and a roof "system" will often be told in dollars. For example, for between $10 and $30 (1997 prices) you can buy simple blocks of foam to attach to a kayak or canoe and then strap the boat to your roof. Or you can buy a fancy system for anywhere from about $90 to $350, depending on how many accessories you buy to customize your rack for canoe, bike, windsurfer, skis, and so on. These are rough figures but they give you the idea . . .

There are several major manufacturers of racks (see the list of a few, below). One good way to deal with this rack/system issue is to speak with friends about their likes and dislikes with their systems. Another is to call a few members of an area paddling group to learn their preferences. Price, availability, and compatibility with your vehicle will lead you to a decision.

Thule, Yakima, and others build fine rack systems, and each has its devotees, but none come cheaply. These manufacturers have designed rack systems for just about any vehicle model. (It used to be that racks were universal—one size fits all—but progress has its consequences.) The manufacturers have booklets in which you can look up your vehicle and determine which rack system is compatible. Unfortunately, that rack is tailored to fit that specific vehicle model, so if you get a new car or truck you'll have to go back to the rack people and look in their little booklet again to see which rack "feet" are compatible with your new wheels.

One manufacturer, Quik-N-Easy, makes aluminum support brackets that you attach to two-by-fours. These brackets currently sell for around $50 (1997 prices). (Two-by-fours are additional.) The catch? *Your vehicle must have rain gutters* into which the brackets fit. Unfortunately, car designers don't, as a rule, take paddlers into consideration when they're dreaming up next year's sleek lines and new doodads—which means most new cars don't have rain gutters. You may want to decide which model car or truck to buy based on whether it has gutters!

Besides buying a rack from a manufacturer, you might try the homemade variety. If you own a truck you can rig up something simple and strong by visiting lumber and hardware stores. Sometimes you can find plans or kits for do-it-yourself racks in the classified ads of paddling magazines. As mentioned above, you can also buy inexpensive foam blocks intended to hold a boat on a cartop. They're okay for occasional boaters, but serious paddlers seldom use them. They've been known to slip and slide, not something pleasant to experience at sixty-five miles an hour on a gusty day as you head across a high, narrow suspension bridge where the oncoming traffic is mostly 18-wheelers.

So, the bottom line on racks is beware . . . you can easily spend hundreds of dollars on a rack and all its accessories. Ponder your options, considering both price and cost—the cost, that is, of losing your expensive boat off the top of your car. And remember, racks are made for any vehicle imaginable. It's really a matter of which rack suits your vehicle—and your pocketbook.

And incidentally, if you have a bad back—listen up. Don't ever lift the entire weight of the boat to get it on the rack. Lift just one end of it to the rack and then *slide* it along. Or, you can invest in a gadget with a swing boom and geared winch that raises and lowers your boat from a Yakima or Thule rack (from Lancelot Company, Millerton, NY; 518-789-4008). And, yes, you'll want to tie your boat down somehow (see Chapter 5 sidebar on knot tying).

Commercial racks:

Jemb Rack Systems, Williston, VT; (800) 272-5362

Mirage Truck Racks, Williston, VT; (800) 272-5362

Quik-N-Easy, (213) 358-0562

Rail-N-Rack, Lewiston, ID; (800) 243-9592

Thule, Seymour, CT; (800) 238-2388 (pronounced "TWO-lee")

Yakima Products, Arcata, CA; (800) 348-9231

Or take a look at some of the small boat trailers:

M.O. Trailers, Goshen, IN; (219) 533-0824

Trailer Lite Corporation, Camarillo, CA; (800) 854-8366

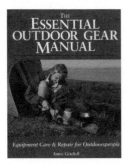

celebrity) 10-year-old Royalex Tripper in a parking lot. The thing had led a rough life: Dings, dents, and gouges nearly obscured its worn-through skid plates; the wood rails were splintery and gray; mildew blackened the cane seats. But the boat was still solid, ready to paddle, and obviously had some stories to tell.

Many paddlers (probably most) could never devote enough time on the water to accumulate that kind of wear. Even so, with some simple preventive maintenance through the years your Royalex canoe will likely outlive you.

SPLIT PADDLE BLADE

Repair split with clear epoxy

Sandwich between wood blocks & clamp evenly.

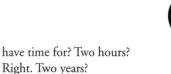

Filling Those Winter Nights—
Build Your Own Boat

Take winter by storm this year—build your own boat. The boat building process will surely blow your mind, build character, cause you to dust off that four-letter vocabulary, and, with any luck, leave in its wake something to paddle. Maybe even something beautiful.

But before you gut the basement and fill your house with sawdust and toxic resins, consider the following:

- What method do I learn from: by watching, by doing, through books, or video?
- What type of boat do I want? How big?
- What types of materials do I want to use? Traditional or fully synthetic, or a combination?
- How extensive a project do I have time for? Two hours? Right. Two years?
- How much space will it take up? And will this project drive any housemates out of the house? If so, is this good or bad?
- How much will it cost?

Get your hands on a number of the books on the following pages. Peruse the pictures. Picture yourself in the midst of such projects, or paddling your own handmade craft, and then finalize your decision. By all accounts, home boatbuilding is rewarding, and taxing, beyond your wildest dreams. But beware: it is also known to be addictive.

Small Boat Building

Boatbuilder's Manual, Sixth Edition

by Charles C. Walbridge

(Birmingham, AL: Menasha Ridge Press, 1987)

That this book has been through six editions over the past twenty years is but one form of testimony to its value to the home builder. Walbridge hits on not only all the aspects of building kayaks and canoes that you would expect (like properties of resins, plugs and molds, laying up, etc.), but also on the less easy-to-find aspects (like safety when working with stinky and sometimes toxic materials, the ethics of copying another design—the word is *don't*—or making spray skirts).

One can still build a boat relatively cheaply using materials mentioned in Walbridge's book. But not so many people are doing this now as were a few years ago. The reason? Materials (plastics technology) have changed as have production procedures. So the question becomes this: do you want to lay down cloth, resin, etc., or would you prefer to lay down a charge card? How do you spend your

REMINDER

Just about all of the books mentioned in this catalog can be obtained by: (a) patronizing a local bookstore; (b) contacting one of the many paddling suppliers listed in Chapter 3 (most have toll-free phone numbers); or (c) inquiring at a library. See also the section in Chapter 1 called "About This Book" for good sources of hard-to-find books.

winter evenings, anyway?

This book has plenty of useful information for the amateur builder. Unfortunately, it was not well edited, so there are plenty of typos. But all in all, if you are thinking of building using reinforced plastics (saving plenty of money), you would do well to take a look at this manual.

Canoes and Kayaks for the Backyard Builder

by Skip Snaith

(Camden, ME: International Marine Publishing Company, 1989)

If you are attracted to projects, especially ones that are not likely to cost you a bundle, then Skip Snaith's book will show you how to build a simple canoe or kayak from a few strips of plywood, a bit of fiberglass and epoxy, and a bit of time. You won't need much more than a few simple tools and a place to work in order to turn out a light and strong craft. And if finished well, even plywood can be attractive.

Snaith calls his technique the "taped-seam" or "tack-and-tape" method of construction. It entails building a simple form (that's what gives a

boat its shape) and bending the long plywood planks or strips over the form, then fiberglassing over the seams to make them waterproof. Finally, you paint it, attach gunwales, and paddle off into the horizon. He estimates twenty to one hundred hours and $150 to $250 to complete the project, depending on lots of variables. A safe bet would be to count on the upper end of these estimates or a bit more—then there are no shocking surprises.

For the simplicity of its method and economy of both time and money, Snaith's book sets an admirable example.

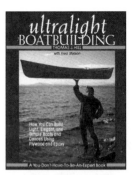

Ultralight Boatbuilding

by Thomas J. Hill

(Camden, ME: International Marine Publishing Company, 1987)

Maybe you remember a popular fashion model in the 1970s named

Twiggy. She was a matchstick of a human being. All the parts were there, but not by much, and there wasn't one extra fat cell on her entire body. If you would like to build a boat, particularly a canoe or skiff, along Twiggian lines, then Thomas Hill has something for you in *Ultralight Boatbuilding.*

The technique involves using plywood in the lapstrake method of construction. There are no frames or ribs in the finished craft. Just a bit of glue holds the whole kit and caboodle together. Not even many tools are needed to build one of these fine, light, somewhat delicate craft. What are needed, as with many projects, are time and patience.

In addition to plenty of good photos, and chapters on lofting, scarfing, planking, and varnishing, there is a "gallery of designs" in which one can sample the range of boat styles to consider building. While it may seem strange that plywood could be associated with beauty, Thomas Hill has proven that it can.

Fifty Plates from William Picard Stephens' "Canoe and Boat Building: A Complete Manual For Amateurs"

by William Picard Stephens
(Mystic, CT: Mystic Seaport Museum Press, 1987)

William Picard Stephens (1856–1946) was well known in canoeing circles during the late nineteenth and early twentieth centuries. His home port was New York, where he was active in the New York Canoe Club, the first club to form in the United States (1871). Nine years later, the American Canoe Association was born.

In later life Stephens became an expert on yachts—he was editor of *Lloyd's Register of American Yachts*, wrote *Tradition and Memories of American Yachting*, and had a keen interest in the America's Cup races. But in his salad days he had focused his attention on canoes and similar craft. The New York Canoe Club was based in St. George, on Staten Island, and it was there that he designed and built sailing canoes.

His book *Canoe and Boat Building: A Complete Manual for Amateurs, Containing Plain and Comprehensive Directions for the Construction of Canoes, Rowing and Sailing Boats and Hunting Craft* was first published in 1885, when Stephens was twenty-nine. It appeared in numerous editions and is now both out of print and hard to find. Fortunately, the Mystic Seaport Museum in Connecticut has reproduced the design plates from that book for those who would like to build from "old school," classic designs. The designs are for a variety of boats, among them open and

Advanced Strokes

Many paddle rafts bomb down rivers relying solely upon forward strokes and backstrokes. You can move across the river's surface much more effectively if you teach your crew drawstrokes and prystrokes. These strokes will allow you to move laterally fast and allow you to navigate narrow passages easier.

—JB & TB

55

covered canoes, sailing rigs, etc. The prospective builder would need to work from these simple drawings of the various boats.

If you are thinking about building a canoe or other small boat, one of the first questions you might ask is, "What type of boat do I want and how and where will I use it?" If you favor an older style craft over a sleek, modern racing boat, you could do far worse than consulting the designs of William Picard Stephens.

Canoe Building

Canoecraft

by Ted Moores and Merilyn Mohr
(Buffalo, NY: Firefly Books, 1988)
Looking for something to keep you in mischief when the snow flies? This book on wood-strip (most often long slender cedar strips) construction will take you from the stage of thinking about it right through to maintenance and repair of your "baby." It goes without saying that this book is for the project-oriented person. The investment will be one of time much more than money, but the finished product will give new meaning and untold dimension to the word dividend. The photographs (some present day, some historical) are well chosen and illustrate the authors' points well; the drawings are at least that

good, if not better. The book includes plans and design details for seven different craft, from the general purpose to flatwater racing-style canoe. If you are thinking you want to get away from your spouse, spend the winter in the basement, and build what this book calls "the poor man's yacht," then there is no hope for you. Get *Canoecraft*.

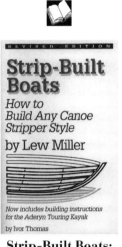

Strip-Built Boats: How to Build Any Canoe Stripper Style

by Lew Miller
(Kirkland, WA: Canoe America Associates, 1992)
This is a bare-bones guide to building using the strip method. If you work well by trial and error, this slim booklet may be enough. But if you like things spelled out in detail, try one of the longer books on the strip building method.

Before you start a project it is a good idea to ask yourself, "How do I learn new things, anyway?" Some people learn best by watching, some by doing, some through books, some by thinking. What method is easiest for you? After you've pondered this question you'll be better suited to proceed with building a boat.

Building a Chippewa Indian Birchbark Canoe

by Robert E. Ritzenthaler
(Milwaukee: Milwaukee Public Museum, 1984)
This is a dandy little forty-page book, liberally illustrated, that shows how to build a canoe out of birch bark, cedar, and other natural materials. There are chapters about gathering the materials, about shaping them, and about how to "sew" the craft together. If you are thinking you might like to try building a traditional canoe from scratch, take a look at this booklet; it will give you an idea of the beauty of the final product, as well as the commitment of time and energy needed to pull it off successfully.

This booklet even has a nice

> *"I believe the reason personal and recreational uses of the canoe increased was because the canoe remained very much the same as it was. Few of man's early inventions have absorbed and survived technological progress so brilliantly; few primitive concepts have come through so clearly."*
> —*Walter Teller, in* On the River (Sheridan House, 1988)

map showing the range over which white birch grows in North America (from coast to coast, including much of Canada and parts of northcentral and northeastern United States), as well as the different regional styles of canoes.

Building the Maine
Guide Canoe

by Jerry Stelmok
(New York: Lyons & Burford, 1992)

If you want to build a very handsome, classic craft you will be proud of for many years, follow Jerry Stelmok's directions. He is a master. The boats he builds become instant heirlooms, and he will show you how to do just that in this book. Books like this one cause one to stop and inquire, "Might we be in a golden age of canoe building *right now?*"

In addition to providing the prospective builder with chapters on virtually every aspect of building a wood-and-canvas canoe, Stelmok has illustrated, with pho-

tos and excellent sketches, many of the details. If you are going to build a traditional wood and canvas canoe, this is *the* book you should consult as your guide.

Another book, by Stelmok and Rollin Thurlow, is *The Wood & Canvas Canoe: A Complete Guide to Its History, Construction, Restoration, and Maintenance* (Gardiner, ME: Tilbury House, 1988). Virtually anyone contemplating this type of construction would do well to read these books. Be the beneficiary of a couple of masters and turn out not only a utilitarian craft, but also a beautiful one.

How to Build
an Indian Canoe

by George S. Fichter
(New York: David McKay Company, 1977)

Fichter's book is an adaptation and abridgment of E.T. Adney and Howard Chappelle's classic *The Bark Canoes and Skin Boats of North America*. As did the classic, Fichter's abridgment details the

BETULA PAPYRIFERA
(Canoe Birch)

by Annie Getchell

*Are the means
primitive or sophisticated
slaughter?
husbandry?
to skin a living thing—
its seed the spoils
for sons to come.*

*Thawing wind swirls fog and
ruffles tendrils on the stiff hide
rolled up raw and seeping
sharp astringent smell.*

*First we'll peel to ruddy inside
then gore and wrap and lace
around steambent ribs
with dusky damp spruce roots.*

*After big rains, we'll follow
the ice
and fill this vessel with
spring harvest of
fiddleheads and lily beds.*

*Gather spruce blood when
we find it
to seal against the seasons
until the brittle skin
grows into forest floor.*

Then we'll hunt one more.

57

OF CANOES AND GEOLOGIC TIME

by Annie Getchell

The bark canoe was plenty sophisticated by the time whites started thrashing around in the new world. Of the craft's evolution there is but little trace, due to the compostable nature of early native prototypes. Birchbark boats of yore modestly disintegrated to duff, each generation's innovation preserved as collective knowledge.

Which isn't a bad thing. In fact, the idea of defunct, inert, modern canoes stacking up across North America is starting to keep me up nights. I dream that some remote Saskatchewan towns are bidding now for the economic privilege of becoming the hemisphere's first canoe repository.

Those fragile and temporary sheets of paper birch have been eclipsed by twentieth-century materials whose half-life has yet to be realized. Under "ideal conditions," a plastic hull will last forever, chirp the manufacturers. Maybe, but how many people *really* store their boats out of the sun, or unscrew wooden rails for the winter? And do we *want* the shrunken corpses of infinite Discos to last infinitely?

Martin Brown, Maine Guide and renowned raconteur, offers true field experience when it comes to assessing the longevity of modern canoe materials. Forever maybe for the average guy, says Martin, but used commercially, a Royalex canoe is viable for about five years. He explains: "Like old people, who are brittle . . . as

long as they don't fall on the ice they'll keep on trucking." Martin also suggests that sandwich construction has become flimsier—not stiffer—over the years. He contends that early Royalex boats, such as the venerable Blue Hole, are outliving more recent models (this may be due more to manufacturers' penny pinching than engineering considerations).

Steve Scarborough, designer and principal at Dagger Canoe Company, with a long history of wooden paddle–building behind him, has another view. "We punish these newer boats more than ever, as our skills have evolved along with the designs. ABS–sandwich boats are made with premium plastic—and canoes and kayaks represent some of the toughest tests for any material."

construction of canoes as it was done by native North Americans. It is nicely illustrated, provides an easy read, is short (ninety pages), and would give a young reader a taste of how it was done (or *is* done for those so inclined). For someone who isn't sure whether or not to take on such a project, this might give some insight into the process, the tools and supplies needed, etc. Ultimately the question becomes, do you want the gist and a quick read, or would you prefer the original version with all the details?

The Weymontaching Birchbark Canoe

by Camil Guy
(Ottawa: National Museums of Canada,
Anthropological Papers, No. 20, 1974)

The Weymontaching Indians live about 150 miles north of Montreal and have been canoe

builders probably since time immemorial. Camil Guy had the opportunity to observe all the details of the canoe building process while studying the Weymontaching in the 1960s. Guy writes of their ingenious use of local raw materials to create an extraordinarily handsome and utilitarian bark canoe. First he discusses the materials and tools— the bark itself, the general-purpose crooked knife, and other necessary items. Then he takes the reader step by step through the building process—assembling the frame, shaping the sides, measuring, lashing with roots, caulking, etc. The booklet is only about fifty pages long but gives the essence of the process. It is well illustrated with drawings and photos.

Despite specialized refinements from clever designers, Royalex springs eternal, even after it has become too floppy to paddle. With this realization comes a new kind of respect for linear polyethylene and—gasp—aluminum canoes, both rendered from recyclable materials. These hulls represent the best choice available today for environmentally savvy canoeists (wood-and-canvas construction included, due to nasty fillers and paints).

Aluminum for aluminum's sake—it already exists, thanks to the military. And canoes are a great and peaceful use for post-hawk (we hope) leavings.

Rotomolded linear polyethylene, albeit not renewable, is thoroughly recyclable, and can be sourced from a witches' brew of second-hand plastic. Credit Paul Farrow, a former environmental cleanup executive, for his ingenuity in this regard. His Massachusetts company, Walden Paddlers, is the first manufacturer to source its compact kayaks from one hundred percent post-consumer and industrial waste. Ironically, some of Walden's raw material originates in Dagger Canoe's Tennessee plant.

Scarborough laughs when I argue that wooden canoes are still better because they are "sustainable." "What's sustainable about cutting old-growth cedar?" he counters. Plastic sources are not limited to petroleum. "Source resins can be vegetable. During a glut, we'll get epoxy from oil," explains Scarborough. "During a shortage, we'll make plastics from soy."

In the midst of these developments, I have always lived in places where paper birch grow . . . greedily gathering curls of chalky skin from the snow as if they were seashells. Blushing sheets of elastic possibility that can be woven or modeled or painted upon. It is not likely that boatbuilders will come to use birchbark again, so my fantasies go up in smoke—how do other people start their fires?

—Annie Getchell, author of The Essential Outdoor Gear Manual, *paddles Kevlar and Royalex canoes whenever possible. She would like a birchbark model.*

59

Building Lapstrake Canoes

by Walter J. Simmons
(Lincolnville, ME:
Duck Trap Woodworking, 1981)

The canoes built by Simmons could easily grace a mantel or find their way into museums. They are works of art. But he would probably rather see them on the water, where they belong. A boat needs the support that water provides.

Simmons' book will help you think about, and then build, a lapstrake-style canoe. He recommends quarter-inch planking of cedar—northern white cedar to be exact. It is workable, bends easily, soaks up comparatively little water in use, and is sufficiently rugged. Furthermore, he writes, "These lapstrake canoes are far and away the easiest of all round-bottomed lapstrake boats to build." Simmons gives the builder all the line drawings, all the practical details, all the coaching needed. He even leaves note-taking space on the pages so one can make additions or comments. Because virtually all of us will encounter different problems and have different questions during the building process, this note-taking business is a fine idea.

Canoes and Canoeing

by Percy W. Blandford
(New York: W.W. Norton & Company, 1968)

If a traditional kayak or canoe built in a traditional style is your calling, scrounge a copy of Blandford's book. He includes plenty of draw-

> "*. . . a good and reliable boat may be built by any one of ordinary mechanical ability in less than a week's time, and at an expense of from five to seven dollars.*"
> *—from* Canvas Canoes; How to Build Them *(1899)*

ings, specifications, and lists of supplies needed. He includes chapters on accessories, making a sailing rig, and more.

Blandford's boat building technique employs wooden frames and a fabric cover. It is an inexpensive style to be sure, but the uses of this type of craft would not likely include big water.

Don't overlook books like

Blandford's. Granted, his technique isn't on the cutting edge, but if that's not where you want to be anyway, he might be able to help you.

Kayak Building

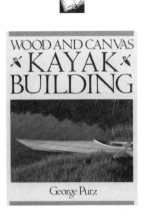

Wood and Canvas Kayak Building

by George Putz
(Camden, ME: Ragged Mountain Press, 1990)

If you lay down a credit card for a sea kayak, your next month's bill will sting a bit. If you listen to George Putz, you'll have yourself a handsome craft of some 17 or 18 feet, a new skill, no shortage of pride, an appreciation of history, and, in all likelihood, a new addiction—sea kayaking. Putz takes even the novice-but-budding boat-builder from soup-to-nuts. And the nice thing is that he does it in just over a hundred pages, so you don't need to spend ten years fathoming the book before you tackle the project. He gives you what you will need, like sources for tools, manufacturers and suppliers of materials, but not a lot of extra fluff.

If a boat building project is brewing inside you and a sea kayak needs to be the result, let George Putz be your guide.

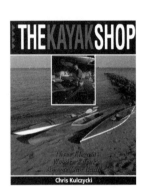

The Kayak Shop: Three Elegant Wooden Kayaks Anyone Can Build

by Chris Kulczycki
(Camden, ME: Ragged Mountain Press, 1993)

Want to build yourself a dream boat? The book's cover alone is likely to bring on pronounced lightheadedness in those thinking about building a kayak . . .

Kulczycki's principle themes in sharing the process of plywood kayak building are: simplicity, lightness, economy, and aesthetics. He gives the building details as well as plans for three craft:

- a round-bottomed, high-performance 16-foot single sea kayak
- a hard-chine 18-foot sea kayak
- a compounded plywood 20-foot double kayak

He also includes other practical things one needs in building—like a list of tools, suppliers, etc. The book is well illustrated, so you can easily see what the process and result are supposed to look like. One very important tip he gives is to use good quality plywoods.

Many a family, many a spouse, many a roommate has had to endure life with a boatbuilder. "Harrowing" would probably be one of the first words to come into the mind of one of these unfortunate souls to describe that relationship. Kulczycki is no exception and his tale is worth reading.

My parents returned home one day to find the patio transformed into a boatyard. Not appreciative of my breakthroughs in naval architecture, they forbade me to launch my first design. But, convinced my craft was as seaworthy as the Queen Mary, I

recruited a friend to help me carry it to a nearby stream for sea trials. We didn't have any oars or paddles, but that didn't matter much since our stream was only 20 feet wide and, fortunately, flowed slowly. In any case my pram leaked too much to go far.

▲

Kulczycki appears to have come a long way with regard to boatyards, naval architecture, seaworthiness, and even oars and paddles. But whether his parents have given up that silly idea of having a patio is another matter. What good is a patio anyway?

Baidarka: The Kayak

by George Dyson
(Edmonds, WA: Alaska Northwest Publishing Company, 1986)

This book is about a man and his passion for a particular type of boat. Baidarka is a Russian word for a specialized, generally long kayak well suited for travel in the northeast Pacific Ocean. George Dyson has had a fascination with the craft for years and has admirably traced its history. He has also been instrumental both through this book and as director of the Baidarka Historical Society (Port Moody, B.C.) in creating renewed interest in this skin-covered craft of the Pacific.

Historically Baidarkas were made of such materials as driftwood, whale bone, and sea lion skin. Dyson's construction technique employs aluminum tubing as a primary material. He explains that there may be one, two, or three hatches for as many occupants of the boat. The length of these craft makes them stable and well suited to the frequently windy,

choppy, tidal archipelagos of the northern Pacific coastal regions.

Baidarka includes plans for building at home, and numerous fine photos and illustrations dug up from libraries and archives across the North American continent. The man did his homework and shares his passion well.

Inuit Kayaks in Canada: A Review of Historical Records and Construction

by Eugene Y. Arim
(Ottawa: National Museums of Canada, 1987)

This is an academic study of the kayak varieties made by Arctic peoples from eastern Siberia to Greenland—no small neighborhood. While there are fifty or sixty distinct models from these regions, this book focuses on three groups: the Mackenzie, the Central Canadian, and the East Canadian. Several scale line drawings are included as well as a number of attractive reproductions of old photos. If you're *really* into the details of kayak history, this book makes excellent reading.

Qajaq: Kayaks of Siberia and Alaska

by David W. Zimmerly
(Juneau, AK: Division of State Museums, 1986)

It would be far beyond the scope of *The Whole Paddler's Catalog* to deal with the history and development of small boats from all the regions of the world. But because *Qajaq* is such a significant and well-done book, touching on numerous aspects of the kayak through history, it is highly recommended.

This book accompanied a 1986–87 exhibit in Alaska. It includes wonderful drawings, plans, historical photos, and touches on issues as varied, yet related, as kayak hats of the early days and kayak construction using skins and other locally found materials. Oh, how times change. Today it's a locally found Visa card that produces a kayak.

Zimmerly did his homework. He traveled from California to Leningrad in search of information on the early history of the Siberian and Alaskan kayaks. If you've got a hankering to learn something of

THE CASE FOR ROCKER

by Chris Kulczycki

Of all the design factors affecting a sea kayak's performance, rocker is the least understood by the average paddler. Rocker is the upward curve of the kayak's keel line over its length. If you were to place on the floor a kayak with pronounced rocker, such as a whitewater kayak, its middle will touch the floor while its ends at the waterline will be several inches above the floor. A boat without any rocker placed on the same floor will touch the floor over most of its length. The amount of rocker designed into a kayak has tremendous effect on its tracking, handling, and speed. And there is too little rocker in most sea kayaks.

Most paddlers know that rocker decreases a boat's ability to track, or hold a straight course. If you were to paddle two boats that were identical except for the amount of rocker in their hulls, the "flatter" hull would undoubtedly track better. If, however, the ends of the more rockered boat were finer, or sharper, than the flat hull, the rockered boat might track just as well. But why add rocker to a hull if we must simply compensate for it? Well, there are a few very significant benefits to rockered hulls.

Rockered hulls are faster. Yes, I know that a few ill-informed kayaking pundits still cling to the notion that rocker decreases speed, but they are wrong; we have only to look at other fast, low-powered hulls to see this. Sailboats, fast pulling boats, even flatwater racing kayaks have considerable rocker. In these boats, as in sea kayaks, there are two main forces that must be overcome when paddling (or rowing, or sailing). The

first is the waves generated as the hull moves through the water. A boat creates a bow wave where it cuts through the water and a stern wave as the water comes together again at the boat's end. The paddler's energy is expended both in creating these waves and in pushing them along. Here the length of the boat is very important; in order for waves to move faster, or easier, they must be farther apart. In fact, a boat's theoretical top speed in knots (a knot is 1.15 mph) is 1.34 times the square root of the length of waterline. This speed can be raised a bit if the hull is very narrow in proportion to its length. So if wave generation were the only factor, kayaks would be shaped like very long pencils. But we estimate that creating and pushing those waves takes only about 60 percent of a sea kayaker's effort. Most of the remaining effort goes toward overcoming hull friction, the second force the paddler faces. Wetted surface area is the term for how much skin area is generating friction below the waterline. The perfect low-wetted-surface-area boat would be shaped like half a basketball, a hull shape with maximum rocker. It's clear that a good compromise between the pencil-like and the ball-like hull will have a fair amount of rocker. A trip to the local boatyard will confirm that boat and yacht designers have known this for centuries.

Rockered hulls also handle better. Imagine a hull without rocker suspended between two waves, its bow and stern buried in those waves while its mid-section barely touches the water. The ends of such a boat can "root," causing erratic tracking.

To compensate for lack of rocker the designer must add additional height and buoyancy to the boat's bow and stern. This creates windage at the worst possible place—the boat's ends. Wind pressure on a high bow or stern compromises handling further and pushes the kayak off course. The ocean is rarely flat, but flat hulls fit only flat water, another reason that ocean-going sailboats, fishing dories, surf boats, and whitewater kayaks have lots of rocker.

As the West Greenland style and other hard-chine kayaks continue to gain popularity, another reason for increasing rocker becomes evident. With hard-chine hulls (those with fairly sharp angles where the bottom meets the sides), drag can be created by water "swirling" around or over the chine. As the hull slices through the water some of the displaced water moves from the low-pressure area under the hull to the high-pressure area alongside the hull. As water flows over the sharp chine, eddies are created that slow the boat. A solution to this would be to design the chine to have the same curvature in plan view as in profile view, but on a 22-inch-wide kayak this would mean 11 inches of rocker, too much even by my standard. Still, it's obvious that adding rocker will minimize those pesky pressure differences.

Admittedly, there are some drawbacks to adding rocker. Drawing a rockered hull that both tracks and handles well takes far more experience and testing than designing a "flat" hull. A boat with a rockered hull will have a limited weight range because it depends on fine ends for tracking; if those ends are not submerged it won't track. So if you want a boat that can be paddled by both your 80-pound niece and your 250-pound brother, get one with little rocker.

So how much rocker should a sea kayak have? My single designs have between 2½ inches and 4½ inches of rocker. They track very well as long as the paddler is heavy enough to properly submerge the ends. They turn easily and do well in heavy seas and wind.

Despite the many benefits and few compromises of rockered hulls, there is still resistance to rockered hulls among some sea kayakers. You really should try out a few properly designed rockered hulls before buying your next boat; you'll be pleasantly surprised.

—Chris Kulczycki is a builder of custom wooden kayaks and kayak kits in Annapolis, Maryland. He writes for SAIL, Sea Kayaker, Cruising World, Ocean Nagivator, *and* Fine Woodworking, *among other magazines.*

---

the background of your cruiser, slalom, or squirt boat, sit down with this slender (one hundred-page) book for an hour or two.

⅄

The Arctic kayak appeals to us on an emotional level beyond that inspired by more prosaic items of material culture. It has a romantic image associated with fur-clad Eskimos silently gliding along, hunting their sustenance or playing like otters in the waves; it illustrates the artistry and ingenuity of man in fashioning a superior means of transportation in an unforgiving climate.

⅄

More Good Books on Building Boats

Building Your Kevlar Canoe: A Foolproof Method and Three Foolproof Designs by James Moran (Camden, ME: Ragged Mountain Press, 1995)

Building the Wood-Strip Canoe by Stephen A. Bolesky (Pownal, VT: Garden Way Publishing, 1988)

The Stripper's Guide to Canoe Building, Third Edition, by David Hazen (Larkspur, CA: Tamal Vista Publications, 1983)

Building a Strip Canoe by Gil Gilpatrick (Freeport, ME: DeLorme Publishing Company, 1993)

The Modern Canoe: A Practical Guide to Woodstrip/Resin Construction by Stephen Pellerin (Toronto: Doubleday Canada, 1994)

The Aleutian Kayak: Origins, Construction, and Use of the Traditional Seagoing Baidarka by Wolfgang Brinck (Camden, ME: Ragged Mountain Press, 1995)

63

To Paddle or Not to Paddle: Making and Rigging Sails and Poles

Getting a free ride courtesy of a little zephyr can be a lot of fun. Whether you jury-rig your canoe or sea kayak by hanging a sheet, poncho, tent fly, or rag on a stick, or prefer something a little "yachtier," something with lee boards and a tiller, it doesn't really matter. Rig up anything you can. It will add a dimension to your experiences on

the water that, if nothing else, will surely give you a good story to tell.

Ditto with canoe poling. Learning to use a pole effectively takes a little time, but it is well worth the effort. When you tire of using a paddle, poling will provide a welcome respite.

Sail Your Canoe: How to Add Sails to Your Canoe

by John Bull
(Leicester, UK: Cordee, 1989)

If you find the idea of living life on the edge (of the gunwale) exciting, you really owe it to yourself to try sailing a canoe. It's a gas. And John Bull has put together a great sixty-page book on how to rig your canoe for some added fun.

John Bull leans toward the fancier end of the spectrum. In *Sail Your Canoe,* he gives all the particulars for tailoring a canoe so it can be sailed with ease. The book is project oriented (plenty of drawings, measurements, blueprints, etc.) with plenty of details. One minor glitch is that the book was published in Britain, so the parts suppliers are also British.

John Bull is not giving you a line of bull when he says "the pleasure to be had from sailing a canoe is out of all proportion to the very modest investment it requires."

Canoeing with Sail and Paddle

by John D. Hayward, M.D.
(New York: Frederick A. Stokes, 1893)

This one from 1893 won't give you the latest in racing rules, sailing techniques, etc. But its photos, sketches, and drawings will amuse you to no end.

The Basic Essentials of Canoe Poling

by Harry Rock
(Merrillville, IN.: ICS Books, 1992)

Harry Rock has won many awards as a competition poler. He can make a canoe behave like a rocket.

Because few books have been written exclusively on poling, this one is a welcome one on the scene and Rock shares with the reader the basic principles of poling plus lots of tips. For example, he points out that an experienced poler might be able to assist in a rescue in ways that a paddler might find difficult; he points out that a pole allows one to navigate very, very shallow water—which any experienced paddler will tell you is damnably hard to do with only a paddle. He speaks of the strengths and weaknesses of aluminum, wood, and fiberglass poles (he favors aluminum). He makes some excellent analogies, such as likening some aspects of poling to skiing—choosing a route and maintaining one's balance are surprisingly similar.

But Rock discusses only one of the two major types of poling. He discusses power or competition poling, sometimes called sport poling. The other major type is classic poling. One key difference between the two is the stance taken. For power poling one stands facing straight forward while for classic-style poling one stands on a diagonal. (Garrett Conover discusses the classic stance in his book *Beyond the Paddle—A Canoeists' Guide to Expedition Skills: Poling, Lining, Portaging and Maneuvering Through Ice,* Tilbury House, 1991. See page 32.)

So, while Rock's book does an excellent job on power poling, it should not be considered the end-all on poling. It could have been improved by the inclusion of a list of sources for poles or the components to make one.

64

Canoe Poling

by Al Beletz and Syl Beletz
(St. Louis, MO: A.C. Mackenzie Press, 1974)

While definitely out of date, *Canoe Poling* is still a good source for much of the background one needs in order to have a basic understanding of poling. The authors are veteran polers, and include in their book the history and lore of poling, techniques, tips, competitive poling, and even poling on ice.

The book looks like something spit out by a 1950s mimeograph machine—the sort of thing your fifth-grade teacher handed you umpteen years ago. The quality of the photos is poor, and the table of contents hard to find, but the information is still useful.

Make a Pole

With a little creativity you can make a pole. In the most basic sense, a canoeing pole is nothing more than a big dowel or closet rod. If you know of a dowel-maker nearby, go pester him or her for something about 12 feet long. Tap a piece of metal pipe onto one end to keep the wood from getting frayed or "broomed." And presto . . . but don't be too impressed, because most really good wooden poles are made of ash or spruce. If you are lucky enough to live near any spruce or ash groves you can take a young sapling (say, 1½ inches in diameter) and attach a piece of copper pipe to one end for the "shoe," as it's called.

If using native materials appeals to you, you will enjoy the following method as told by Lynn Franklin in the November/December 1982 issue of *WoodenBoat* magazine:

"You can fashion your own pole, although a canoe pole is made by God who grows it on the north side of a slope in an even-age stand of stunted black spruce. The spruce will have grown slowly—rings close together. Much of it will be dead from lack of light. Herb Hartman swears the best black spruce is dead because it was pissed on by a moose. There are plenty of moose in Maine. That's

what you want, a dead spruce.

"A live pole will be sappy and crack when it dries out. You would have thrown it away by then anyway because it was too heavy. Choose a straight, dried out, black spruce and cut out a 10' piece about the same bigness both ends.

"Shave it to 2"diameter, more or less. Taper it ever so slightly. Now this is the important part: When you pole, your hands get wet and stay wet and get soft. So sand the knots until there is not a blister left in them.

"Salvage a couple of rings of copper pipe to fit your ends. Cut a slot in the ends, work the rings over them, wedge the slot. Then wipe on a couple of coats of boiled linseed oil.

"Now you have an end-over-ender's pole to walk on the bottom going up and to hold your canoe safe and slow coming down.

"See you on the river."

If you don't want to deal with dead spruce or moose pee, you can go to a local metal warehouse and hope to find finished aircraft-grade tubing (sometimes simply designated "round aluminum tubing"), but this can be tricky. Look for grade "6061-T6," the technical specification for the type most often used. One source is the Aircraft Spruce & Specialty Company of Fullerton, California (800-824-1930, or FAX 714-871-7289). If you do find a good source for tubing, then plug the ends with a hard plastic called Delrin, or with wood. Wood, though, tends to "broom" with use and is second-best compared to Delrin. Harry Rock attaches each of his Delrin pole ends with a bolt, which is inserted

---

Good Cockpit Fit

The most important safety feature of a sea kayak is how it fits you. A wide boat might feel stable in calm water, but if you rattle around in the cockpit you won't be able to lean the boat into waves effectively. Concentrate more on fit than a particular width. Make sure you can't slide around sideways in the seat very much, and can brace your knees against the underside of the deck while working the rudder pedals. Don't hesitate to customize the cockpit and seat by shaping and glueing in foam blocks or pads.

—JH & RH

into a tapped-and-drilled hole in the Delrin; the head is cut off the bolt.

Some suppliers of poles, or pole pieces and parts:

Edward Hayden, 1796 Route 85, Oakdale, CT, 06370; (202) 442-1170. Mr. Hayden makes 12-foot poles of aircraft-quality aluminum tubing (1⅛-inch diameter, and wall thickness of .058 inch). They weigh three pounds when plugged. He plugs the ends with either wood or Delrin.

Peavey Manufacturing Co., Eddington, ME; (207) 843-7861. Peavey makes poles of white ash in 10-, 12-, 14-, and 16-foot lengths, and in diameters of 1¼ and 1⅜ inches. They will also sell you just the metal shoe.

Brell Mar Products, Inc., Jackson, MI; (601) 922-9815. Brell Mar sells a telescoping (6- to 12-foot) aircraft-grade aluminum pole with a variety of "foot" attachments. The brand name is "Git-A-Long." These would be best suited for light-duty use, muddy river bottoms, etc.

UP THE CREEK WITHOUT A PADDLE

by Harry Rock

"Hey, you're going the wrong way!" "Don't you know you're not supposed to stand in a canoe!" "Look at him, he's going to fall out!" And so on and so on. These are the comments a canoe poler is subjected to from floaters who know little more about their craft other than one end is tougher to sit in than the other. Yet this esoteric sport is gaining popularity with people who are interested in another dimension of canoe sport.

The greatest lure of poling is the total sense of independence and self-sufficiency one feels by not having to depend on a shuttle or a partner to have a rewarding experience on the river. I used to think of river canoeing as a weekend sport because it was so hard to find a partner to help with the shuttle during the week. For myself, there is nothing better than heading to the river to play in the rapids after a tough day in the office. The desire to just get away frompeople after dealing with them all day is reason enough to turn to pushing the big stick. I simply love dropping the boat in the water and heading upstream to work out the daily stress and become one with nature, even for a short while. The quiet gurgle of gliding through the flats or the exhilaration of climbing up drops and surfing waves is the perfect way to end the day, especially with no "booze cruisers" to listen to.

Poling is also the ultimate low-water sport. Often there is enough water to float a canoe but not enough to keep the paddle from turning into a trimmed-off broom stick . When most canoes are creating shade on their racks because of a lack of water for paddling, poling extends the season.

Two distinct schools of poling have emerged over the years: the classic Maine backwoods style, and the more modern freestyle power poling form preferred by the competitive ranks. The primary difference is that the classic style uses a diagonal stance with an ash or spruce pole, while freestylers use a squared-off stance and a lightweight aluminum pole. While each style has it disciples, it is generally accepted that freestyle is easier to teach and to learn. The primary reason is balance, which is enhanced when the poler pulls the forward foot back and squares off the stance. This allows the boat to rock from side to side in rough water with out any feeling that the boater is going to be pitched out. The squared-off stance also enables the poler to freely use both sides of the canoe for propulsion and correction while the classic stance relegates the person to just one side. The aluminum pole has also bettered the wooden pole based on weight and double-ended capacity, allowing a quicker turnover of plants and improved control. While this view will surely generate protests from the traditionalist, competitors all agree that the freestyle form of poling is more stable and generates more power and speed.

One limiting factor of the sport has been the lack of adequate poles. There are no commercial producers of aluminum poles—they are usually manufactured by private canoeists who have access to the stock plus the tool-and-die equipment to make the plugs for each end. Others start off with a closet pole purchased from the local lumber yard. Closet poles unfortunately are weak, springy, and prone to breakage; however, commercial producers such as Shaw and Tenney produce fine poles of spruce or ash. Most Maine Guides make their own pole by finding a good tree and then shaving it down. Hours of

4

Expanding Your Horizons

ᴏʀ

How to Get Specialized

"Fortune brings in some boats that are not steered."

—*from Shakespeare's* Cymbeline

Fast Lane:
Resources for Racers

You may be drawn to the idea of making your canoe, kayak, or raft go fast in a race. Or you may be drawn to just *watching* others race—it's worth observing racers if for no reason other than to see where technology has taken boat materials and shapes, and to see how paddlers learn to be efficient and conserve energy in the interest of arriving at the finish line first. It is always worth watching people who are experts at something "do their thing." You can almost always learn something. That same principle applies to paddling as well as to dancing (is there a difference?); to negotiating a boulder-strewn river drop as to skiing through the moguls; to

finding the fastest-moving water as to finding the absolute fastest path to run a marathon.

But whether you follow every race or an occasional race, aim for the Olympics or next year's regatta, here are a few of the books that concentrate on getting you to go fast. Read them and you'll learn a few tricks of the trade and you'll surely go faster. Whether or not you'll win . . . now that is another matter.

painstaking work results in a beautiful stick that is a pleasure to look at and just plain feels good to hold on to. The down side of wood, however, is that it is heavy and prone to absorbing water, which is counterproductive to efficiency and quickness.

The greatest limitation to the distribution of existing poles has been the prohibitive cost to shipping because of the length, which generally is 12 feet. There are no readily available collapsible poles which can be shipped more easily because of the difficulty of designing a strong joint and the high cost of production.

Once a person has pole in hand, the next challenge to overcome is the issue of balance. The poler should stand one to two feet behind the center thwart to create a slightly stern-heavy trim. This picks the bow stem up so that it doesn't track in the oncoming water when moving upstream, thus improving control. Feet should be spread as wide apart as possible, right up against the chine of the canoe and under the plane of the shoulders. An excellent balance exercise is to start to slowly rock the canoe back and forth, weighting and unweighting each leg much like a downhill skier does from turn to turn. The upper body should be motionless, letting all motion come from the waist down. As the poler becomes more comfortable with the motion, accelerate the action so that each gunwale kisses the water surface while creating large waves. The next step is to fully weight one side so that the canoe is motionless with one gunwale touching the surface for several seconds and then alternate to the other side. As you get more comfortable, you will be able to pick the unweighted foot off the hull. These balance exercises should be done each time one stands in a canoe regardless of ability. A final step to stability is to ensure a clean surface with no mud or sand, to prevent slipping. Feet should always be washed off before stepping into the boat. Rubber soles provide excellent traction on ABS canoes; Kevlar and fiberglass canoes require some type of nonskid surface such as graphite or nonskid tape.

As there is not enough space here to go into detail on technique, remember three things. First, in deep water use the pole as a kayak paddle. It will produce surprising speed and power. Second, in shallow water, generate thrust by pushing off the bottom. Make sure the pole is always planted behind you with at least a 45-degree forward angle on the pole to generate proper leverage and propulsion. Third, remember that poling is nothing more than an application of angle and leverage, regardless of whether it's creating power, correcting direction, reading water, or playing the intricate rock garden. Study the forces you are trying to create or overcome and learn to work with them, not against them. The river is a relentless source of energy which will wear you down if you don't learn to interpret it and become its partner. In poling, exactly one half of the trip is always uphill against gravity, so efficiency, grace, and finesse are required to be successful.

—Harry Rock is a ten-time overall national poling champion, with eleven national slalom titles and ten national wildwater titles; he's won eighty-one straight races over ten years. He is the author of The Basic Essentials of Canoe Poling *and is an active educator in the sport of poling.*

**Canoe Racing: The
Competitor's Guide to
Marathon and Downriver
Canoe Racing**

by Peter Heed and Dick Mansfield

(Syracuse, NY: Acorn Publishing, 1992)

Whether you are a beginner and interested in racing, a veteran paddler,
or even a veteran racer, you can
probably learn something from
Heed and Mansfield. Their book is
up to date, so the comments on
training, materials used in construction of boats, etc., is all very
current. The authors give excellent
tips on finding races around the
country, equipment, technique, that
all-important topic of training,

WHERE ARE THE RACES?

Maybe your mind is made up . . . this is the year you'll race. You've got the
equipment, the mind-set, the racing partner, but, where's the race? Here's a
quick strategy for finding out.

- Paddling magazines print calendars of upcoming events, including races.
- You will likely find race schedules on some of the paddlers' on-line ser-
  vices, bulletin boards, discussion groups, etc. See Chapter 2 for more on
  Internet resources for paddlers, including the address for the Paddle-Comp
  mailing list (for racers).
- Ask at a local paddler equipment supplier.
- Contact nearby paddling clubs.
- Contact one of the paddlers' associations listed in Chapter 2.

actually reading the river and choosing a course (the fast lane), portaging, general racing strategy, and a
glossary of specialized terminology
used by racers. To all this they append

a handy list of other resources like
books, magazines, and videos.

ᘄ

*There is no more important part
of a canoe race than the start. While*

Photo courtesy of the Library of Congress, Prints and Photographs Division, Washington, D.C.

Photo courtesy of Maine State Museum.

you will not win the race at the start, you may lose it there. You can be guaranteed of this: at the start of any race it's going to be fast and it's going to be wild.

Most canoe racers will want to be in front or at least with the front pack at the start because otherwise, it's a major disadvantage to have to cope with the wakes and irregular waves of the leading canoes. The closer you are to the front after the start, the fewer energy-sapping irregular wakes you will have to deal with. Good racers go hard off the line, so if you want to be competitive, you're going to have to go hard as well.

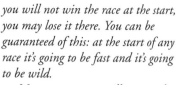

The Ultimate Run: Canoe Slalom at the Highest Levels

by William T. Endicott
(Baltimore: Reese Press, 1983)

This book is for none but the most serious of racers. It includes loads of detail on race gates, strokes, and the variety of problems racers encounter. A significant portion of the book is devoted to physiological principles and training. Still another portion consists of case stud-ies based on interviews with several world-class paddlers. If you are thinking seriously about the Olympics (not attending, but participating!) or simply gobble up *anything* about racing, then read *The Ultimate Run.* But you will need to be committed—the book weighs 2½ pounds and is more than five hundred pages long.

The River Masters: A History of the World Championships of Whitewater Canoeing

by William T. Endicott
(Washington, DC: Endicott, 1979)

Bill Endicott has been active in racing circles for decades. He has been both a successful racer and coach of racers. He has written many books about the racing scene, among them *The River Masters* (Endicott, 1979), *The Ultimate Run: Canoe Slalom at the Highest Levels* (Reese, 1983), and *The Danger Zone: Downriver Canoeing at the Highest Levels* (Endicott, 1985).

These books are for serious racers, history nuts, and other gluttons for detail. They are well done. *The River Masters* is a compendium of information covering the early days of serious international whitewater competition, including the World Championships, Europa Cup, Pre-World Championships, and the Olympics. It includes an index of competitors from 1949 through 1978, World Championship course maps, and a photograph album.

The Danger Zone: Downriver Canoeing at the Highest Levels

by William T. Endicott
(Baltimore, MD: Endicott, 1985)

Here is a book for the serious C1 or kayak racer. It includes plenty on paddling technique, on the body, muscles, and working out, and a few case studies. The case studies are of prominent world-class paddlers, what they did, how they trained, why they won, etc. This book is long on detail, so consider it of interest to any serious, ambitious paddlers.

A PADDLER'S IDITAROD

In Alaska each March, mushers drive their dogs for 1,160 miles over some incredibly rugged country for the sake of a good race. On "the outside," as Alaskans call everywhere else, there is a 1,000-mile annual paddler's race that starts in Chicago and ends in New York City.

The paddler's race is administered by the American Canoe Association.

The course is run over a period of about thirty days, during which "mini daily races" are held, each covering thirty or forty miles and each inching closer to New York. The course takes paddlers through four of the five Great Lakes, through the Erie Canal, and down the Hudson River to Battery Park at the southern tip of Manhattan Island. The winners make big money (recently the top four all made $10,000 or more, with first place taking $25,000).

If you are very serious about endurance, are passionate about racing, and have a kayak or canoe that wants to be taken on a long trip, consider racing in the world's longest paddlesport competition. To get up-to-date information on the next race, contact the American Canoe Association, 7432 Alban Station Blvd. Suite B-226, Springfield, VA 22150-2311; (703) 451-0141, FAX (703) 451-2245; (awa@rahul.net).

Canoeing: An Olympic Sport

by Andras "Andy" Toro
(San Francisco: Olympian Graphics, 1986)

If you are determined to represent your country in the Olympics, this book will give you a clue as to whether you are up to it. It includes information for both kayakers and canoeists. No stone is left unturned.

Andy Toro has been an Olympic competitor and has studied both naval architecture and marine engineering. He is well qualified to speak about biomechanics, hydrodynamics, advanced training, and racing strategy. He draws on physical principles, statistical data, and relevant formulas to make his points. You might say this book is not for the occasional weekend racer.

There are also several appendices of useful information, such as the results of canoeing and kayaking events in the Olympics from 1920 through 1984.

This book would make an excellent choice for any serious racing coach or racer. But as time goes on, it will need to be supplemented with information about newer ideas, techniques, and materials.

Photo by Ken Jewett.

More Good Books about Racing

Whitewater Racing: A Comprehensive Guide to Whitewater Slalom and Wildwater Racing by Eric Evans and John Burton (New York: Van Nostrand Reinhold, 1980)

Sprint Racing Canoeing, Level 1, Coaching Certification (Ottawa: Canadian Canoe Association, 1984)

Book of Champions of the Canadian Canoe Association, 1900–1984 by C. Fred Johnston (Ottawa: Canadian Canoe Association, 1988)

Canoe and Kayak Race Management: Marathon and Whitewater Open Canoe (Connecticut Canoe Racing Association, United States Canoe Association, and American Canoe Association, 1985)

Canadian Canoe Association National Championship Manual (Vanier, Ontario: Canadian Canoe Association, 1981)

Performance Sea Kayaking: The Basics . . . and Beyond (Performance Video and Instruction, Inc., Durango, CO; 970-259-1361). This is a video, but it should prove useful to the sea kayaker who wants to learn more about going fast.

72

1936 OLYMPIC REQUIREMENTS

"The body of the kayak must be constructed of wood, though the boat may be with or without canvas covering. Another important point is that the rudder equipment must not be fixed in the case of the single seater kayak. . . . Canoes must be made of wood, with or without canvas covering, and can be quite open or covered at the front 100 cm and at the back 75 cm, measured from the bow's head to the farthest point of the deck extending backwards or forwards respectively. Side decks and washboards are prohibited."
—from Canoeing *by William G. Luscombe (1936)*

Feminine Touch:
Resources for Women

☯

Women have always struck out on their own and excelled in adventure sports, from climbing to sailing to paddling. Trouble is, much of the published resources in sports are written by and directed at men. But according to several outdoor retail associations, women comprise more than half the retail sales in sports such as climbing and paddling.

Following are some resources for women who want to meet other women in paddling or other outdoors sports, find out about women-only trips and associations, as well as some good books by women paddlers.

Associations and Outfitters for Women

Adventure Associates, Seattle, WA, (206) 932-8352

Her Wild Song, Brunswick, ME, (207) 721-9005
Rainbow Adventures, Bozeman, MT, (800) 804-8686
Women in the Wilderness, St. Paul, MN, (612) 227-2284
Woodswomen, Minneapolis, MN, (800) 279-0555

Books about Women and Paddling

Rivers Running Free: Canoeing Stories by Adventurous Women

edited by Judith Niemi and Barbara Wieser

(Seattle, WA: Seal Press, 1992)

A wonderful collection of more than thirty selections from the diaries and journals of women who have paddled throughout North America. In the preface the editors write, "This is a book about adventurous and exploring impulses in women, about traveling in wild places by canoe. Many of these women have traveled great distances, but the real stories are the journeys of mind and spirit."

They are stories of urban trips and wilderness trips, of short and long duration, of just a few years ago and of a hundred years ago, of younger paddlers and of some elder paddlers, of solo trips and of group trips. The editors have sprinkled the text with some useful maps and delightful photos. It also includes a list of books by and about women on the water. This book would be great to read aloud around a campfire.

In April of 1985 nine feet of snow fell on Prince William Sound

---

"I have never seen Mrs. Hopkins so hearty in my life . . . canoe traveling agrees with her."

—a comment made by Mr. Edward Manley Hopkins, husband of Voyageur artist Frances Anne Hopkins, to a friend in 1864

in one week. So is May 10th too early for a sea kayaking excursion in Alaska? Not for this hardy group. Why May? Because Ginny and I, who organized the trip, are both wilderness guides, too busy in the summer for our own personal trips.

"It's all old ladies," I explained to Denis when he called to book the earliest possible trip. "Just my speed," he retorted. He joined, and added spice to the group. Ginny and her pals,

---

The Double Oar Turn

You can turn a raft by pulling or pushing on one oar at a time, but double-oar turns—executed by pulling one oar while pushing on the other—are much more efficient.

—JB & TB

Celia from Fairbanks, and Helen B. from Wisconsin, are all 67 years old. My paddling partner Wendy and I are both in our mid fifties. Elizabeth from Anchorage and Denis from New York are in their forties.

—from the chapter "It's All Old Ladies"

SPEAKING WITH . . .
JUDITH NIEMI

It was about 1960 when Judith Niemi realized that the canoe beckoned her. Now in her mid fifties, with about thirty-five years of experience under her belt, she guides adult women's trips and is an energized person if there ever was one. She has a *feeling* about canoeing that is infectious. Over the course of her life, she has taught canoeing, guided trips, taught women's history at the college level, paddled in Alaska, Minnesota, Florida, Labrador, and Ontario.

If you ask her what advice she would give to other women, based on her thirty-five-ish years of paddling, these are among the things she will say:

- Don't get stuck in the bow! In other words, often women (especially when paddling with men) will end up in the bow seat. That may be okay to learn bow paddling, but one should not become a permanent fixture in the bow. *Learn stern!* Paddling from the stern is different than the bow, and everyone should be exposed to both in order to develop confidence in paddling from both positions.
- Try solo paddling—women who do generally love it.
- Be smart, pack smart, think about what you're doing, and what you're taking along.
- Don't go for mileage on the water, go for a quality experience no matter how much distance is involved.

BIG TIPS FOR SMALL PADDLERS

by Roseann Hanson

The Inuit say *mik-shrok*. "Small is sufficient."

I like that concept, because I am a small person, and I like being small. But as an active outdoorswoman, I have struggled for years with finding sports equipment that fits me properly, from boating to biking to backpacking. I first came across "Mik-Shrok" as the christened name of a Mariner Coaster sea kayak belonging to a Seattle woman, one of many small paddlers across the country with whom I talked for this story. It was apparent to me by her carefully chosen boat name that she, too, has walked the frustrating path of many small people in a quest for appropriate equipment.

My first sea kayaking setup, as I look back after a three-year, sometimes-frustrating search for properly fitting equipment, was ludicrously disproportionate to my body size. I'm of the small-but-tall variety, weighing in at about 107 after a fully-clothed wet exit, and topping out at 5'7"; I have an average trunk height, long thighs but narrow hips and shoulders. So there I sat in a 17-foot, 24½-inch beam boat, wallowing in a PFD that rode up to my chin and chafed my armpits, enshrouded by a huge spray skirt that puckered and sagged in the middle and let a steady drip-drip-drip into my lap from the pooled water, and flailing away with a 240-cm large-bladed paddle.

No wonder that I was always bringing up the rear of the group, but, hey, I figured it was because I was simply smaller and weaker, right? Frustration mounted, however, especially in rough water, because my small hips rattled around in the large seat and my back became sore from compensating for the lack of bracing power. It was also, I realized as my novice status wore off and I became more educated in kayaking, very unsafe; because my boat did not fit I tired much too easily and I could not execute an eskimo roll (I'd pop right out of the large cockpit) or maneuver quickly in challenging seas.

This prompted a three-year search through retail stores, visits at two trade shows with a dozen boat and accessories manufacturers, and talks with other small paddlers. Today I paddle an Eddyline Raven, a 16-foot, 9-inch LOA boat that has a 22½-inch actual beam (carrying a total of two hundred pounds the waterline length is 14'9" and waterline beam is 21⅜ inches). Because virtually all of my paddling is extended cruising, I needed a boat that was as high-capacity as possible that still fit my small body. My kayak is narrow by North American standards, but wider than many kayaks by British designers. It has roomy bulkhead compartments fore and aft, large hatches, and expedition-oriented options like bungees and a compass. Though not designed specifically as a boat for small people, it fits my hips and knees snugly, and the low coaming at the sides allows me to paddle confidently without hitting the sides of the boat with the paddle, even with my narrow shoulders and short reach.

Some people told me long, narrow boats are best for advanced paddlers because they are less initially stable, but I found the opposite to be true if you are a person of small stature and the boat is not enormously long (14 to 17 feet is fine). Because my center of gravity is much lower than a person of the 5'10"/180-pound average-male variety, the boat is perfectly stable, and since it fits me well in width, it is responsive and playful. And most importantly, for the first time ever I am a powerful and efficient paddler. My thighs fit firmly but comfortably on the braces, my hips are snug and my lower back presses firmly into the seat; my strokes, unimpeded by a wide and tall coaming, are now perfectly efficient. I have paddled my fully loaded Raven twenty-five miles in one day without problem, and I now set the pace with a group rather than bring up the rear.

Rounding out my equipment purchases are a custom-made spray skirt that fits my tiny torso (30 inches under the armpits) and has a shortened tube (9 inches from armpit to waist); a youth PFD; and two 220-cm paddles with narrow blades.

Based on my experiences during a three-year shopping odyssey, here are some tips for a small paddler's shopping trip:

- Be prepared to deal with the notion that if you are short or small, you need a short, fat boat.
- Likewise, be prepared for endless opinions about which boat types are best, much of which is contradictory. "Narrow boats are unsafe." "Beamy kayaks are barges." "Speed is safety." "Stability is safety." "The best bow lifts over the waves." "The best bow cuts through the waves." And on and on.

- The best defense is to go forth prepared with three solid sets of knowledge: Know your body, know your kayaking goals, and know some basic boat hydrodynamics.
- If you don't know your kayaking goals, you're probably not ready to buy a boat. Wait until you have some experience under your belt, either from guided trips paddling singles or, better yet, a good school.
- While shopping, make lists if you need, then stick to them. Don't let pushy boat designers or salespeople convince you that you're wrong. "Appropriate" is a good buzzword: make sure your purchase is *appropriate* not only for your body type but also for your intended kayaking voyages.
- Make an effort to understand a little about small-boat hydrodynamics. For an excellent source, reference *Sea Kayaker* Magazine's boat review series, running from Winter 1993 through Summer 1994.
- As a general rule, small paddlers should stick with around 220-cm paddles, probably no longer. Narrow blades are preferable, and buy the lightest paddle you can afford.
- Regarding PFDs and spray skirts, go for fit, fit, fit. Extrasport offers what I think is the most broad variety of styles and sizes, including XS adults and youths, both long and short lengths. Snap Dragon spray skirts will sew a skirt to your height and chest sizes if necessary, or even change the tube placement if you've had to alter your seat position, as you might for shorter legs.

Most kayak manufacturers are responding to market demands by introducing boats specifically for small paddlers. Some kayak industry statistics indicate that there are three women to every two men going on guided trips, and about half of retail kayak customers are women, so it's not surprising that there are now more boats available for paddlers smaller than the "average male." This is good news for small men as well.

Keeping your mind on appropriate fit and performance relative to your needs is the most important thing to remember in looking for a boat. Frustration and confusion will only lead to a rash purchase, and that could lead to uncomfortable and unsafe paddling. For further opinions, talk to fellow paddlers who are similar in stature to yourself.

And remember: mik-shrok.

—Roseann Hanson is a natural history writer and editor who has paddled her Raven kayak in Sonora and Baja, the Arctic, and the Pacific Northwest. She lives near Tucson, Arizona. This essay was adapted from an article published in Sea Kayaker *Magazine, December 1995.*

Water's Edge: Women Who Push the Limits in Rowing, Kayaking & Canoeing

by Linda Lewis
(Seattle: Seal Press, 1992)

These are the stories of several women who have made waves on either the paddling or rowing scene. They have won Olympic medals, been on very long voyages, or otherwise provided inspiration for fellow women paddlers and rowers.

Paddlers profiled are: Marcia Jones, Francine Fox, Gloriane Perrier, Traci Phillips, Cathy Hearn, Valerie Fons, and The Back River Seven.

Rowers profiled include: Ernestine Bayer, Anita DeFrantz, The 1984 Eight (Olympians), Kris Karlson, and Lou Daly.

The Lady's Country Companion

by Jane Loudon
(Bungay, UK: Paradigm Press,
reprinted 1984, from original 1845 edition)
While hardly devoted to women of
the river, this "companion" is sure
to knock your socks off, if not your
farmer johns. The author moved
from the city to the country and
wanted other women to be able to
make the adjustments she was able
to make. On boating, she wrote:

⋎

*"If you have a boat on your water,
take care, when it is chained up in the
boat-house, that it floats in water, and
does not lie in mud. Pleasure boats
should be painted every year, and always kept perfectly clean and dry in
the inside. They should never be exposed for any length of time to the heat
of the sun, and if the smallest opening
is perceived it should be mended immediately. Great care should be taken,
in a small pleasure boat, to stand up as
seldom as possible; and never be
tempted, by the wish of seeing any particular object, to rush suddenly from
one side of the boat to the other."*

⋏

But she advises:

⋎

*You will observe . . . that though
I have mentioned a few sporting
terms, with the meanings that are, I*

PADDLING WITH WOMEN

by Dorcas S. Miller

What's so great about a women's trip?

For starters, I learned how to paddle with women, and I found out right away that I had to take my turn carrying the canoe, paddling stern, and navigating. I had no opportunity to slough off, saying, "I'm too small. The canoe is too heavy. You're better at navigation—you do it." There were no big strong males to save the day, so we "girls" did everything. Along with bug bites and blisters, I gained an independence and a love of the North Woods that I have nurtured ever since. Not only can I paddle "manless," but I often do.

Paddling with women lets me stretch my limits. On one trip—a long time ago, when my knees had fewer miles on them—Beth and I tackled the nine-mile Grand Portage along the U.S.–Canada border. Ten minutes with the canoe; switch; ten minutes with the pack; switch. Continue for a total of fifty minutes, then rest ten minutes of every hour. And those were the days when we carried 80-pound canoes, when

light-weight Kevlar canoes were still a gleam in someone's eye.)

I like the ebb and flow of conversation on a women's trip, where we can talk freely about periods, PMS, and menopause. We can nab a tampon and some hand lotion from a tent-mate. We can be silly and subtle and sad. In some ways, it is easier to talk about emotions, but this may be because I've been paddling with some of my women friends for nigh onto twenty-five years.

Sometimes these conversations lead to amusing situations. A few summers ago, four of us were standing in the ranger's office to register for our trip into Canada's Quetico Provincial Park. Nancy and I gave the ranger our party's names, addresses, and itinerary. As he filled out the forms, we reminisced about a trip on a river in Canada's Northwest Territories.

"Remember that day on Aberdeen? The lake's as big as an ocean and the wind is whipping up waves four feet high. I didn't want to go out on it but got outvoted, five to one."

"Yeah, and as soon as we went out there, we wished we'd voted 'No,' too."

"There were times when I couldn't see your boat at all."

"And we got pushed past the turn-off to Schultz and wound up at the east end of the lake and had to portage overland to get to where we wanted. But it was pretty in there."

Meanwhile, our paddling cohorts Susie and Mary were sharing experiences of another sort.

"I resolved to do it after the divorce. I was feeling low and the grey hair didn't help my self-image."

"I thought about it a long time and decided that I looked a lot older than my age, and so I went ahead and had it done. It is a hassle dealing with the roots, though."

The ranger shuffled forms and asked about our canoeing experience. "We've been paddling in the Quetico since the early 1970s," we said.

"I'll spare you the usual reading of the rules," he responded. He gave us our permit, and we headed for the waiting lake. As I left, I wondered how the ranger was processing the two conversations—one about a seven-week trip across the Barrenlands in northern Canada and the other about grey hair. Does he get

believe, generally assigned to them, I would advise you never to make use of them in conversation; as nothing can be more unfeminine than for a woman to use terms only apted to manly amusements. I am sure your husband would dislike to hear you ape the sportsman; as men, with very few exceptions, always feel disgust at a masculine woman.

Whew! Even Lake Wobegon never sounded quite like that. But this book is *sure* to provoke lively after-dinner conversation.

The Wen, the Botany, and the Mexican Hat: The Adventures of the First Women Through Grand Canyon on the Nevills Expedition

by William Cook
(San Bernardino, CA: The Borgo Press, 1987)
Okay, so this one is written by a man.

But it's a great story. In 1938, botany professor Dr. Elzada Clover and graduate student–cum-botanizing companion Lois J. Cutter descended more than six hundred miles of the Colorado River. Because they were the first women to successfully make the run, they received plenty of notoriety. This is the story of that run in their boats the Wen, the Botany, and the Mexican Hat.

---

many women's groups coming through his station? Are any of the women old enough to be dealing with the question of grey hair? Did he think that our raven-haired friends were along for the ride?

If he did, he was dead wrong. Susie is a wilderness veteran—in the lower 48 and Alaska. At each portage, when it was her turn to carry the canoe, she put on a pack with her personal gear, picked up the canoe by herself, and then trotted on down the trail—in sandals. And Mary, though with less experience, took her turn in the stern and with the canoe on portages.

Of course I cast an envious eye on couples who paddle together. It's fun to have someone right there, in your very own kitchen, with whom you can pore over maps on a winter evening. It's easier to have someone at hand to help make decisions about food and gear. And sharing the shimmering sunsets and doing the black fly boogie together can strengthen a relationship. If you're both paddlers.

Let me say that my husband is unequivocally a climber. Although

we put in our time learning how to climb together—and get out regularly—we discovered early on that paddling a tandem canoe required more marital energy than we were willing to devote to the activity. The breakthrough came when we got separate boats (sea kayaks, since we live in Maine), and the world of the water lay at our little neoprened feet. But still, when it's time for a wilderness canoe trip, he says, "Have a great time!" and packs me off to paddle with my women buddies.

So when I see a man in the stern and a woman in the bow, I wonder how they got there—if they went by weight (the rule of thumb is, "Heavier in the stern"), ownership (usually it's his boat), control (stern person steers), or tradition (male in the stern). Has the woman always paddled bow? Does she always carry the pack? Does she know or care that she can paddle stern and carry the canoe?

Maybe they've got it worked out to their satisfaction. Maybe they negotiated their roles and don't want to entertain changes. But even contented bow paddlers should spend some time in the stern, if only to

understand what goes on back there and develop skills that could come in handy should the stern paddler become sick or injured. And the question of weight isn't insurmountable. It's easy enough to reposition the packs or, for a day trip, throw a little extra ballast in the stern.

Here's my advice: If you'd like to paddle stern but don't get the chance, if you enjoy taking your turn cooking on trail but don't want to do it every night, and if you think it would be fun to hang out with your women friends for a few days, then get busy and organize a paddling trip. You won't be sorry you did.

—Dorcas S. Miller has been plying her paddle for twenty-seven years as an Outward Bound instructor, Maine Guide, and private citizen. She helped found Women Outdoors, Inc., and has written several natural history books as well as Good Food for Camp and Trail. *She is currently working on* Stars of the First People, *a book about Native American star and constellation myths, and* Profiles of American Outdoorswomen, 1870s–1920s.

Georgie White: Thirty Years of River Running

by Georgie White Clark and Duane Newcomb
(San Francisco: Chronicle Books, 1977)

An autobiographical account of the life of a spirited and prominent commercial rafting guide. She was one of the early ones, and is legendary in the annals of modern whitewater rafting.

More Good Books about and by Women Paddlers

Keep It Moving—Baja by Canoe by Valerie Fons (Seattle: The Mountaineers, 1986). Chronicle of her voyage with Verlen Kruger, whom she had just met, down North America's west coast from Canada all the way around Baja.

Deep Water Passage: A Spiritual Journey at Midlife by Ann Linnea (New York: Little, Brown and Company, 1996)

Paddling My Own Canoe by Audrey Sutherland (Honolulu: University Press of Hawaii, 1978). Sutherland has paddled all over the Pacific alone in her inflatable kayak.

Down the Wild River North by Constance Helmericks (Boston: Little, Brown, 1968)

Breaking into the Current: Boatwomen of the Colorado by Louise Teal (Tucson, AZ: University of Arizona Press, 1993)

Women Outdoors: The Best One Thousand Nine Hundred Books Programs & Periodicals by Jennifer Abromowitz (Williamsburg, MA: J. Abromowitz, 1990). An extensive list of books about women and the outdoors; includes a section on paddling.

Adventures in Good Company by Thalia Zepatos (Portland, OR: Eighth Mountain Press, 1994). A resource book for adventure trips for women only.

Other Resources for Women

Canoe & Kayak Magazine sometimes runs a column called For Women Only. Guest columnists offer essays, advice on technique, and other insights useful to women paddlers. And this magazine is among the best at featuring technical articles written by woman experts. Regular contributing editors include Elizabeth "Boo" Turner and Kristi Streiffert, and the entire staff of technical editors is female: Laurie Gullion, Shelley Johnson and Claudia Kerckhoff-van Wijk.

Beyond Diapers:
Resources for Families
☺

Chances are that if you are into paddling and you have or are about to have a family, you will want to include everyone in your passion. Canoeing, sea kayaking, and rafting lend themselves particularly well to family participation. In fact, family paddling might be the fastest-growing segment of some types of paddling.

But how do you get started? Before you strap the playpen onto the oar frame and begin the search for Hypalon diapers, you might start with some of the books below. And try searching the Internet and canvassing clubs for members who paddle *en masse* with their families—you can learn alot by talking with people who have tried it before.

Photo courtesy of the Library of Congress, Prints and Photographs Division, Washington, D.C.

Starting Small in the Wilderness: The Sierra Club Outdoors Guide for Families

by Marlyn Doan

(San Francisco: Sierra Club Books, 1979)

There are times when Mom and Dad want to get away from the kids, and times when taking them paddling provides everyone with great satisfaction. *Starting Small* is reserved for the latter. If you are new to parenting and want to share the pleasures of the outdoor world with your kids, then this book would be an excellent starting place.

There is a useful chapter on equipment for children, and a chapter titled "In Camp with Children" which even includes a section on "toileting children."

More Good Resources for Paddling Families

Kids Outdoors: Skills and Knowledge for Outdoor Adventurers by Victoria Logue, Frank Logue, and Mark Carroll (Camden, ME; Ragged Mountain Press, 1996). Includes a chapter on canoeing, but has a wealth of other information written for kids ages 11 to 15.

Adventuring With Children by Nan Jeffrey (San Francisco: Foghorn Press, 1992)

Canoeing by Laurie Gullion (Champaign, IL: Human Kinetics Publishers, 1994). Includes sections of interest to family paddling.

The Essential Sea Kayaker by David Seidman (Camden, ME: Ragged Mountain Press, 1993). Includes a chapter on paddling with kids.

Paddle America: A Guide to Trips and Outfitters in all 50 States by Nick Shears (Washington, D.C.: Starfish Press, 1994). A useful book that also includes a state-by-state overview of paddling opportunities, including good rivers for family outings.

Five Easy Paddles Video Series including *California 1, California 2, Florida, Hawaii, Boundary Waters West,* and *Along the Lewis & Clark Trail* (Placid Videos, Simi Valley, CA; 800-549-0046). Trip accounts of places to paddle that are especially well suited for beginners or families.

Books for Kids

ADVENTURES

Stuart Little by E. B. White (New York: HarperCollins, 1990, originally published in 1945). The adventures of the debonair mouse Stuart Little as he sets out to find his dearest friend, a little bird who stayed a few days in his family's garden.

Paddle to the Sea by Holling Clancy Holling (Boston: Houghton Mifflin, 1941). A young Indian boy carves an Indian figure in a small canoe and sends himself on a long, adventurous journey through the Great Lakes to the sea.

L.L. Bear's Island Adventure by Kate Rowinski (Camden, ME: Down East Books, 1992). A young bear paddles his sea kayak on an adventure to a nearby island, finding several of his animal friends along the way.

FAMILY RAFTING

by Jeff Bennett and Tonya Bennett

Rivers are corridors through time— passages that reveal the earth's geological past in water-hewn cliffs and gauge the passing of the seasons with ice, drought, and flood. And rivers can tie generations with a common bond: our universal primal fascination with the unbridled emotion of moving water. Whether you're seven or seventy, rivers run through your soul, touch your heart, and stir your imagination. They draw you in, fulfill your senses, and call you back time and time again.

There is perhaps no better way to bring generations and families together than to experience rivers from the dry, inviting cockpit of a raft. These delightfully spacious and forgiving vehicles provide ample room for both fidgety kids and comfort-craving adults to share a front row view of the world from a safe and enjoyable environment.

Traveling with children is not without its tribulations. What family outings lack in whitewater intensity, they make up for in logistical challenges. Parents guard the gates between safety and danger and bear final responsibility for the success of their river adventures. With each oarstroke, parents can bring families closer to a more perfect union, or drive them deeper toward frustration and calamity.

We're referring here to children aged five to eleven. Sure, there's plenty of room for debating suitable ages and maturity levels for rafting trips, but I've seen thirteen-year-olds tackle Class V rapids that sent me slithering toward the nearest portage route. In any event, size up your children and read on—you may be entering a whole new realm of family fun.

Evaluate Your Children Honestly

Let's say your kid has snuck through his developing years while avoiding any body of water bigger than a bathtub. Chances are his reaction to river running is going to be something quite different from that of a seasoned swimmer. While a gung-ho water rat will be chomping at the bit for some real whitewater, a more apprehensive child may perceive the next rapid as his last.

Before planning your first family river outing, evaluate your child's skills, motivation, and confidence level honestly, then choose a trip that will match his or her interests perfectly.

Psyche 'em Up

Kids are masters of reading their parents' moods and convictions. If you want your first trip to be successful, you've got to exude confidence and veil any anxieties. Next, pick the psychological ploy that works best with the young ones. Turn the river into nature's playground, a natural rollercoaster, or an endless water slide. Play upon your child's inherent sense of adventure with tales of Indians and explorers, and keep his or her imagination reeling.

Planning a Safe Outing

Of paramount importance in any family outing is safety. Not only must you utilize top-quality rafts and rafting equipment, you must outfit the entire family with personal gear sufficient to keep everybody warm and protected. Let's start with a quick trip to the local paddling shop.

Contemporary lifejacket designs allow for a nearly custom fit for children as small as twenty pounds. Snug, well-fitted lifejackets can help children keep their heads above water after a dunking and provide a safer trip through small rapids. Properly sized helmets that cover a child's head, forehead, temples, and nape of the neck also provide a margin for safety that is welcome in even the most docile river environs. Helmets allow parents a measure of calm when their klutzy antics result in banged heads or when their child lunges toward the river in search of fish, ouzels, or floating sticks.

If you haven't been able to find a river sufficiently warm to avoid having to wear insulating clothing, make sure your child also dons a wet suit, paddling jacket, and whatever additional outwear may be necessary to ward off the chilling effects of cool water. Remember, your kids don't have the same experiences and sensibility that you have and they're less likely to know how to help themselves if they go for a swim.

Finally, bring along some extra items that you may not otherwise feel are necessary for short outings. For example, a first aid kit is a must. And, an extra paddle or two can come in handy when your child drops one overboard.

Starting Easy

Kids and water usually mix splendidly. However, long days on any river can drive any kid to the brink of a tantrum.

Pick a short, warm, gentle river for your first trip. It should be challenging enough so that it will whet your child's appetite, but tame enough so that your child won't associate rivers with fear. A three- or four-hour trip—with some breaks for lunch or exploring side creeks and canyons—can be perfect for first timers. Look beyond that first trip to the future, and make it your goal to have your children reach the take-out begging for more. With any luck, you'll have turned them into instant river addicts and converts to your love of whitewater rafting.

Pick the Right Group

Family trips may fill your heart with pleasure while searing the nerves of others. Make sure your children are truly welcome on a group family trip and that every member of the trip is OK with having children along.

Safety on the River

Make more conservative decisions while floating the river. Why roll the dice on making it through a Class IV or V rapid when you can just as easily portage? When bouncing through Class II or III rapids, have your kids hold on and stay low in the raft. They'll share the same thrill they'd be getting sitting up higher, but have the added safety margin of keeping

their weight inboard. Finally, always have another raft along just in case you run into any trouble. The other raft's ability to assist in any rescue situation may prove invaluable.

Let Your Child Call the Shots

If timed correctly, any family-style river trip should allow ample opportunities to float, relax, and soak up the scenery. This should also allow you an opportunity to give your child some say in how fast or slow your trip should be going. If your child wants to explore river banks and side canyons every forty-five minutes or so, it may be more fun to do that than to convince your sulking youngster to keep paddling.

Play Games

Another way to make rivers interesting is to make up games along the way. Give points for spotting wildlife, birds, or yellow boats and reward your children with something special at the end of the trip. Let them try rowing or paddling on gentle riffles, or let them swim in calm pools.

Snacks

Boy, if there's one thing that'll put a smile on a kid's face in no time flat it's food. Whether your child's taste leans toward BLTs or PB&J, take what he or she likes to eat. Snacks can eat up a lot of time (no pun intended)

and keep your child's mouth and mind occupied during less interesting sections of river. A few nutritious granola bars can be a fitting reward for making it through a Class III rapid or a simple pleasure to be shared while watching the banks slide by.

Remember, you are the guiding hand that dictates your child's whitewater destiny. Choose a path that will make them happy and appreciative of rivers.

—Jeff Bennett has been an avid kayaker, inflatable kayaker, and rafter for more than a decade. A frequent writer and photographer for both Paddler *and* Canoe & Kayak, *he is also the author of numerous books on whitewater travel including* The Complete Whitewater Rafter, The Complete Inflatable Kayaker, Rafting, Class Five Chronicles, *and* A Guide to the Whitewater Rivers of Washington.

Tonya Bennett's paddling career began in 1984 with a trip down Oregon's Deschutes River. Since then, she has run rivers from northern British Columbia to central California. She has edited such books as Class Five Chronicles *and* The Complete Whitewater Rafter, *and her articles have appeared in* Paddler, Canoe and Kayak, Adventure West, *and other magazines.*

Photo of Jeff Bennet by Linda Shaull.

The Wind in the Willows by Kenneth Grahame (New York: Viking, 1983, originally published in 1980). The escapades of four animal friends who live along a river

in the English countryside—Toad, Mole, Rat, and Badger.
Three Days on a River in a Red Canoe by Vera B. Williams (New York: Scholastic, 1992). Mother,

Aunt Rosie, and two children make a three-day camping trip by canoe.
The Singing Canoe by Eva-Lis Wuorio (New York: World Publishing

Co., 1969). Between daydreams about taking trips in his new canoe, Mickey teaches himself to swim so that he will be allowed to take the boat out alone.

Jem's Island by Kathryn Lasky (New York: Scribner, 1982). Jem goes on his first overnight kayak trip with his father to an island.
Sleepy River by Hanna Bandes

(New York: Philomel, 1993). A canoe ride at nightfall provides a mother and child glimpses of ducks, fireflies, bats, and other wonders of nature.

THOUGHTS ON A CHILD'S FIRST RIVER TRIP

by Ken Wright

This is our third day on the river, and it is fantastic. Every bend in the canyon is a new and grandiose display of earthworks. This corner reveals huge horizontal bands of white sandstone cut with half-shell alcoves and amphitheaters; back there we were dwarfed by river-to-canyon-top stair-stepping talus slopes. A half moon hangs above it all like God's grin. My wife, my young son, and I silently watch worlds unfold at the river's pace.

I lean on the oars, unnecessary for most of today's floating. The blades dry in the desert air. I just study, listen, smell. Sarah sits on the front right tube of our cataraft. She leans back on the seat, knees up, arms folded, face shaded but peering from a slot under her straw hat. Webb stands behind me. He is above my head, and when I look up I see his small face backdropped by big blue sky. He, too, stares off somewhere, until he looks down at me looking up. His round cheeks and blue eyes and white-blond curls comprise a serious, pensive face. He holds my look. I smile, and he smiles back.

For young Webb, this late-spring float of Colorado's Dolores River is his first multi-day river trip. Looking back over these three days of floating, riverside dinners, and nights filled with fat stars, I would say this venture has been blessed and inspiring and therapeutic. Certainly it has been those things for me and my wife, and for Webb I believe it has been some child's equivalent of those. But I also must admit that as splendid as this venture appears from this third-day vantage point, the decision to take Webb along was not an easy one for Sarah and me. It's not that we didn't want him here—wilderness trips and river running lie at the heart of my and Sarah's life together, and we want him to share in that life—but Webb is only one year old.

As we pondered the idea in the weeks before the trip, the risks gnawed at us like ulcers. Even on a flat and slow stretch of river such as this one, there is danger in wilderness when you're away from doctors and phones and pharmacies. Wilderness isn't child-proofed; a lot can happen to a crawling and curious child surrounded by such a new world. There is water, storms, insects, and rattlesnakes. There can be illness and tumbles and broken limbs. There will be campfires, cookware, and river running equipment.

And the risks weren't all we worried about; our selfish selves had something to say. Part of the reason we take wilderness trips is to break the demands of our daily routines. But how relaxing will it be for us, we wondered, to deal with our nuclear-powered one-year-old on a 16-foot raft for three days? As any parent can tell you, a toddler is not so much a person as it is a circumstance. People or pets you can negotiate with or at least train, but a small child is more like the weather; there's no use arguing with or trying to change what is presented. You just deal, continuously. We could picture the gory details: first he'll want to throw his toys in the river; next he'll want to crawl somewhere, anywhere, off the boat.

It didn't look good. It didn't seem smart. Our friends, once they stopped laughing and realized we were serious, urged us to stay home and rent a movie instead. Still, we decided to test our little-boy-on-the-river theory, so we took an afternoon's shakedown cruise down a languid, meandering stretch of river near our house. On a clear and dazzling Saturday afternoon, under sparkling Western skies and alongside cottonwoods and broad meadows, we floated through Hell. Webb got sunburned and frantic and cried. A lot. Sarah and I got exhausted and short-tempered and cried. A lot. Our friends got annoyed, even though they were vindicated, and haven't called us since.

We decided to go for it.

The risks still called for Alka-Seltzer. We talked a lot about those risks, and concluded that danger is a part of life, ours and Webb's, and there's no use letting it anchor us to the living room. The river, we decided, won't be much different from the other camping and road trips we had taken and survived. We would be careful and aware; we would let Webb be absorbed by and wander (as much as a one year old can) this great, big, dangerous world he has inherited, but we would watch him vigilantly. As for the parenting challenge, we opted for strapping a portable playpen to the rear cargo frame, offering the life-jacketed Webb room to play and crawl, or a place to just stand and watch the canyon roll by.

And, remarkably, that is what he has done for three days now. He has even napped, snoozing to the subtle slosh of the river in the shade of a tarp bungee-corded around the playpen's top. This is not to say that these three days haven't been work for me and Sarah; they have been. We have put in our time rowing hard upstream to retrieve his bath books and balls and yellow rubber duckies. We have passed hours entertaining him with lengthy and animated explanations of sedimentary geology and Anasazi history and other things he won't understand for years. We even let him read the river guide book for a while, which he did thoughtfully for nearly forty-five minutes. Or so we thought, until we realized he had pulled out all the relevant pages. We never found them.

It's been challenging, but we have survived. The trip has been injury-free and has been no more work, really, than chasing Webb through his normal days at home. I dare say Sarah and I are even having a great time, even though we have spent our nights at camp crawling

with Webb through sand and mud and into tamarisk, while our companions in the other boats sipped cocktails and took exploratory hikes. That's okay; we can live with that small sacrifice to be out here on the Dolores River together, with our son.

Still, there is something more. Last night, as we savored some time alone together after putting Webb to bed, after we were done congratulating each other, after we thought we had overcome the little-boy-on-the-river quandaries, we were disturbed to find another stream of thought flowing to some deep questions: who remembers anything they did when they were only a year old? I asked Sarah. Why suffer the risks and hassles when he won't even recall being here? Will our little one-year-old get anything out of this river trip?

I have pondered those new quandaries all day today. After rewinding and playing back these three days on the river, I conclude this little man has gotten something from this river trip. I sense he has learned and experienced from it, and even enjoyed it. This is hard to prove, of course, and the only evidence I have is his tiny laugh from the dark as Sarah and I said good night through the tent screen, his awed squeal "'Dee!" and finger pointing in the direction of a canyon wren's song, his two-toothed smile and hinged-finger wave to beached boats we passed, and his furrowed brow as his tiny fingers examined beach sand and splashed water while we bathed him in a warm side creek.

Will he remember this trip? Maybe not as the "this happened and then we did that" recollections we adults

conceive of as memories. Children are *feeling* critters, with soft and malleable spirits, and I suspect that over these three days something of his personality was sculpted by wind, shaped by the flow of the river, and colored by soil and bedrock.

Was it worth the risks and hassles? Today, as the river slides us along, now past a side canyon where narrow red walls bend away toward some unseen other world, I tally the costs and benefits. There were tears and bumps and meals later than he would have liked. Sarah and I passed on walks and swims and late nights around the fire we would have liked. Still, like all the experiences of raising a child, this venture was more work than expected but more rewarding than we could have hoped for. Although Webb may not talk or walk, he is a living, experiencing person, and we saw him breathe in the wilderness, the real living world. And this changed us all.

I squint up into the sun again and see Webb has returned to his toddler's study of the canyon's walls. He leans, his little face scrunched up against his little fingers that grip the crib's side. I am joyous beyond words. Perhaps bringing a child into this, immersing him in life and land, risk and hassle and all, is all a parent can do. Perhaps it is the best we can do.

—*Ken Wright is a writer, teacher, river guide, and father (not necessarily in that order). He lives in Colorado's San Juan Mountains with his wife, Sarah, and their children Webb and Anna. This essay is from his book* A Wilder Life: Essays from Home *(Kivaki Press, 1995).*

83

Face to Face: A Novel by Marion Dane Bauer (New York: Dell, 1993). Picked on at school by bullies, thirteen-year-old Michael confronts his fears during a trip to Colorado to see his father who works as a whitewater rafting guide, and whom Michael has not seen in eight years.

BOATS AND SKILLS FOR KIDS

White Water Rafting by Marty Nabhan (Mankato, MN: Capstone, 1991). Describes the history, equipment, and techniques of whitewater rafting.

River Thrill Sports by Andrew David (Minneapolis: Lerner Publications, 1983). A guide to the equipment, skills, and safety precautions required for rafting, canoeing, and kayaking. Also includes a glossary of pertinent terms and the international scale of river difficulty.

Canoeing is for Me by Tom Moran (Minneapolis: Lerner Publica-

tions, 1984). Two brothers describe basic canoeing skills; then they take a day-long trip during which they practice these skills.

Amazing Boats by Margarette Lincoln (New York: Knopf, 1992). Text and photos provide an introduction to the history of boats, from simple floating logs and dugout canoes to high-tech fishing boats, icebreakers, and floating airports.

Canoeing by Donna Bailey (Austin, TX: Steck-Vaughn, 1991). Readers learn the fundamental skills, techniques, and safety precautions of canoeing and kayaking.

Whitewater Kayaking by Jeremy Evans (New York: Crestwood House, 1992). Provides information about canoeing and kayaking, covering safety, equipment, paddling techniques, and more.

Danger! White Water by Otto Penzler (Mahwah, NJ: Troll Associates, 1976). Text and pho-

tographs explore the challenge of whitewater canoeing and kayaking, the equipment involved, and the skills needed.

Kayaking by Alan Fox (Minneapolis: Lerner Publications, 1993). Discusses the equipment, techniques, competitions, and other aspects of kayaking.

ENVIRONMENT FOR KIDS

The Clean Brook by Margaret Farrington Bartlett (New York: Cromwell, 1960). Shows how a stream in a natural state filters out things like mud, leaves, bugs, etc.

The River by George Maxim Ross (New York: Dutton, 1967). Two trickles of melted snow meeting on top of a mountain are the beginning of a mighty river that ends in the ocean.

Rivers and Lakes by Theodore Rowland-Entwistle (Morristown, NJ: Silver Burdett, 1987). Describes the characteristics of different kinds of rivers and lakes, and their importance to the surrounding plant, animal, and human life.

Paddling in Offshore Winds

When paddling along a coastline in an offshore wind (a wind coming from the land), don't be tempted to paddle close to cliffs, thinking it might be calmer there. Wind can shear over the cliff edge, punching the water below with gusts from unexpected directions.

—JH & RH

THE WISE MEN OF GOTHAM

Three wise men of Gotham
They went to sea in a bowl;
And if the bowl had been
stronger,
My song had been longer.
            —*from* Mother Goose

The Stream by Naomi Russell (New York: Dutton, 1991). A picture book that explains the water cycle by following the journey of a small mountain stream.

River Life by Barbara Taylor (New York: Dorling Kindersley, 1992). Examines, in text and photographs, the animals and plants that live in and along a river.

Water: A Resource in Crisis by Eileen Lucas (Chicago: Children's Press, 1991). Discusses how human activities and carelessness are polluting the earth's water supply and what must be done to clean it up.

Games— Not Just for Kids

Don't listen to those dour, pasty-faced adults who tell you that having fun is for kids, for the immature, for the irresponsible. Let them huddle into clusters to discuss the proper use of finger bowls, golf etiquette, and irregularity. Meanwhile, you can be having a little fun on the water. These books may provide you with a few ideas for fun.

Canoe Games

by Dave Ruse
(London: A & C Black, 1986)

This book is primarily for teachers of kayaking and canoeing. Have you ever tried playing "Frisbee white water" or "sandwich" or "kiss chase?" Here's your opportunity to be silly in your boat—this book is loaded with ideas for both the sane and mad. And if you never lay eyes on Ruse's book, make up your own games.

Be advised that while some of the games mentioned would be fun, others will strike you as idiotic, ridiculous, or foolhardy. For example, "Ice Carrying: This game can only be carried out when most of the ice has disappeared and there are a few isolated pieces left. The challenge is to carry back as many pieces as possible to the base without losing them." Editor's comment: no comment.

Games (and more!) for Backpackers

by June Fleming
(New York: Putnam Publishing Group, 1983)

If you never grew up, or you take your kids along on your trips, and would like some fresh ideas for entertainment, then June Fleming can help you. These games work as well for paddlers as for backpackers. Fleming hits on everything from making a plant press to a wooden harmonica, from feather collecting to juggling, from playing the spoons to cat's cradle and other string-figure games.

Some of these games will take you back to your own childhood; some others will bring out the child in you today. Either way you win and you and your friends and children will have plenty of fun sharing tales of games played, uh, how many years ago now?

85

Getting Able:
Resources for People with Disabilities

Paddling offers new worlds to explore for people with some physical disabilities—especially those with limited leg mobility. Here are a few resources and books for people who would like to explore those paddling possibilities.

Canoeing and Kayaking for Persons with Physical Disabilities

by Anne Wortham Webre and Janet Zeller
(Newington, VA: American
Canoe Association, 1990)

While this manual was written primarily for instructors of the disabled, it would make good reading for other paddlers as well. It covers a variety of useful topics, like equipment for the paddler, a checklist for the instructor, adaptations (such as back rests, customized grab loops, rear view mirrors, etc.), and rescues. There is also a good source list for adaptations (commercial firms that sell them) and a list of other books. This book is available from the A.C.A. and a useful addition to the literature of paddling.

More Good Books for Disabled Paddlers

An Introduction to Kayaking: For Persons with Disabilities by John H. Galland (Loretto, Minnesota: Vinland National Center, 1981)
Water Sports For the Disabled by the Water Sports Division of the British Sports Association for the Disabled (Wakefield, West Yorkshire, UK: EP Publishing, Ltd., 1983). Includes information on canoeing, water skiing, sailing, and many more water sports.

ACA DISABLED PADDLERS COMMITTEE

The American Canoe Association maintains a list of groups that provide programs, services, etc., for the disabled. They also maintain a list of trained paddling instructors who work with the disabled. Latest info can be obtained from the Disabled Paddlers Committee, American Canoe Association, 7432 Alban Station Blvd., Suite B-226, Springfield, VA 22150-2311; (703) 451-0141, FAX (703) 451-2245; awa@rahul.net (http://world.std.com/~reichert/aca.html).

The Essential Sea Kayaker by David Seidman (Camden, ME: Ragged Mountain Press, 1993). Includes a chapter on paddling resources for the disabled.

Leading the Way:
Resources for Trip Leaders and Instructors

☞

If your job is to teach paddling or to guide people on paddling trips, you might find the following useful:

The Wilderness Educator: The Wilderness Education Association Curriculum Guide

edited by David Cockrell
(Merrillville, IN: ICS Books, 1991)

The recent growth of adventure travel unfortunately has created an excess of guides with inadequate training. Poorly trained guides cause otherwise avoidable situations, including damage to water environments (poor campsite selection, littering, inadequate sanitation facilities, etc.), leadership problems in groups, and accidents. The Wilderness Education Association has done something toward solving those problems by getting this book out.

If you are already in a leadership role, or thinking of becoming a rafting or kayaking guide, then read this book. Because it's not light and fluffy reading, it's not for everybody. However, if you

are responsible for an outdoor expedition, be it a day trip or a three-month expedition, then you are probably going to need to know something about group dynamics, expedition behavior, personal growth of members of the party, and, surely, group safety.

This book includes nine chapters on topics as varied as emergency procedures and backcountry conservation, basic wilderness skills and decision-making ability.

The Guide's Guide: Reflections on Guiding Professional River Trips

by William McGinnis
(El Sobrante, CA: Whitewater Voyages/River Exploration Ltd., 1981)

As the title suggests, this book is for you if you work for an outfitter, or want to work for one. It includes checklists, do's and don'ts, and suggestions for handling a guided party. There is plenty of attention to safety, a paramount concern of any guide. Anyone working for a river guiding service would be well served by becoming familiar with the contents of this book, though it could use an update.

Canoeing and Kayaking: Instruction Manual

by Laurie Gullion
(Newington, VA: American
Canoe Association, 1987)

This is the "official" instruction manual put out by the American Canoe Association.

The good news is that it is comprehensive, always puts safety first, and gives the instructor or future instructor an excellent introduction to the peaks and valleys of teaching paddling. It should be required reading for anyone who is teaching paddling or for river guides who need to acquaint greenhorns with both the pleasures and dangers of river travel. There are chapters on a wide variety of topics such as safety, lesson organization, conditioning for paddling, strokes, maneuvers, river reading, rescue, and competition.

The bad news is that it reads like a dry textbook or a methodical Army manual for cleaning your M-16. But generally the good outweighs the bad, so if you want to teach paddling, you would do well to read it.

*Elements of a Teaching Progression
The National Instruction Committee recommends that instructors use these elements in their paddling lessons:*

*1. Orientation to paddling
2. Introduction of paddling strokes*

*3. Practice of paddling maneuvers
4. River practice site with moving water
5. River trip with multiple whitewater practice sites*

Crucial to learning new skills is a progression of activities that encourages students to develop solid skills.

SPEAKING WITH . . .
PAUL PETZOLDT

Now in his late eighties, Paul Petzoldt, author of *The New Wilderness Handbook* (W.W. Norton, 1984; this book is reviewed in Chapter 5), has had more time than the average lover of the outdoors to think about its meaning, its significance, and the problems we bring to it. In several ways he is not happy with what he sees.

He has observed many people get in over their heads. By doing this, he says, they put themselves *and others* at risk of life and limb. This is selfish, irresponsible, creates rescue problems for others, and draws unnecessarily on the public coffers. Things must change, Petzoldt believes.

A good rule of thumb, he says, is "If you don't know, don't go!" By this he means that a person or a party should be educated about *risks*, should learn to use *good judgment*, learn not to harm the land and waters where one travels, to have *knowledge* of one's whereabouts, to have planned ahead, and, generally, to think about what one is doing rather than to act impulsively.

Those who don't do this he calls "salmonheads." He says they're like spawning Alaskan salmon in that

they go and go and go, not knowing when to stop. The salmon proceed up, up, upstream no matter whether their flesh comes off, they lose an eye, or whatever—till they spawn—it's in their blood. But humans are supposed to be wise, to know what is beyond their capabilities, to exercise good judgment in realizing when to turn back. But too many of them are like the salmon, losing skin, breaking bones unnecessarily, and losing sight of when to stop.

His solution? In a word, education. People going out to climb mountains, descend rivers, cross oceans, or otherwise spend time in the wilds need to learn some basic skills before doing so. Mr. Petzoldt is active in and an advocate for the programs of the Wilderness Education Association. Its purpose is "to promote the professionalization of outdoor leadership and to thereby improve the safety and quality of outdoor trips and enhance the conservation of the wild outdoors."

Paul Petzoldt takes the long-term view. He wants to protect places that are wild, and have them used sensibly by people who are responsible and who care for them. Suppose just for a moment that something *you* did made you one of his "salmonheads." How might your behavior on the water change for the long-term protection of the wilds?

The varying needs of students will affect the nature of the progression . . .

. . . The purpose of an organized progression of activities, where one component builds upon another, is to help paddlers experience a sense of accomplishment and improvement. Stronger direction by the instructor at the outset speeds the introduction and practice of skills. The direction of specific activities also allows the quick spotting and immediate correction of errors. Participants expect constructive criticism in a lesson, and they are looking for guidance in improving their skills.

The Canoe Guide's Handbook: How to Plan and Guide a Trip for Two to Twelve People

by Gil Gilpatrick
(Yarmouth, ME: DeLorme Mapping Company, 1983)

This book includes comments on provisioning for a guided trip, checklists so you won't be embarrassed by forgetting to bring the canoes, and a variety of other suggestions and tips for the river guide.

"As the core is to the apple, so is judgment and decision-making ability to outdoor leadership."
—*from* The Wilderness Educator: The Wilderness Education Association Curriculum Guide

More Good Books for Instructors and Trip Leaders

Sprint Racing Canoeing, Level 1, Coaching Certification (Ottawa: Canadian Canoe Association, 1984). For any canoeing coach who wants to get "up to speed" on racing basics, terminology, and rules and regulations, this would make useful reading.

A Canoeist Manual for the Promotion of Environmental and Ethical Concerns (Hyde Park, Ontario: Canadian Recreational Canoeing Association, 1983). This manual is a teacher's guide—a must for every paddling instructor or even trip leader.

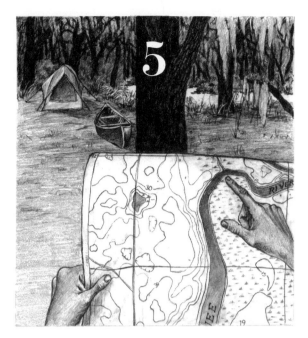

Voyaging

OR

How to Get Out of the Armchair

"One way to avoid adversity is to stay home."

—*Bill Mason in* Song of the Paddle
(NorthWord Press, 1988)

Navigation, Maps, and Atlases

⊕

Have you ever cursed yourself for not carrying the right map as you aimlessly drove around looking for your put-in? Have you ever arrived at your put-in carrying a chart of another region or, worse yet, another country? Have you ever wondered if there is *any* map at all that gives the detail you would need to run a river, cross a lake, or thread through the islands of a bay?

Whether you're paddling from your own backyard or flying all of your equipment to another continent for an extended trip, maps will be crucial to the success of your trip. Charts and maps will help you plot a course, choose campsites, arrange the best begin-ning and ending points, and more.

So, where do you get started? Begin by thinking *big;* buy yourself a world atlas. Granted, over the coming weekend you probably won't be on the Danube or the Nile, but who knows about the *next* weekend? Moreover, you will find that an atlas will get you *wondering*.

Next, think *small*. Look at your own backyard. What maps include the very spot where you are right now? It won't take reading your local map for long to see what it tells you about *water*. Have you got an ocean on that map? How about a lake? A river? A tiny brook? If none of the above, take a look after the next heavy rain and then think about what a lucky man Noah (of ark fame) was.

Next, begin collecting maps and charts. Also, visit a map library. Sound like a strange idea? Then save this one for winter, but try it. Toy stores have nothing over map libraries. And there are loads of these around the country, but begin looking at major university libraries.

There are a few other things you will want to investigate if you haven't already. One is to find a store near you that sells topographical (or "topo" for short) maps. These are put out by Uncle Sam (the U.S. Geological Survey) in the United States, as well as the Canada Map Office in Ottawa and the Mexican Geological Survey in Mexico City, but there are dealers all over that sell maps of their respective regions (stores in the northern United States are more likely to carry Canadian maps, while those in the southwestern states may stock Mexican maps). Sporting goods stores and outfitters sometimes sell them. If you are not near a sporting goods store, ask at your local library—they may have some you can copy (you can only copy maps that are in the public domain, such as those of the U.S. Geological Survey; privately produced maps are protected by copyright laws). You can also call the USGS Earth Science Information Center in Reston, VA, at 1-800-USA-Maps (1-800-872-6277). The people there know their maps and are helpful. The Map Link Company of Santa Barbara, CA, distributes maps of many map publishers in North America as well as around the world. Map Link prints a directory of maps in their inventory; they can be

BETTER THAN THE NORTH STAR

It probably goes without saying, but if you don't already have one, get a simple compass and learn the basics of using it. You may find it handy getting around the Everglades, circumnavigating Manhattan Island, or descending the Saskatchewan River through Saskatoon. Some compasses are sold with a simple manual that tells you about all you need or, if not, try these good books for orienteering basics:

The Outward Bound Map & Compass Handbook by Glenn Randall (New York: Lyons & Burford, 1989). This book is only about a hundred pages long, but it gives a good overview of using both maps and compasses.

Be Expert with Map & Compass by Bjorn Kjellstrom (New York: Collier Books, 1994). This provides a good introduction to the topic.

Land Navigation Handbook: The Sierra Club Guide to Map and Compass by W.S. Kals (San Francisco: Sierra Club Books, 1983)

Especially for paddlers, there is:

Fundamentals of Kayak Navigation by David Burch (Old Saybrook, CT: The Globe Pequot Press, 1993). The author, David Burch, has written an excellent synthesis of all a paddler would need to know about navigation. Contrary to the title, this is not a book for just kayakers, but one for any paddler—kayaker, rafter, canoeist, for any small-boater. For those who prefer the old-school approach, Burch covers compass use, dead reckoning, getting maps and charts, etc. For those who want to go high tech, he gives an overview of electronic navigation. Whichever method you prefer, this book would make an excellent addition to your library.

Above all, remember that developing an *appreciation* for maps and charts is free. You will rely on them to tell you where a body of water is and whether it can be paddled at all, or the size of a river's watershed and rate of its descent (what rapids might you expect to find).

reached at (805) 965-4402.

One of the first things to get, after the topographic map of your locale, is the *index or catalog* of topo maps to your state or province. The index or catalog will tell you the names of the many maps for your region and provide ordering information as well. In short, the index will be the key to

broadening your geographic horizons. It will also get you wondering about that stream in the next county, that lake up north, or that coastline just over there.

"Give me the map, there."
—*King Lear*

The Map Catalog: Every Kind of Map and Chart on Earth and Even Some Above It (Third Edition)

by Joel Makower

(New York: Tilden Press, 1992)

This thorough book will show you how to get topo maps, river maps, tide and current maps, bicycle route maps, aerial photographs, county maps, geologic maps, military maps, and plenty more.

You might call *The Map Catalog* a source book, because it doesn't include the maps themselves but exposes you to what is out there and how to get ahold of it. This is the sort of book that will get you sending a lot of post cards for further information and traveling to your nearby library to see if they have such-and-such. If you like maps, this book will lure you deeper and deeper into the world of cartography.

Raven Maps

Raven Maps in Medford, OR, produces some gorgeous maps (800-237-0798). This company specializes in physical maps—shaded so that relief (mountains,

river valleys, etc.) is highlighted. Raven Maps paints the shading in rich hues of brown and blue. For the paddler, these maps are *much* more interesting than political maps—Raven Maps accentuate the sorts of things that paddlers like to know. For example, the way the Columbia River Gorge slices through the Cascade Mountain Range near Portland really stands out on Raven Maps. The Ozarks practically leap off the page, as do the Badlands and the broad Hudson River valley. Raven Maps' selection includes many U.S. states individually and one map of the whole United States.

PLASTIC RAISED RELIEF MAPS

Using any map requires a little imagination—a map is nothing more than a grouping of symbols that suggest some things about a place; it is up to you to interpret the rest. There is somewhat less interpretation with a plastic raised relief map, because they are three-dimensional as well as tactile—you can actually feel the mountains, valleys, and other landforms. A good source for raised relief maps is Hubbard Scientific of Fort Collins, CO; (800) 523-5485, FAX (303) 484-1198. A common raised relief map scale is 1:250,000, so each map covers an area measuring roughly 100 by 70 miles. Hubbard produces maps for U.S. areas that have significant relief—most all of the West, and the Appalachian mountain states of the East, but none at this scale for Canada. You can order Hubbard's index first, to get an idea of their offerings.

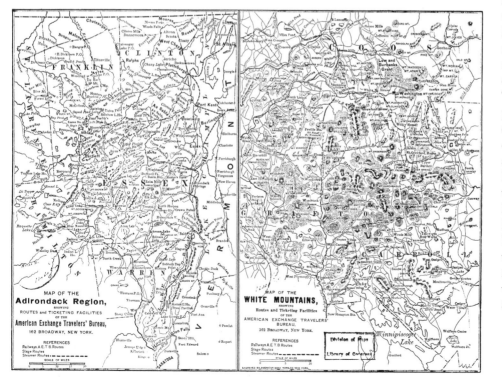

91

How to Lie with Maps

by Mark Monmonier
(Chicago: University of Chicago Press, 1991)

Never completely trust any map; after all, they are only *representations* of what is really out there. A few chapter titles give the flavor of this book: Blunders that Mislead; Maps that Advertise; Maps for Political Propaganda; Development Maps (or, How to Seduce the Town Board).

Imagine it. Having to deal with map deception before you even get to the water. What is this world coming to? What is the moral of this story? Always consult *at least two* maps of any given area. That way you see the views of two cartographers rather than one. But you also increase the likelihood of being doubly deceived . . .

The purpose of this book is to promote a healthy skepticism about maps, not to foster either cynicism or deliberate dishonesty. In showing how to lie with maps, I want to make readers aware that maps, like speeches and paintings, are authored collections of information and also are subject to distortions arising from ignorance, greed, ideological blindness, or malice.

The crowd diminishes according to the square of the distance from the nearest road and the cube of the elevation above it.
—attributed to David Brower

NEED A CANADIAN MAP?

If you are having trouble finding a store near you that offers a good stock of Canadian topographic maps, you can easily order them over the phone. Dial up the Canada Map Office in Ottawa (1-800-465-6277) and order the *index* for the area that interests you. With the index you can read them a map number, they will mail you the maps you need, and you will live happily ever after. Easy as pie.

Other Canadian resources include the Canadian Recreational Canoe Association (1029 Hyde Park Rd., Suite 5, Hyde Park, Ontario, Canada N0M 1Z0; 519-641-1261, FAX 519-473-6560). The CRC sells guidebooks and maps through their *Paddling Catalogue*. Ask them to mail you a copy.

Use a Barometer

A barometer (or altimeter, which is just a barometer with elevation marks) is a useful tool for sea kayakers, especially those who do long crossings. A rising barometer is one sign of steady or improving conditions; a falling needle might make one think twice about tackling a twenty-mile hop between islands.

—JH & RH

The Mapmakers

by John Noble Wilford
(New York: Knopf, 1981)

Although this book has nothing directly to do with paddling, it does offer something about the history of mapmaking and cartography. It is interesting to learn the background of our modern maps (topos, river, and other thematic maps, etc.). Wilford covers many of the heavy hitters in the history of cartography, from Ptolemy to John Wesley Powell, from Ortelius to NASA. Whether you are interested in the ancient or the modern, Wilford will take you there.

Atlases

Water Atlas of the United States

by James J. Geraghty, et al.
(Port Washington, NY:
Water Information Center, 1973)

This is a paddler's atlas if there ever was one. Water this, water that, water, water, water. It contains about 125 maps, 86 of them covering water issues in the conterminous 48 states and the remainder in Alaska and Hawaii. The editors call it a "visual guide to the water situation in the United States." It is sad that, in a time when water is becoming more of a precious commodity, this atlas has gone out of print. You will need to visit a library to turn up a copy.

Among other things, it includes:

• principal rivers and drainage basins

- precipitation (in inches) by state
- area (in square miles) covered by inland water
- surface-water runoff (average annual, in inches)
- normal distribution (by month) of surface-water runoff
- distribution of precipitation
- major reservoirs and dams
- water transfers between river basins
- navigable inland waterways

The last publishing date of this atlas is 1973 but it is still useful; keep in mind that nearly every aspect of water use has in-

CD-ROM MAPS

Planning a paddling trip to the American West? A software company called Coldbay produces a great set of maps on CD-ROM—its title is Rocky Mountains Recreation Maps. It is a database of topographical maps for Montana, Wyoming, Utah, Idaho, Colorado, and northern New Mexico. You can zoom in on any area of the 1:100,000 scale maps, and choose to display relief in 100-, 200-, 500- or 1,000-foot contours. You can also create elevation profiles and ask the program to estimate distances. Your PC system must be a minimum of a 386DX with 3MB RAM, 10MB HD, operating with DOS 5.0 or Windows 3.1 or higher. Suggested retail is $39.95.

tensified and since changed. There is a real need for an update to this useful atlas.

National Atlas of the United States of America

U.S. Department of the Interior, Geological Survey (Washington, DC: Government Printing Office, 1970)
It is a shame that this atlas isn't updated every five years or so. It was a tour de force if there ever was one, and luckily for paddlers, quite a bit of it is still useful and interesting. You can't buy a copy of it these days, but it is widely available in libraries. No paddler would regret having put his or her nose among its pages for a while.

Here is a sampling of the types of maps included among its four hundred–plus pages:

- physical features of the land
- natural resources of the country
- human activities
- relief maps
- land form maps
- tide range maps
- average snowfall maps
- monthly precipitation maps
- surface water maps
- floods and droughts
- water use maps

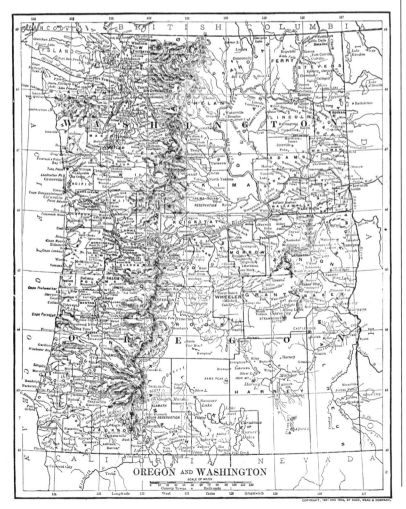

OREGON AND WASHINGTON

THE DELORME ATLASES

It goes without saying that any paddler needs decent, up-to-date maps of an area to plan shuttle arrangements, to calculate the length of a particular trip, or for a host of other reasons. If you covet maps, if you have an insatiable appetite for them, then you should get topo maps for a trip as well as others that are available. Definitely don't pass up atlases produced by the DeLorme Mapping Company.

The DeLorme atlases are done state-by-state, and although not every state has been completed, most of the frequently paddled ones have. For example, most western states now have an atlas, as do most eastern states. Many of the midwestern states are also completed as are a few of the southern states. They say they are "mapping America's back roads one state at a time."

One of the reasons these atlases are so useful is that they include not only the detailed maps of each state, but also a lot of information useful for the person heading outdoors. For example, the gazetteer, as they call it, for each state usually includes river trips, natural features of the area, hiking routes, scenic drives, bike routes, historic sites, parks, campgrounds, and more. If you want to find out if your state has been completed, call DeLorme at (800) 227-1656.

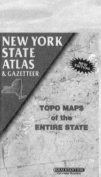

Most of the information has been superimposed on maps of the nation, revealing, for example, flood-prone areas, tide ranges all along the coasts, and where precipitation is concentrated. The scope of this atlas is exceedingly broad. It includes a lot of dated information about the economy, business, culture, and history. So although one needs to be careful in using it, paddlers can still find plenty here of interest and value.

Atlas of Environmental Issues

by Nick Middleton
(New York: Facts on File, 1989)

Do you know any kids who have an interest in paddling and their environment, and who like maps and atlases? This atlas offers maps on a variety of topics like rivers, big dams, acid rain, alternative energy, and soil erosion. It is a slim sixty pages, and strong on graphics and color, so should appeal to lots of younger paddlers.

Atlas of United States Environmental Issues

by Robert J. Mason and Mark T. Mattson
(New York: Macmillan
Publishing Company, 1990)

If you are fond of atlases, you might want to take a look at this

> "Heracleitus likens the universe to the current of a river, saying that you cannot step twice into the same stream."
> —Plato, ca. 375 B.C.

Planning and Provisioning

There is no question that a little planning goes a long way for a paddler. It is always terribly inconvenient, for example, arriving at the river's edge and discovering you have no paddles. Oh, darn. If you run quickly through a checklist prior to departing, you can avoid this sort of inconvenience. If you are going out on an extended trip, planning is all the more important. In addition to equipment, you will need to plan things like put-ins and take-outs, caching food, and emergency options.

Here are some good books for paddlers on trip planning and provisioning.

The Paddler's Planner

by Patricia J. Bell
(Eden Prairie, MN: Cat's-paw Press, 1989)
Bell's book includes various checklists, including repairs, cooking

equipment, safety, etc. But 150 of the 190 pages of this book are nothing more than a trip log where you write down the date of the trip, the starting and ending point, weather conditions, and what you had or plan to have for breakfast, lunch, and dinner. Yes, you could do the same with a spiral notebook, but the lists are handy, and buying such a book might get you started keeping trip logs, which are very handy for future trip reference.

The Complete Wilderness Paddler

by James West Davidson and John Rugge
(New York: Vintage Books, 1983)
The authors of this book take a unique approach to demonstrating paddling and trip planning. The gist is that they paddle a river (the Moisie in Canada) and take you, the

one. It includes a wide range of maps and accompanying text of interest to paddlers, including water use and quality, parks, recreation, wildlife, the Wild & Scenic Rivers System, the interstate highway network, and a few other pleasant surprises. This is no ten-minute atlas; you will want to sit down and get comfortable with it in your lap.

The Atlas of Natural Wonders

by Rupert O. Matthews
(New York: Facts on File, 1988)
This special atlas will surely put most paddlers happily in dreamland. About fifty areas are highlighted, each given about four pages of background text, photos, maps, and drawings. There are a few places that most any paddler would know, such as the Amazon, Niagara Falls, and the Grand Canyon, but also thumbnail sketches of lesser-known areas, such as Lake Baikal (Commonwealth of Independent States), Lake Titicaca (Peru/Bolivia), Lake Vanern (Sweden), and Milford Sound (New Zealand).

95

reader, through the entire journey from soup to nuts, start to finish, inside and out. Each chapter is devoted to a different aspect of the trip, from finding where to go to general planning, securing maps,

dealing with winds, portaging, whirlpools, food, disasters, and about everything else imaginable. For anyone planning an extended trip, or for someone who simply wants a very broad look at all the

things to think about prior to taking a trip, this book would be worth its weight in freshly panned river gold.

Going With the Flow

There are several good, near-instant sources for data on rivers,

---

HOW TO PACK A SEA KAYAK

by Jonathan Hanson

How Not to Pack

My worst packing experience occurred on the second trip of my sea kayak guiding career. I met a group of six in Bahía Kino, Mexico, and we caravaned to the launch point at Punta Chueca, a Seri Indian village. We were a bit late and I had some business to attend to with the Seris, so I decided to let the group—self-proclaimed experienced kayakers—pack their own boats, after they assured me they were "almost" within my guidelines of three dry bags per person.

When I returned they were finished. But virtually all the community gear—food, stove, water, etc.—was stacked by my boat. With no time to argue I stuffed and strapped and piled on deck until my poor 17-foot single resembled a garbage scow. When we launched, my view over the bow looked like one of those films taken from a submarine's conning tower, shortly after the "dive" klaxon has sounded. It appeared I had slightly exceeded the design displacement of my craft, and the effect was alarming—but we made it to our destination on Tiburon Island and set up camp.

The group had actually done a

really good job of packing their gear. A colorful beach umbrella was well wedged into a front compartment, along with two folding chairs and a multi-sport whiffle-ball set in a string bag. The rear of a double held the other four chairs, several sleeping bags that looked to be good to at least 40-below-zero, and an enormous dome tent. Another single held the volleyball net and poles. I suppose they could have saved some space if they'd deflated the volleyball itself, since they had prudently brought along a sturdy metal pump anyway. Two roll-up tables and an equal number of soft coolers filled with unmentionably cheap beer completed the kit. As the three couples frolicked in the sand, it became obvious where they had scrimped in order to bring so much recreational gear: clothing. Throughout our stay Seri fishermen frequently cruised by offshore to admire the scene, which I christened Venice Beach II.

The moral of the story is, don't start your own guiding business. The sub-moral is, don't take more stuff than you need.

Safety First

The most important parameter to keep in mind when packing a sea kayak—or any boat—is safety. There

are several aspects to this, including weight distribution, load control, windage, flotation, and access.

The heaviest items in your boat—water containers, canned food, and the like—should be kept *low* and *centered*. This more than anything else will determine how the boat handles on the water. Placing heavy objects low helps the stability of the craft immensely. Keeping weight away from the ends of the boat does a couple of things: it helps the bow and stern climb waves rather than punch through them, and it makes turning easier (this is why the best sports cars are mid-engined; in engineering terms, the desired effect is called a *low polar moment of inertia*). Weight should be centered from side to side as well—an easy detail to overlook, but a boat canted even a little to one side will want to turn in endless circles.

Once the weight is in its proper place, make sure it doesn't go elsewhere. The cargo in your front and rear compartments should be immovable. Usually this is not a problem on long trips, since the boat will be packed full. If there is loose space, it can be filled with a spare dry bag, rolled to capture air—which serves the double purpose of providing extra flotation. As your food and water

particularly flow levels, available at paddlers' fingertips.

Waterline National River Gauge Reports is not a book, but a 900 (toll) phone service. Here's the gist: First you dial (800) 945-3376 to order lists of gauge codes (six-digit numbers) for the regions of the country that interest you. Each code number is for a different gauging station. You look over the list of rivers for which you would like a gauge reading, then dial (900) 726-4243 (with the appropriate six-digit number in hand) and listen to a recorded voice tell you that the level from such and such gauging station is 4.02 cfs or 6.59 cfs or whatever for that date at whatever time the reading was taken.

The good news is that the reports are current, cost maybe a couple of dollars apiece (around $1.25/minute of connection time), and may help you plan where to go, what to expect for water, etc. The bad news is that you've got to

volume decreases throughout the trip, more air can be added to the bags to keep things tight.

When the boat starts filling up, it's tempting to strap gear on deck. But not only does this decrease stability, it creates windage that can prove quite hazardous in a blow. Try to limit the deck load to a small bag in front of you, for cameras, snacks, and radios or other emergency gear.

Many people assume that their "watertight" compartments will keep the contents dry and provide flotation in the event of a capsize. But much can happen to destroy the integrity of those spaces: hatches can come off, bulkheads can come loose, or the hull can be punctured. And almost all compartments will leak a little over the course of a bouncy trip. So keep *all* your gear in dry bags, thus providing both protection and flotation. It's surprising how little trapped air it takes to turn a dead weight into a flotation device.

Organizing

Buy your dry bags in as many colors as you can find. This allows easy segregation of kitchen gear from clothing, etc., and recognition at a glance. Transparent bags are wonderful for this, but they aren't as durable. Medium-sized bags are more useful than large ones; they are easier to fit through hatches and into empty spaces, and easier to sort through. It also helps to have different configurations; long, thin ones for the bow and stern, shorter, fatter ones for amidships. Laminated tags are helpful to specify contents.

It is extremely helpful to practice loading your boat at home before a trip, but I don't know *anyone* obsessive enough to actually do such a thing (of course, for a serious expedition the rules change, and trial packing at home becomes a necessity). The best alternative is to have plenty of time at your launch point to go slowly and pay attention to the rules listed under "Safety First."

If the boat is going to be heavily loaded, pack it as close to the water as possible, to avoid long drags. A corollary of this: beware when loading hard or sharp-edged objects. Keep them away from direct contact with the hull, as they can create a wear point or even a puncture.

Keep in mind your itinerary. Camping will be the last thing you do each day, so the tent, which is a good bow-filler and fairly light, can go in first, followed by sleeping bags and clothes. Keep snacks and/or lunch items easily accessible. And do *not* pack away any safety devices such as first aid or survival kits, radios, or flares. These should have well-secured spots in the cockpit, on deck, or on your person.

One of the most helpful things I've learned is to make a diagram of my load arrangement each trip. This allows me to replicate the loading sequence painlessly each morning, and also to know where any particular bag is in the boat, in case I need something odd—such as the whiffle ball set or the beach umbrella.

—Writer Jonathan Hanson of Tucson, Arizona, has been exploring North America by sea kayak for over ten years, from Baja to the Arctic. For several years he operated a sea kayak touring company in Mexico's Sea of Cortez.

Backpaddling

No matter how strong your arms are, the river is stronger. One way to backpaddle effectively is to use your hip as a fulcrum. Place the paddle shaft against your hip and pull your upper hand toward you during the stroke. Beware of submerged rocks and powerful hydraulics.

—JB & TB

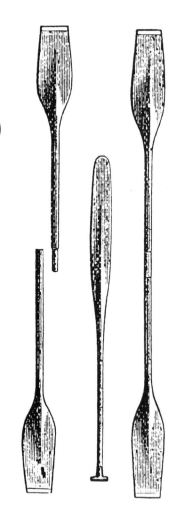

know what those numbers mean. Is a particular reading high, medium, or low for that river? If you don't know what the numbers mean, the information is about as useful to you as knowing the depth of snow in Siberia. But there are plans to issue something that puts the numbers in that all important *context*. So stay tuned.

Another source is the American Whitewater Affiliation's Internet web page. Their River by State listing is updated frequently and will give you the latest information on access, dam release schedules, and conservation. The AWA River by State information is at http://www.awa.org/awa/river_project/states.html.

The New Wilderness Handbook

by Paul Petzoldt
(New York: W.W. Norton, 1984)

Paul Petzoldt first climbed the Grand Teton about seventy years ago, so one could safely say that he's had time to reflect on outdoor recreation and its increasing popularity. He has taken the time to think deeply about it and both how we use and abuse the outdoors. Fortunately he has written down, in *The New Wilderness Handbook,* many of his ideas on enjoying, appreciating, and not ruining those places we love to visit. He includes chapters on equipment, leadership, clothing, survival, outdoor ethics, and a lot more. To all this he appends several useful checklists of equipment and supplies. And, while this book is not directed specifically at paddlers, there is much of use to any

paddler, but especially to trip leaders, professional river guides, and commercial outfitters. Having this book in your personal camping/paddling library would add the voice and wisdom of *years* of experience to your understanding of what it's all about.

The Canadian Canoeing Companion: An Illustrated Resource Guide To Paddling Canada's Wilderness

by Alex Harvey
(Winnipeg, Manitoba: Thunder Enlightening Press, 1988)

The title is a bit misleading here. This is actually a trip planner's book that discusses trip planning, paddling skills, rescues, care of equipment, a large chapter on making your own equipment, and other related material. A lot of the book has nothing to do with Canada, but the section on maps does discuss getting Canadian maps and the resource lists at the end include many Canadian organizations, sources for information, equipment suppliers, schools, and more. But the sources will grow increasingly out of date as time goes on.

The Expedition Cookbook

by Carolyn Gunn
(Denver: Chockstone Press, 1988)

While not particularly oriented toward paddlers, *The Expedition Cookbook* still offers a great deal to anyone planning a major trip. Expedition nutrition is a world unto itself, and this book would give the first-time expedition party a good bang for its buck.

GETTING ALL TIED UP

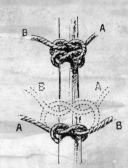

A word of wisdom: avoid having your raft, kayak, or canoe run rapids with no people in it—*tie* it to a tree or stake it as you scout downstream. Your life will be so much better this way.

But before you even hit the water, you will likely need to tie your boat to a vehicle to get there. Then you will need to tie in your gear before you take off. You'll also need to tie a painter (bow and stern line) to your boat to prepare it for pulling, for lining around bad drops, or tracking up others. Get the picture? In short, it is advisable to learn a few skills with ropes and knots. It isn't absolutely necessary, but it is useful.

There are as many ideas about knots, lines, and ropes as there are paddlers. Some people master two or three good knots and do just fine, others like to become experts at every conceivable knot known. Still others don't really know how to tie knots, they just make do with quantity. Artist, author, and paddler Bill Mason used to tie a *lot* of knots when something needed to be secured. Here's what Mason wrote of knots in his *Song of the Paddle* (NorthWord Press, 1988): "I don't know how to tie knots . . . when I'm tying a really important one—for example, when I'm filming out of a helicopter and I'm leaning halfway out the door and if it comes undone I'm dead—I tie a lot of knots. Like maybe a hundred of them. But I've never been killed because I don't know how to tie knots. . . . If you want to talk about rope, that's another matter. I know a lot of things

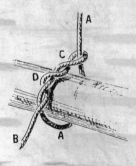

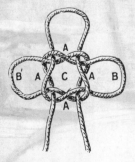

about rope. For example, ropes are always too short or too long . . . another thing about rope is that you always have less than you thought you had."

Many of the books on canoeing, kayaking, and rafting include chapters dealing with rope work, and here are a few books that cover the highlights and then some:

The Morrow Guide to Knots (for Sailing, Fishing, Camping, Climbing) by Mario Bigon and Guido Regazzoni (New York: William Morrow and Co., 1982). A marvelous little book with many color photos that clearly show the simple way to tie most any knot.

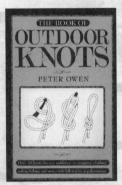

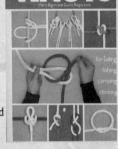

The Book of Outdoor Knots by Peter Owen (New York: Lyons & Burford, 1993). A fine book including sections on manufacturing rope, choosing rope, caring for rope, and selecting knots. Its excellent diagrams make easy work of first-time knot tying.

The Basic Essentials of Knots for the Outdoors by Cliff Jacobson (Merrillville, IN: ICS Books, 1990)

Knots & Splices by Cyrus L. Day (Camden, ME: International Marine Publishing Company, 1995)

Ashley Book of Knots (New York: Doubleday, 1993, originally published in 1944). This tome is a comprehensive classic.

66

Elements of Camping, and Camping Elements

Paddlers who are on the water for as short as a weekend or as long as a lifetime have to come to grips with the elements. In the old days, the elements consisted only of earth, air, fire, and, luckily, water. Nowadays the list is expanded to include hydrogen, oxygen, bismuth, rubidium, and a special one for paddlers, palladium. Besides these, there are loads of other ones, but one doesn't see them along the riverbanks very often.

Some of the elements that this section is really about, though, such as insects and rain, must be prepared for or they could cast a pall over your adventure. It is always better to cast a tarp over your campsite than a pall over it; this way, the rain is less bothersome and your friends are more tolerable.

What follows represents a sampling of the thinking on how to deal with life when your shelter is of the portable rather than the permanent

sort. With luck, they will help you to improve your camping skills and enjoy your outings more and more.

Canoeing and Camping: Beyond the Basics

by Cliff Jacobson
(Merrillville, IN: ICS Books, 1992)

This book is for the person who likes to read everything available about canoeing and camping. The author often uses a conversational or chatty tone, or sometimes the tone of a lecture, but all in all it is a useful book.

Woodcraft and Camping

by Nessmuk (George Washington Sears)
(New York: Dover, 1963, reprint of 1920 original)

Just as Thoreau, John Muir, Aldo Leopold, and Rachel Carson are key figures in the history of conser-

vation, Nessmuk is for camping and love of the outdoor life. Nessmuk was hardly a fan of buildings, pavement, and cities. His preface to *Woodcraft and Camping* consists of the following short poem:

100

For brick and mortar
breed filth and crime,
With a pulse of evil
that throbs and beats;
And men are withered
before their prime
By the curse paved in
with the lanes and streets.

And lungs are poisoned
and shoulders bowed,
In the smothering reek
of mill and mine;
And death stalks in
on the struggling crowd—
But he shuns the shadow
of oak and pine.

Nessmuk writes of campfires, outdoor cooking, fishing, getting lost, hatchets and knives, and plenty more. Although the materials have changed a great deal since this was written, there is still much to recommend it. If nothing else, it would be great fun to read a selection among friends on your next outing. Try his concoction for dealing with those pesky, bothersome, vile, wretched, foul, annoying, irksome, hellish, disturbing, unpleasant, biting insects: "Three ounces pine tar, two ounces castor oil, one ounce pennyroyal oil. Simmer all together over a slow fire, and bottle for use."

Surely we don't enjoy the bugs any more today than Nessmuk did eighty years ago. But today we apply goo to our skin that eats through some types of plastic. Hmmmm.

Lots has changed about the ways we camp versus the way it was done in the past. We don't trench around our tents; we don't make bough beds; in many places we don't build fires. If you want to learn how to camp by today's standards get ahold of Laura and Guy Waterman's book

HAVING A "PLAN B"

One of the things no one ever tells you when growing up is that you'll need a lot of "Plan B"s. Because Murphy's Law is alive and well, your paddling plans will undoubtedly encounter problems of some sort. When this happens, actually *before* it happens, it pays to have thought of what you would do *if* . . .

Try these things to at least begin thinking about this "Plan B" stuff:

Start by using checklists. They are developed by people who have, at one time or another, forgotten everything that's on the list.

Try to anticipate everything that could go wrong on your trip—bad weather, rising water, no water, uncooperative animals, gear failure, access problems to put-ins or take-outs, civil war—and have an *alternative* ready.

Talk with friends about what they have done to cope with problems that have arisen while on their trips—strategies for raising sunken boats, repairing damaged equipment, what to do if someone is injured, etc.

Try not to put all your eggs in one basket—spread the eggs around so that if the basket goes swimming there is another basket with some eggs in it. For example, to continue the food motif, make sure all the trip's food is not packed in the one boat that is lying at the bottom of those rapids . . .

Remember that when "Plan A" falls through, you will have a good story to tell sometime in the future (another good reason to keep a trip log or diary).

101

Backwoods Ethics (The Countryman Press, 1993; this book is reviewed in Chapter Eight), but if you would like some entertaining reading on how it was done a few years back, read Nessmuk's little classic. He won't let you down.

Landing Through Surf

When landing through surf, remember that waves come in sets. Watch from offshore for a few minutes; you'll soon find the pattern of large waves followed by smaller ones. Then you can time your landing to ride in on a small wave.

—JH & RH

THE OUTWARD BOUND®
CANOEING HANDBOOK

PAUL LANDRY
&
MATTY McNAIR

The Outward Bound Canoeing Handbook

by Paul Landry and Matty McNair
(New York: Lyons & Burford, 1992)

The Outward Bound people do good work. Add this book to their catalog of achievements. Outward Bound helps people develop leadership skills, confidence in themselves and their abilities, a compassion for

WHY A SHOTGUN OR PEPPER SPRAY IS ON MY EXPEDITION EQUIPMENT LIST

by Alan Kesselheim
On a number of expeditions, even into well-known bear country, I've been swayed not to take a gun or pepper spray. I believe that clean camping practices and careful avoidance of obvious bear territory will eliminate all but the extraordinary encounters. If I don't bother them, they won't bother me. But it's exactly those extraordinary encounters that decided the issue for me. In years of wilderness travel through bear country, I've had only two confrontations, but they were enough to convince me for life.

In the first instance, six of us in three canoes descended the final miles of the Seal River in northern Manitoba, wending through delta channels before reaching Hudson Bay. Paddling around a bend, we suddenly faced an impressive polar bear, just in the process of climbing into the water. Our initial reaction of awe, and a scramble for camera gear, was closely followed by nervous consternation, as the white bear swam directly toward us, blocking our progress.

Retreating to a far shore, we spent an agonizing ten minutes pinned down by a bear that exhibited curiosity without fear. It patrolled back and forth twenty yards away, and was completely unfazed by our shouting, pan banging and whistle-blowing. Finally, the bear swam far enough to one side to allow our hurried escape, but had it been more aggressive, a gun or pepper spray would have been our only hope of real defense.

The second confrontation involved a black bear in northern

Alberta, and ended on a more sobering note. My partner and I had camped at the beginning of the Grand Rapid portage on the Athabasca River, and spent the next morning navigating the mile-long carry. Returning after the first load, we found that a bear had been into

our equipment, ransacking packs for food. While we assessed damage, the bear reappeared, probably assuming that it had equal claim to this windfall. Our shouts did nothing to scare it off. Only retrieving the 12-gauge shotgun and firing into the air drove the tormentor away. But just tem-

porarily. It returned twice more while we packed up, each time running off when we fired shots toward it.

We escaped from the campsite with all our equipment, and managed the long, densely-vegetated portage, only to have to wait out a thunderstorm at the far end. While it rained, the insistent bruin accosted us again, having doggedly pursued us for over a mile. Running out of the woods, it charged to within fifteen feet before I shot and killed it.

I am not a hunter, and garnered no satisfaction from killing a vital wild animal, but I did experience an overwhelming sense of relief. Suddenly that shotgun seemed a whole lot less cumbersome. I am far from an expert on guns, but my choice of a 12-gauge for bear protection has been endorsed by people who live in bear country. When defensive protection is the gun's main purpose, and short-range confrontations are the most likely scenario, there are few more effective weapons than a 12-gauge shotgun loaded with slugs. While handguns have some proponents, and are less

burdensome, their effectiveness is dubious, and they are illegal in some countries such as Canada.

I purchased a used 12-gauge "riot gun" at a gun shop, and have been pleased with its characteristics. The magazine can hold over a half dozen shells, which can be fired rapidly if necessary. Some people choose to alternate rounds of large buckshot with slugs, believing that if one ammunition doesn't prove effective, the other will. I assume that in last-resort circumstances I'll want the most lethal combination possible, and so favor slugs.

More recently, canisters of pepper spray (capsicum is the potent active ingredient) have come on the market. I've largely replaced the shotgun with the canister on most forays into bear country. The pepper spray is lightweight, compact, and convenient by comparison. A holster allows you to strap it on your belt during portages or day hikes, and the spray is reputed (through many testimonials) to stop charging or insistent bears cold.

I can't claim personal experience

with the spray, and I admit to a certain nervousness about a product with an effective range of thirty feet (pretty close to a charging bear!) I also worry about windy conditions and bears that are so enraged that nothing short of a freight train will stop them. Even so, the pepper spray strikes me as a viable and reasonable, not to mention less deadly, alternative.

Many people travel repeatedly in bear country without a gun or pepper spray and never have problems. More power to them. Much as I abhor any Rambo connotations, I've come to feel about self defense in bear country the way I feel about seat belts in a car. When the statistics catch you, its value is pretty hard to refute.

—Alan Kesselheim avoids bear confrontations but regularly faces three charging children in Bozeman, Montana. He is the author of four books and numerous magazine articles. This essay is adapted from his article published in Canoe *magazine, July 1988.*

---

the land and waters, and much more. This book provides a good, short introduction to what this paddling stuff is all about. One of the best things about *The Outward Bound Canoeing Handbook* is that the portions on equipment, technique, and safety are all very simply written—not an abundance of jargon and technical this-and-that. It's very easy to follow and the drawings help illustrate the key points. Note though, that this book covers

basics; it doesn't get into advanced whitewater technique, high-tech materials, and the like.

⋎

Lightning is a powerful force, carrying a current of up to fifty million volts and reaching temperatures of fifty thousand degrees Fahrenheit. Each year in the United States lightning is responsible for over one thousand injuries and two hundred to three hundred deaths. Seventy to eighty percent of the people struck by

lightning survive. To reduce your chances of getting injured by lightning, learn what to do so you will not find yourself on the water during a thunderstorm. . . .

When you first see lightning or hear thunder, you should think seriously of getting off the water. . . . Once off the water, seek a place which has minimum chances of attracting lightning. The best shelter is in a clump of trees that are shorter than the surrounding trees. Tall trees are dangerous, as they act as lightning rods. When a tree is struck by lightning, the electricity runs down the trunk and out through the roots. You can insulate yourself from possible ground currents by sitting on your PFD. . . .

Harsh Weather Camping in the Nineties: Secrets, Suggestions, Tips & Techniques

by Sam Curtis
(Birmingham, AL: Menasha Ridge Press, 1993)

Who hasn't been outdoors when the heavens opened? When it happens, it tends not only to soak clothing but also to dampen spirits. Look at it this way—it gives you new story-telling stock. Paddlers don't always have fish stories, so a little rain, intense heat, bitter cold, or other such pleasant miseries provide you with anecdotes for the

104

DEAR DIARY . . .

Some folks like to keep a journal of their trips. Journals or logs can be fun—to review a year or five years or twenty-five years later—and also useful—a place to look up favorite campsites, good or bad take-outs, that brand of sock that worked so well, etc.

If you record a trip, here are a few things you might like to note:

- name of destination (river, lake, ocean, bay, etc.)
- trip members
- dates
- put-ins, take-outs, and distance covered
- flow, river ratings and gauges to watch, or tides, etc.
- dams or breakwaters
- portages
- shuttle information
- problems encountered and what to do differently next time
- positive experiences
- weather
- history and anecdotes
- pollution or water quality
- campsites
- maps and guidebooks

folks back home.

Sam Curtis tells us that "a rainy day is mainly a state of mind." The trick, he says, is to be prepared for it both in your mind and with the proper equipment. In *Harsh Weather Camping*, Curtis deals with all sorts of weather conditions. He covers such topics as the right footwear, good rain pants, socks, hats, sleeping bags, tarps, gaiters, food, wind, hypothermia, underwear, and plenty more. He has included a synopsis of the strengths and weaknesses of both natural and synthetic materials used by wet

weather clothing manufacturers. He touches on how to avoid having that large pond build up around your sleeping bag at midnight, how to choose clothing and equipment that don't steal either all your comfort or good spirits. He even gives a few tips on watching weather, "reading" clouds, etc. This book is a handy collection of tips on how to enjoy camping under conditions widely varying and frequently encountered on earth.

More Good Books about Camping

Simple Tent Camping: The Basics of Camping by Car or Canoe by Zora and David Aiken (Camden, ME: Ragged Mountain Press, 1996).

Backwoods Ethics, Second Edition, by Laura and Guy Waterman (Woodstock, VT: The Countryman Press, 1993). This fine book is reviewed in Chapter Eight.

How to Shit in the Woods: An Environmentally Sound Approach to a

Lost Art by Kathleen Meyer (Berkeley: Ten Speed Press, 1994). Although this sounds like a satire, this book actually has some useful information in it (see the review in Chapter Eight). Must reading for all campers.

and seeds of several sorts. If you are a sage and your friends Rosemary and Basil are cumin along, you'll have a dilly of a thyme with this salt-of-the-Earth gang.

Fuel for Paddlers
☺

Most of us have ended up on a trip on which someone else was in charge of the food. If you were lucky, the cook was a paddling gourmet and concocted a never-ending stream of sumptuous fare, from poached trout to stuffed wild mushrooms in a lemon-herb sauce. Or, you may have been extremely unlucky, and your cook was no cook at all, but a fan of those little brown packages found at Army surplus stores. The ones marked: Meal, Ready to Eat. Don't ask questions.

While MREs may meet your basic caloric requirements, and certainly are not very much trouble, learning a few camp cooking tricks, as well as planning your meals ahead of time, will add new dimensions to your camping experience. Don't they say that variety is the spice of life?

River Runners' Recipes

by Patricia Chambers
(Seattle: Pacific Search Press, 1984)
There is nothing like a specialized cookbook for river rats. Who would want a crummy carrot salad

when you can have Westwater [River] Carrot Salad? Or plain old egg salad when Youghiogheny Egg Salad is available? Anyone for Tuolumne Rellenos? Wolf River Yogurt Cake? Inner Gorge Bean Dip? King's River Spinach Salad?

Besides plenty of recipes for breakfast, lunch, dinner, hors d'oeuvres, breads, veggies, sweets, and more, Patricia Chambers gives the river cook numerous planning suggestions and tips in the early chapters of this handy book. Her list of spices is extensive: not just paprika and pepper, but also celery

Good Food for Camp and Trail: All-Natural Recipes for Delicious Meals Outdoors

by Dorcas S. Miller
(Boulder, CO: Pruett Publishing Company, 1993)
Look at it this way: aren't you going paddling in the first place because you enjoy it, because it's peaceful, exhilarating, healthy, etc.? Well, if you are what you eat, why not stop eating bologna and start eating well. Your body will thank

105

you. Dorcas Miller will make that easy and won't overwhelm you with do's and don'ts. In the first half of her book, Miller lists recipes; in the other half she discusses planning meals, nutrition for the active person, buying trail food locally and through mail-order houses, etc. Miller offers plenty of practical advice. She sums it up when she writes, "The two most important aspects of a trip are the food and the weather. You can't do much about the weather, but you certainly can do a lot about the food."

This is certainly among the best of a new breed of outdoor cookbooks.

❧

Gorp: Good Old Raisins and Peanuts (5 cups)

Gorp has as many recipes as granola does. You can mix various nuts and seeds, dried fruit, and chocolate in whatever combination suits your taste.

Gorp 1 (without chocolate)

1 C. peanuts, 1 C. walnuts, 1 C. raisins, 1 C. coconut, 1 C. chopped dried fruit. At home: mix ingredients and bag. Nutrition per ½ cup: 288 calories, 8 grams protein, 30 grams carbohydrate, 18 grams fat.

Gorp 2 (with chocolate)

1 C. peanuts, 1 C. walnuts, 1 C. raisins, 1 C. chocolate bits. Nutrition per ½ cup: 365 calories, 9 grams protein, 36 grams carbohydrate, 24 grams fat.

Unimportant afterthought: Lexicographers haven't been able to crack the gorp nut. Some think it is derived from the word glop, some say good old raisins and peanuts, bureaucrats think ground operations re-

view panel, some just shrug their shoulders. The shoulder shruggers may be on to something . . .

❧

Wanapitei Canoe Trippers' Cookbook

by Carol Hodgins

(Cobalt, Ontario: Highway Book Shop, 1982)

Readers are told in the foreword to this book that the author is the trip stores director for a wilderness canoeing organization on Lake Temagami in Ontario. It is clear not only that she has experience feeding people in the wilds, but that she has done her nutritional and economic homework.

SPEAKING WITH . . .
DORCAS MILLER

It doesn't take much paddling experience to realize that what gets expended in energy must be replaced with food. This is one of the fundamental laws of physics.

Dorcas Miller will tell you that the food you eat outdoors becomes an even more important part of your day there than it does on the home front. Because she has learned that she can't control the weather, she puts planning time and energy into deciding what foods would be best for a trip.

Among other things, she recommends asking the following food-related questions prior to heading out:

1. How much energy will this type of activity require? If you don't take enough food you are *far* more likely to end up looking trouble in the eye.
2. What style will this group like? We're not talking about the world of fashion here, but whether the group wants simple, easy-to-eat fare or enjoys the ritual of cooking, eating, and socializing.
3. Ask group members what they like. This may sound ridiculously simple, but sometimes the little things in life can be the big things. If someone in your group *really* likes chocolate, bring some along; it will do double duty—first as energy, twice as psychological boost.

Why settle for a wasteland of a meal like ramen noodles, she says, when, with just a little effort, you can do some simple baking or drying of foods, and be a much happier, infinitely better nourished camper?

The book is about ninety pages long, the first third consisting of a summary of nutrition for the paddler, costs, packing, preparation, cooking, flexibility when things go wrong, etc. The other two-thirds of the book consists of recipes—and she includes variety. For example, there is a recipe for basic pancakes, but also for crepes; there is quick-fried rice and vegetarian shepherd's pie; there are butterscotch bars, gorp, brownies, and white cake. And that's just a taste!

Remember the old saying "you are what you eat"? Well, if you're not eating as well as you might, why not let paddling introduce you to the world of good nutrition? Then you will not only get a respectable day's exercise, but also eat well and maybe even have an extra penny in your pocket at day's end.

NOLS Cookery
(Third Edition)

edited by Sukey Richard, Donna Orr,
and Claudia Lindholm
(Mechanicsburg, PA: NOLS
and Stackpole Books, 1991)

The National Outdoor Leadership school (NOLS) in Lander, WY, has given a lot of thought to much of what we do outside. Cooking is no exception. In this handy and brief (about one hundred pages) book they offer all kinds of practical advice to the cook or would-be cook. Suggestions are made for planning for large and small groups; then there is a discussion on cooking; and finally about fifty pages are devoted to hearty, nutritious recipes.

The NOLS approach may be different from what you are accustomed to. Instead of planning each

IN PRAISE
OF CAST-IRON COOKING

The art of cooking in a cast-iron Dutch oven is fortunately alive and well among the paddling community. Some of us think a Dutch oven is one of the better reasons to choose paddling over backpacking . . . if you've never savored steaming dumplings over sumptuous stew, or hot and spicy apple cobbler, you are missing out on some of life's greater pleasures.

Some tips on Dutch ovens and cooking in them:

- Don't be tempted by lighter aluminum varieties, which burn food more easily.
- A true Dutch oven will have legs, and a slightly domed, lipped lid with a handle.
- Dutch ovens are sold by inches-in-diameter. Common sizes are 10 (4 quarts), 12 (6 qts.), 14 (8 qts.) and 16 (12 qts.). Twelve- and 14-inch ovens are most useful.
- Season a new cast-iron oven by coating the inside (after washing with soap) with vegetable shortening or bacon fat and heating it in a 400-degree oven for about an hour. Wipe down, cool, and repeat. Never use soap or harsh scouring pads on your oven again (it takes the seasoning off). A properly seasoned and cared-for Dutch oven will last nearly forever.
- Start learning to cook with a Dutch oven by using charcoal briquettes; they provide even, easy-to-manage heat. A rough guideline for guesstimating temperature in a 12-inch oven is as follows: for 350 degrees, use 8 coals under, 16 on the lid; for 450 degrees, use 10 coals under, 20 on the lid. (Dutch oven recipe books tell you how many to use; once you get the hang of it, you can adapt your home recipes in the field.)
- Every time the lid is removed, cooking time should be extended by five to ten minutes.
- Useful accessories: a "gonch" hook to lift the oven and lid (a pair of sturdy pliers will do); a lid stand, to keep it out of the dirt when checking on dinner (try a ring cut from a coffee can); and a pair of tongs for handling coals.

Here are two good Dutch oven cookbooks:
The Outdoor Dutch Oven Cookbook by Sheila Mills (Camden, ME: Ragged Mountain Press, 1997)
The Old-Fashioned Dutch Oven Cookbook by Don Holm (Caldwell, ID: The Caxton Printers, 1970)

107

meal beforehand, they practice "bulk rationing"— calculating how many pounds of food the average active camper needs per day multiplied by the number of days out. This approach lets the cook of the

day decide what to cook based on such things as (a) what do people feel like today? (b) what is the cook capable of? (c) what needs to be used up? The beauty of this approach is that you always have *options*—you are not locked into a rigid daily planner.

The editors are honest and don't beat around the bush. They speak of freeze-dried foods as tasteless, expensive, and ridiculously high in salt. Moreover, they recommend that if the directions say "serves six," count on three; "serves two," again, halve it. Having said all that they realize that, at times, particularly when weight is a factor, freeze-dried foods are a viable alternative.

Canoe and Camp Cookery

by Seneca
(New York: Forest and Stream
Publishing Company, 1885)
Definitely not the latest in cookbooks, nor one with the very healthiest of recipes, but definitely worth looking at. At the very least, it is entertaining. This book is a fine example of the wealth of wonderful older things written about paddling. Of course, you won't find

REMINDER

Just about all of the books mentioned in this catalog can be obtained by: (a) patronizing a local bookstore; (b) contacting one of the many paddling suppliers listed in Chapter 3 (most have toll-free phone numbers); or (c) inquiring at a library. See also the section in Chapter 1 called "About This Book" for good sources of hard-to-find books.

this book on the shelves of your favorite bookstore, but ask your library to find you a copy and you'll be delighted and amused.

Woodchucks and Porcupines

When properly cooked, are little inferior to any game. They must be thoroughly parboiled before cooking, and then may be roasted or stewed. A young woodchuck or porcupine may be baked in the ground with the hide on, after having been drawn, and is very palatable.

Camp Catering: Or How to Rustle Grub for Hikers, Campers, Mountaineers, Packers, Canoeists, Hunters, Skiers, and Fishermen

by Louise and Joel Hildebrand
(Brattleboro, VT: Stephen Daye Press, 1938)
While you probably shouldn't go looking here for the latest information about nutrition and dietary needs while outdoors, *Camp Catering* has aged surprisingly well. There are sections on all the regulars: beverages, breakfast recipes, dinner suggestions, etc. But there are also suggestions for finding "natural foods" (foraging), cooking in the ground, seasoning, cooking trout, and a good deal more.

There's even a chapter titled, "The Ski Camper's Cuisine." Where else would you find that? Even the illustrations have a light touch.

Gorp, Glop & Glue Stew: Favorite Foods From 165 Outdoor Experts

by Yvonne Prater and Ruth Dyar Mendenhall
(Seattle, WA: The Mountaineers, 1982)
You might call this an "eater's digest" of cookbooks because its a digestion of some of the favorite recipes of some veterans of the wilds. Some of those veterans are paddlers, some are hikers, some rock climbers, and so on. All are cooks, and they've practiced their culinary skills from the Peace River to Patagonia, from Virginia to Vladivostok. They admit to having had both kitchen triumphs and culinary catastrophes. Now you can be the beneficiary of their collective experience.

There is usually a paragraph or two accompanying each recipe that gives background on the cook or some insight into the cook's approach to working in the camp kitchen. This adds a pleasant dimension to the cookbook.

Their camp kettles have received foods from supermarket and nettle beds, from mountaineering shops and mousetraps. *Some cuisine reflects gourmet creativity; much shows practicality, or lack of interest in eating compared with other pursuits.*

Kayak Cookery: A Handbook of Provisions and Recipes

by Linda Daniel
(Old Saybrook, CT:
The Globe Pequot Press, 1988)

A handy book for *any* paddler, really, not just kayakers. It is divided into two parts—the first a collection of the wisdom, experience, and pointers of a veteran outdoor cook, and the second a collection of recommended recipes. Author Daniel pays particular attention to the space limitations of paddlers, mentioning that it is best if almost anything brought along can serve at least two purposes. And she does it with a light touch.

Daniel includes chapters that you would expect—planning, provisioning, and drying of food. She also includes, among her extensive offering of recipes, "dinners that travel *up to* a week" and "dinners to eat *after* a week."

I have seen kayaks that looked like produce barges, with carrots, cabbages, celery, onions, and oranges in the bilge. (I have also seen the look on the face of a paddler when he remembered the cabbage he had stuffed up into the bow five weeks ago . . .)

"I would even eat the stuff at home."
—*from* Kayak Cookery *(1988)*

More Good Books on Fuel for Paddlers

The Portable Baker: Baking on Boat and Trail by Jean and Samuel Spangenberg (Camden, ME: Ragged Mountain Press, 1996). This book will introduce you to baking outdoors—surprisingly easy with Dutch ovens, Outback Ovens, and more. Bread never smelled so good.

The One Pan Gourmet: Fresh Food on the Trail by Don Jacobson (Camden, ME: Ragged Mountain Press, 1993). A good cookbook for shorter trips (weekends) and people who like meat. Recipes designed for backpackers, canoeists, kayakers, bicyclists, and boaters.

Trailside's Trail Food edited by John Viehman (Emmaus, PA: Rodale Press, 1993). A book with plenty of useful information for *anyone* active outdoors—backpacker, paddler, or even scuba diver—and especially those interested in nutrition.

The Lightweight Gourmet: Drying and Cooking Food for the Outdoor Life by Alan S. Kesselheim (Camden, ME: Ragged Mountain Press, 1994). Good tips on drying your own food, including plans for building a dehydrator.

Wilderness Cuisine: How to Prepare and Enjoy Fine Food on the Trial and in Camp by Carole Latimer (Berkeley, CA: Wilderness Press, 1991). This wonderful book will teach you as much about a way of life as how to prepare a variety of wonderful concoctions.

Health and Safety

OR

How to Stay of Sound Mind and Body

"In a great river great fish are found but take heed lest thou be drowned."
—a 17th-century British proverb

110

Medicine and the Paddler

✚

Here you'll find a sampling of medical manuals that are available for a paddler to keep in a first aid kit or medical reference library on the home front or in the first aid kit. These are just a few, but the point worth remembering is that any paddler would be wise to have a basic understanding of the health and medical problems we're most likely to encounter while out on the water.

Hypothermia: Death by Exposure

by William W. Forgey, M.D.
(Merrillville, IN: ICS Books, 1985)
Odds are that at least some of the water you paddle on will be cold. Whether that frigidity has its source in a Canadian glacier, the spring melting of a Tennessee snow, or the bottom of Lake Powell (created by the huge Glen Canyon Dam), it's all the same stuff when it contacts human skin. And not only is it uncomfortable, but it's unsafe to be in it for very long without some form of protection

like a wet or dry suit. If you've never been for a swim in bitterly cold water, imagine someone giving you a good hard wollop on the chest with a baseball bat—that will give you a general idea of the shock you might experience with a cold-water dunking.

Dr. Forgey did his homework before writing this book. There has been a lot written about this subject and he synthesized it and presents it thoroughly for paddlers and other outdoor aficionados. Every

> *"In running rapids or shoal places the canoes should proceed one at a time, and not too close together, so that in case one man hangs on a rock or sticks on a shoal place the next man will not run into him. A collision between canoes is as much to be avoided as is a collision between bicycles."*
> —*from* Manual of the Canvas Canoe: Its Construction
> *(1898)*

paddler should have the "101 course" in hypothermia. This book offers more than that, so would be particularly important reading for guides and trip leaders.

Simon & Schuster's Pocket Guide to Wilderness Medicine

by Paul G. Gill, Jr., M.D.
(New York: Simon & Schuster, 1991)

The good news is that Dr. Gill has pulled together some of the most important medical information for the paddler, or anyone venturing away from "civilization." The bad news is that because the book is tall and slender (roughly 3 x 7 inches) and tightly bound, it wants to slam shut no matter what page you have it open to. You probably won't need medical attention when it slams shut, but after it does it a few times you may need psychological counseling to calm your nerves.

Actually the book is quite good; it provides short summaries of what to do in the event of burns, hypo-

thermia, near-drownings, stings, dental emergencies, imbedded fishhooks, and a lot more. And the book is small enough that it could be tucked into most medical kits. (An updated edition of this book, now titled *The Ragged Mountain Press Guide to Wilderness Medicine and First Aid*, will be published by Ragged Mountain Press in June 1997; ISBN: 0-07-024552-5).

The Onboard Medical Handbook: First Aid and Emergency Medicine Afloat

by Paul G. Gill, Jr., M.D.

(Camden, ME: International Marine, 1996)

Dr. Gill has written this book with the yachting crowd in mind, but for the serious ocean paddler there is plenty to be reaped. In the preface Gill writes that "boating enthusiasts are, as a group, nuts-and-bolts people who want to know how things work and enjoy using their analytical skills to solve problems. With that in mind, in this guide I have gone beyond the simple 'signs, symptoms, treatment' formula and have explained *how* the various illnesses and injuries disrupt the normal anatomy and physiology. I trust the reader will find this ap-

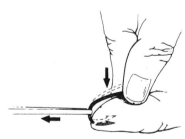

*Fishhook removal:
the "string" technique*

The HELP (Heat Escape Lessening Posture) position

proach more satisfying than a cookbook-style catalog of maladies and stock treatments." Gill then discusses a very broad range of problems one may encounter on the water, among them: CPR and the Heimlich maneuver; removing a fishhook; removing a foreign object from an eye; dislocations; dentistry; seasickness; sunburn; lightning; and even what to do about insomnia, sleep deprivation, and fish poisoning. To all of this he

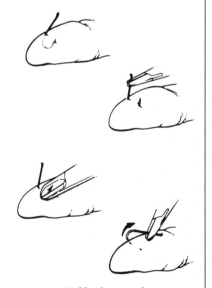

*Fishhook removal:
the "push-and-snip" technique*

appends an excellent and complete list for a medical kit.

Dr. Gill mentions three things he believes are supremely important and worthy of consideration by anyone:

- Maintain your composure.
- Administer to the sick and injured in a humane and compassionate manner.
- Obey the Golden Rule of medicine: "First, do no harm."

NOLS Wilderness First Aid

by Tod Schimelpfenig and Linda Lindsey

(Mechanicsburg, PA: Stackpole Books, 1992)

This is a good, thorough book on the problems one might encounter when out in the wilderness. Whether a dental emergency, a dislocated bone, or a near-drowning, this book gives a good layperson's background on what the problem is and what to do about it. Moreover, its format (each chapter has a useful, brief introduction and summary) and illustrations clarify and enhance the content of the book. Paddlers will find much of use, particularly the chapters that include information on dislocations, cold-water immersion, and water purification. There is also an appendix titled Emergency Procedures for Outdoor Groups. This chapter and this book generally would make good reading for virtually any trip leader.

Another good thing about *NOLS Wilderness First Aid* is that it doesn't concentrate only on first aid; prevention of injuries and attention to safety of everyone are recurrent themes. In other words, avoid injuries if you possibly can. It's so much easier to think, to plan

Commonsense Outdoor Medicine and Emergency Companion

by Newell D. Breyfogle
(Camden, ME: Ragged Mountain Press, 1993)

ahead, and to be cautious than to deal with serious injuries far from professional medical attention. It's less expensive, too.

Medicine for the Outdoors: A Guide to Emergency Medical Procedures and First Aid

by Paul S. Auerbach, M.D.
(Boston: Little, Brown, 1991)

You would be hard-pressed to find a better text for outdoor survival than this one. Any professional

guide would do well to own a copy as would anyone else who is seriously interested in the health and well-being of themselves or their friends in the outdoors. The book would make an excellent companion to an outdoor first aid course. It is directed at the layperson, so it isn't overloaded with medical jargon, although it does give sufficient information on almost any conceivable problem one is likely to encounter—from an imbedded fishhook to the value of sunscreens, from Lyme disease to frostbite. There is an appendix of drugs and drug doses, and a glossary for those terms for which one may need quick definition. Its only possible drawback is that, at four hundred pages, it is about an inch thick.

Call this handy book a companion, a handbook, or a *vade mecum,* because it includes a wide range of medical and other information. As one would expect from its title, this book includes chapters on all the frequently encountered medical problems— shock, dealing with wounds, heat and cold, burns, bites and stings, sprains, strains, dislocations, and a lot more. That's all in the section on "commonsense outdoor medicine." Another part of the book consists of "outdoor reference" material—map and compass use, clothing needs, nutrition, predicting weather, and evacuations. In addition to all that, there are appendices that cover topics such as communicable diseases, use of prescription medications, and basic first aid.

From a book with a scope as broad as this one you shouldn't expect much detail on any topic, but no outdoor medical compendium could realistically be a substitute for a medical professional. The point is this: understand the basic

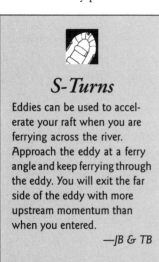

S-Turns

Eddies can be used to accelerate your raft when you are ferrying across the river. Approach the eddy at a ferry angle and keep ferrying through the eddy. You will exit the far side of the eddy with more upstream momentum than when you entered.

—JB & TB

issues covered in a book like this one, and you may be able to help when you or someone in your party gets into trouble.

Emergency Medical Procedures for the Outdoors

by Gordon A. Benner, M.D. et al.
(Birmingham, AL: Menasha Ridge Press, 1987)
For those folks interested in making good decisions when that unfortunate moment arises, this book could either get you out of a pickle or even be a lifesaver. It's arranged in a flow chart/decision tree format and is a very useful book. It is small enough to be tucked into the bottom of a lot of first aid kits.

Backcountry First Aid and Extended Care

by Buck Tilton
(Merrillville, IN: ICS Books, 1993)
They don't make books much smaller than this one without calling them miniatures (about 4 x 5 inches and some fifty pages). But don't let the size discourage you. In fact, Tilton does a respectable job of touching on many of the health problems you're likely to encounter when in the backcountry. And while it never goes into great detail, it would go into even the smallest of first aid kits.

Tilton encourages the reader to learn about pains, strains, sprains, and to use brains in dealing with them. Or if you've got problems with toes, a nose, or snows, he'll set you straight.

Medicine For the Backcountry

by Buck Tilton and Frank Hubbell
(Merrillville, IN: ICS Books, 1994)
There is hardly a shortage of medical books available to outdoorspeople, but this one ranks up there with the better ones. The coverage is broad, including these sections: (1) Patient Assessment; (2) Trau-

matic Injuries; (3) Environmental Injuries; (4) Wildlife Hazards; (5) Medical Emergencies; and (6) Common Backcountry Medical Problems. Within each section Tilton and Hubbell give the reader background information and notes on treatment for such varied problems as shock, strains and sprains, dislocations, drowning and near-drowning, bites and stings, seizures, and blisters. And if a paddler encounters still other problems (poor soul), they, too, are probably covered in this book. The language is not overly technical and there are numerous easy-to-remember maxims:

- On splinting: when in doubt, splint!
- Evacuate anyone knocked unconscious.
- When in doubt, treat the worst possible injury.
- Never create a second victim.

Medical specialists are certain to disagree on some of the details regarding treatment of various injuries. For those of us without advanced medical training it makes sense to (a) read what you can; (b) be CPR and first aid certified; and (c) use your noggin. *Medicine for the Backcountry* will get you going in the right direction.

The Outward Bound Wilderness First-Aid Handbook

by Jeff Isaac and Peter Goth
(New York: Lyons & Burford, 1991)

They don't make 'em much better than this one. In their preface, Isaac and Goth write, "We want the reader to understand why problems happen, how to recognize both the obvious and the subtle clues the body gives to reveal its condition, and how to devise and implement practical, flexible and effective treatment plans." They are strong advocates of quick, informed action.

Some of the key issues in this excellent book are:

- Understand normal body functioning.
- Attempt to understand changes brought on by illness and injury.
- Learn how to assess a problem; gather and review information, analyze it, and finally make a diagnosis.
- Devise a treatment plan.
- Continue to monitor the situation, remain flexible, and revise the treatment plan as circumstances require.

A thorough reading and digestion of this excellent book would be time very well spent for any paddler. It's not loaded with a lot of medical jargon, its diagrams are sharp, simple, and understandable, and its authors have clearly thought a lot about the types of medical problems one may encounter where, as they say, there is no 911.

Fitness and Health

Many paddlers realize the importance of being fit in order to optimize time on the water—but how many of us actually stick to a daily fitness program and practice sound health habits? Or how many of us realize that a safe paddler is a fit and healthy paddler?

The scope of this catalog will not allow a detailed look at the zillions of books out there on fitness, but here are some good books worth looking at to help you maintain your state of health and well-being, both on and off the water.

Stretching

by Bob Anderson
(Bolinas, CA: Shelter Publications, 1980)

If you're at all serious about paddling, you will want to stay fit. In addition to the usual healthy habits—eating well, getting sufficient sleep, and practicing technique as much as possible—you should learn to s—t—r—e—t—c—h out properly. Bob Anderson's book will show you many ways to limber up. Arms, legs, stomach, back—he's got advice for stretching them all.

You will feel better and perform better if you follow Anderson's advice. Moreover, you will minimize the chances of an injury that could put you out of the paddling scene for a season or more.

Facilitated Stretching

by Robert E. McAtee
(Colorado Springs, CO: Human Kinetics Publishers, 1993)

Every paddler will have exercise strategies that suit him or her best. The point is not necessarily to swear by a single technique or book, but to be open to changing what you do in the interest of improving performance and reducing the risks of body damage. Here is another fine book on stretching and massage technique that you shouldn't overlook.

Sports Health: The Complete Book of Athletic Injuries

by William Southmayd, M.D.,
and Marshall Hoffman
(New York: Perigee Books, 1984)

No, this isn't a manual on how to injure yourself. This book is a very useful guide for both identifying and treating, as well as preventing, sports injuries. Pulled muscles, tender tendons, or aching backs put all paddlers out of commission once in a while. This book will help you learn more about your body during sports activities so you can (a) prevent injury, or (b) treat those injuries so that (c) you can get back on the water sooner.

More Good Books on Health

Good Health Handbook by the editors of Consumer Guide (Lincolnwood, IL: Publications International, 1995)
Natural Health, Natural Medicine: A Comprehensive Manual for Wellness and Self-Care by Andrew Weil, M.D. (Boston: Houghton Mifflin, 1990)

Other Good Sources for Fitness and Health Information

Paddlers' magazines such as *Sea Kayaker, American Whitewater,* and *Canoe & Kayak* regularly feature columns on fitness and health. *Sea*

THE NEED FOR SLEEP

We've all heard it a thousand times, but there's a special truth in it outdoors. *Get a decent night's sleep.* If you want to be safe while paddling, you'll need to be fresh and up to speed. That means if you need an especially warm sleeping bag, take it along. If it means needing to have a fine sleeping pad, save your pennies and get one. It will pay off. The likelihood of your surviving will be greatly improved and your traveling companions will find you make much better company if you sleep once in a while.

Now get a load of how our forebears managed this:

"The mattress should be of the best hair, although corn or husks will answer the purpose and will be cheaper; but hair is lighter, less bulky and much more comfortable. The mattress is made in the shape of three cushions, each twenty inches long, eighteen inches wide and with a one inch boxing. The cushions are stuffed pretty full of hair and well tacked, being about two and one half inches thick between tacks. The cushions are joined together at one edge, making a continuous folding mattress eighteen inches wide and five feet long. A well oiled bag of heavy drilling or eight ounce duck should be provided in which to stow it, and in cruising the mattress serves as a seat, two of the cushions being folded and placed on the camp stool, which is laid flat on the floor, while the third cushion stands upright against the back rest. The mattress should not cost over from $3.50 to $4."

—from a 19th-century guidebook

Kayaker is particularly good, with their Health and Technique columns written by paddling experts. *Canoe & Kayak*'s Technique and Fitness series are very good reading, usually written by well-known experts such as Laurie Gullion and Shelley Johnson.

Princeton University operates a fine department for training professionals in outdoor recreation. The Outdoor Action Program is recognized as one of the finest sources in the world for wilderness health and safety information. The best way to peruse their program is via their excellent Internet web site, at http://www.princeton.edu/rcurtis/oa.html.

INCOMMUNICADO

It wasn't really *that* long ago that the Pony Express was a mighty fast way to get word to someone a long ways away. And not too long after that the Italian engineer Marconi was playing around with something called wireless telegraphy. Well, speed is a relative thing. These days you can phone, fax, or e-mail messages anyplace on the globe anytime, instantly. But what in heck does this have to do with paddling? These days people are more likely to venture into the watery wilds with cell phones in their sea kayaks, radios on their rafts, or computers in their canoes.

Some people will argue that life has improved because risks are lessened by better communications—rescue is just a phone call away. Others will engage in diatribes against the invasion of the wild lands and waters by more noise, plastic, and such trappings of the modern civilized (?) world.

Well, gang, this ain't likely to be an issue that will disappear. So, just consider that a cellular phone or VHF radio is no substitute for proper fitness, planning, outfitting, and safety training. And consider that others may not want the noise and techno-intrusion of a phone—or a VHF radio, or notebook computer satellite rigged to surf the Internet while surfing the shore—into *their* wilderness experience. Mental health is important, too.

Safety, Search, and Rescue

This is the tough stuff. When things really go wrong in a big way, when Murphy's Law reigns with vigor, when the Grim Reaper lurks, knocks, or comes into full view, you'll surely need help. The books and comments that follow may help you prepare for the tough times. If you are lucky you won't need all the knowledge, skills, and understanding contained in these books, but if you're on the water enough, you are likely to experience some kind of trouble eventually.

Whitewater Rescue Manual: New Techniques for Canoeists, Kayakers and Rafters

by Charles Walbridge and Wayne A. Sundmacher, Sr.
(Camden, ME: Ragged Mountain Press, 1995)

This book presents the best techniques for self-rescue and rescue of your companions on the river. Sub-

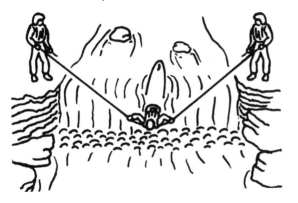

jects include equipment safety, rope-handling skills, swimming rescues, recovering a pinned or runaway boat, and first aid. Walbridge is to river safety as the truffle is to the dessert connoisseur—approaching the status of God.

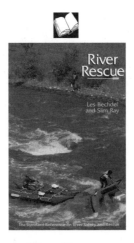

River Rescue

by Les Bechdel and Slim Ray

(Boston: Appalachian Mountain Club, 1989)

In the foreword to Bechdel and Ray's *River Rescue,* Charlie Walbridge—a well-known paddling safety guru who has written extensively about river safety and is chair of the River Safety Task Force of the American Canoe Association—writes, "The skill level of the average paddler today is higher than ever before in all areas but one: the ability to make effective rescues." Given the phenomenal increase in the number of paddlers over the past twenty-five years, this is a troubling thought. *River Rescue* aims to do something about that.

River Rescue is, beyond question, one of the best, most useful books for virtually any paddler to own—a must for every paddler's library. But don't stop there. After reading it the first time pick it up sometime later on and reread any chapter. Chances are you'll learn something new each time you pick it up.

The authors really cover the safety waterfront here. There is a chapter on developing a "river sense" for sniffing out safety. There is one on equipment, one on use of ropes, and one on entrapments and extrications (better to have read about it first than witness a drowning). There are nine appendices, including the International Scale of River Difficulty, Universal River Signals, useful knots, and a cold-water survival chart. *River Rescue* gets the absolute highest of recommendations.

Wilderness Search and Rescue

by Tim J. Setnicka

(Boston: Appalachian Mountain Club, 1980)

For the professional search-and-rescue (SAR) team, or for the individual with an interest in safety and rescues, this book has no equal. It is long (more than six hundred pages), thorough, comprehensive, and full of interesting and useful photos and illustrations.

While its audience is largely climbers, there is much of use to paddlers and rescuers of paddlers. There are chapters on planning, strategy, tactics, and use of ropes, knots, and slings. One chapter (about thirty-five pages) is devoted specifically to whitewater SAR.

More Good Sources for Safety Information

Periodically the American Canoe Association issues an installment in its series, *River Safety Reports.* These consist of fatal accident reports, near-miss reports, and river safety information and ideas. For many years the reports have been collected and edited by Charles Walbridge,

the ACA safety chairman.

Likewise, each issue of *Sea Kayaker* Magazine features a Safety column, written for many years by George Gronseth. It is one of the more well read columns in the magazine. Gronseth features a paddling accident in excruciating detail, so that we might learn from others' mistakes (many are fatal). It pays to read subsequent *Sea Kayaker* issues to follow readers' debates on how the accidents might have been avoided. Subscribe by contacting *Sea Kayaker* Magazine, Seattle, Washington, (206) 789-9536.

All paddlers would be well served by reading about on-the-water accidents. Both the ACA reports and Gronseth's reports can be emotionally difficult to read—they are sometimes gruesome tales in which paddlers have encountered severe problems, often involving loss of life. The circumstances of the accidents are discussed and analyzed so that the paddling community can learn something about how the

accidents happened, and how similar circumstances might be avoided.

Typically the ACA gathers incidents from a three- or four-year period before publishing the results. Recent compilations include 1989–91, 1986–88, and 1982–85. These are available for a small fee from the ACA, Springfield, Virginia, (703) 451-0141; acadirect@aol.com (http://world.std.com/~reichert/aca.html).

Of all the types of paddling in North America, sea kayaking is the least regulated. In fact, it is practically unregulated—there is no national organization to dictate structure and content of instruction, to oversee uniform safety codes, and to control when and where kayakers can paddle or likewise to help paddlers protect access to places to paddle. Like climbing, sea kayaking in North America is pretty maverick. But a few people are making waves by suggesting that North American kayakers should be organized in the same manner as

British kayaking instructors and guides, for example, who operate under fairly rigid control of the British Canoe Union. This has some people, like John Dowd, frothing under their PFDs.

WHO'S TO SAY WHAT'S SAFE FOR YOU?

by John Dowd

As sea kayaking grows from a fringe activity into an industry with serious economic potential, the political soup thickens and you don't need to look far to see that the control personalities have started to wriggle into a position from which they can manipulate their fellow paddlers. You might argue this is just human nature and is inevitable, but it is also the nature of some humans to resist unwarranted controls—particularly in an activity chosen for its freedom. I would like to suggest some solutions to the specter of what I consider to be unwarranted regulation intruding on sea kayaking, but let's start by looking at some "motives" behind the urge to control:

1. idealism ("It is my duty to protect others from themselves.")
2. a pathological need to control others
3. market control for financial gain
4. social/political positioning
5. any combination of the above

If there is a unifying emotion among would-be controllers, it is probably fear—fear of uncertainty, fear of anarchy on the high seas, fear of the democratic process, fear of competition, even fear of open spaces. The vehicle for the entry of these controllers usually involves issues of safety and the positioning of selected ideas. The clumsier individuals can be seen lying in wait, prepared speech in hand, for some tragedy or near-miss. When it occurs (and it will), they will immediately cry: "The solution is to regulate and standardize," and from their back pocket they will produce their manifesto.

Controllers are frequently the people who sing the same song in other fields and, when their solutions fail, will call for more of the same, harder, longer, stronger. The so-called war on drugs is an example of this. I'd wager that, if we spent half the money on education and addressing causes that we spend on fighting the pushers (and cranking up the street price), the problem would be greatly reduced.

There is little we can do about the first two motivating urges for control of sea kayaking other than shun those with the most chronic stages of the disease and gently discourage symptoms when they appear in our friends. Often these people are very well-meaning and do a great deal of good, helping new paddlers get safely on the water, and volunteering personal time, but their urge to regulate others needs to be watched.

To shore up a weak personal position, controllers will sometimes cultivate links with existing power structures such as the Coast Guard, land management organizations, insurance companies, even police, or they will form alliances with the trade, offering moral righteousness to an organization whose reason to exist is simply to limit competition or manage a protected area.

Does that mean that all standardization and regulation is bad? I don't believe so, as long as the organization is flexible, responsive to the wishes of the paddling community it will affect, and is structured to prevent entrenchment of individuals or dogma. A useful feature is to have the organization self-decapitating on, say, a three-year basis, and subject to regular policy reviews. This inhibits the ascendance of controlling personalities, or at least hobbles them somewhat, and makes the organization more difficult to hijack ideologically.

Political positioning is probably the one that concerns me most, since it is usually achieved through ideas or more precisely, by the limiting of the ideas of others. I consider that the present profusion of ideas is a sign of the vitality and health of the sea kayak industry. The flip side of this benefit, of course, is that some really silly ideas are floated by eager experts. That is the cost! Power in this case is gained by having one's ideas entrenched as dogma and in the tacit authority that gives a controlling association.

North American sea kayaking is mercifully still free of any monopoly of ideas, but the battle is on. The hope for the majority of us is that there will be so many competing organizations pushing their agendas and staking out their ideological turf that we will actually have a fairly good choice at the end of the day, and that with a discerning, critical kayaking community silly ideas will not flourish.

A recent survey of instructors at most of the leading sea kayaking schools in North America was encouraging in this way, revealing that many took all the courses offered by wannabe regulating bodies and simply picked what made sense to their situation. The reason they still have that choice is that the monopoly has not been established—yet. And with vigilance, it won't be.

Sometimes in the jockeying of ideas, the options become downright dangerous. This could be in the advocacy of a flawed self-rescue technique, or the promotion of a type of boat or attitude inappropriate to a situation. Totally contradictory "expert" advice appears in respected publications, such as one article, which appeared in *Sea Kayaker* Magazine, advocating a low paddle stroke in high wind (makes sense to me!), while a few issues later another advocates a high stroke. The answer to this is not to entrench a standard "right way" but to subject all ideas to tough peer scrutiny and common sense.

In the early eighties, I received a letter from a well-known British kayak author claiming that doubles were not really kayaks at all; in Britain at that time, double kayaks were given scant consideration. Indeed, the British experience is a great case in point for how *not* to organize kayaking, if organize it you must. During the first fifty years of this century, kayaking (or canoeing, as the Brits still call it) was big in Britain. Masses of people paddled on a regular basis in a wide range of decked "canoes." They paddled on the sea and on canals, lakes, and rivers. Mostly they used lath-and-canvas home-built or kit boats. Big names in kayaking included Granta, Tyne, and others, some of which were producing kayak kits at the same rate plastic manufacturers are turning out boats today.

But all that changed in the sixties with the establishment of a controlling body for manufacturers which defined "safety" standards along with what a kayak was and was not, as well as the establishment of a governing body with a rigid, entrenched hierarchy to define what should and should not be taught—and to make money, not so incidentally.

The result was that the number of people paddling in Britain dropped precipitously over a period of about ten years (some estimates run as high as ninety percent), and I believe that, without the North American influence, British kayaking would have been frozen in time back in the sixties, its practitioners believing that the only real kayak was a single with an 18- to 21-inch beam, and that the river techniques they had embraced were appropriate for the sea.

So what are the alternatives? I believe the antidote to those who wish to regulate kayaking (or anything else for that matter) is education and experience. A fully informed paddling community will not accept unwarranted restrictions on their activities. It is my hope that at the end-user level, if not the commercial level, the paddling community will resist any organization that is exclusive or hierarchical and stand advice from experts against a stiff measure of common sense. If someone tells you to shove your paddle high into the air during a strong wind, engage common sense mode and suggest an appropriate place where they might try shoving *their* paddle.

—John Dowd started paddling in 1961 as a schoolboy in New Zealand. He has worked as professional diver in the North Sea, photographer, and writer, with stints as instructor at a number of Outward Bound schools around the world. In 1979 he settled in Vancouver with wife Beatrice and in 1980 founded Ecomarine, North America's first specialty sea kayak store. He was a founder and president of the Trade Association of Sea Kayaking and, in 1984, a founder and editor of Sea Kayaker *Magazine. John Dowd is the author of* Sea Kayaking: A Manual for Long Distance Touring, *now in its fourth edition.*

7

A Sense of Wonder

OR

How to Become One with Your Surroundings

"One can learn much from a river."
—*Siddhartha*

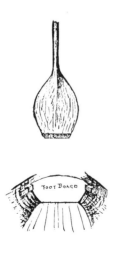

Dust Off Your Sense of Wonder

❄

Things get more interesting when you have an understanding of your surroundings. The alternative is to zoom down a river or along a coastline like a racehorse with blinders on, hell-bent on getting from point A to point B. If your object is to win a race, that strategy may prove best, but if it's to relax and enjoy the paddling, then learning about and appreciating the natural history of your aquatic destinations seems a bit more sane.

First, get out there on the water as much as possible. This may seem like the ridiculously obvious, but it is often forgotten. Familiarity with the flora and fauna will come only with time.

Second, travel when you can with people who stop to smell the daisies, those wonderful nature nerds who carry a magnifying glass to examine plants they haven't seen before, who use their binoculars to spy on birds, who carry a pad on which to sketch a scene or a spider, or who point out the constellations late at night.

Third, collect a few natural history field guides. They are worth their weight in gold. There are field guides on a huge range of topics of interest to paddlers: shells, butterflies, birds, bird nests, mammals, animal tracks, rocks, minerals, ferns, trees, shrubs, reptiles, amphibians, insects, wildflowers, stars and planets, pond life, weeds, wetlands, coastal areas, intertidal zones, whales, mushrooms, fish, edible plants, land forms, grasses, sedges, rushes, lichens, mosses, fossils, spiders, and more. You don't need to carry a whole library in your boat, but two or three field guides on your favorite subjects are well worth the effort of taking along. Anyone interested in a naturalist's approach to the strengths and weaknesses of various field guides can look up "A Guide to the Field Guides" in the May 1987 issue of *Natural History* magazine. Although dated, it will give you some good advice.

Fourth, go on your trips with an open mind and in the spirit of inquiry and knowledge. We appreciate more those things that we understand.

Here are a few titles—some field guides, some picture books, some instructional books—that might help you gain insight into the wonderful world of water, and more.

Wonder of Water

At the Water's Edge: Nature Study in Lakes, Streams, and Ponds

by Alan M. Cvancara
(New York: John Wiley & Sons, 1989)

and

At the Water's Edge: The Secret Life of a Lake and Stream

by Stephen Dalton and Jill Bailey
(New York: Portland House, 1991)

Luckily, there is lots of water and a fair amount of land on planet earth,

DISCOVERY OF A NEW LAKE.

> *"There is magic in rivers, beyond their gleaming beauty. They are unending rhythm; even when winter closes over them, in the mind, like remembered verse, they are still flowing."*
> —from the introduction to the Rivers of America *series of books, published by Farrar & Rinehart in the 1930s and 1940s*

so there is quite a bit of edge—apparently enough for two books called *At the Water's Edge*. Cvancara's is more of a guidebook, while Dalton and Bailey's is a photo essay.

Cvancara's book is a refresher in freshwater ecology, covering things like the water cycle, what wind and clouds do, which flora and fauna to look for, and very basic physics, chemistry, and natural history. Don't be frightened off by that though—it's much more of a guidebook than a dull textbook.

Dalton and Bailey's beautiful book belongs on a coffee table. The text is broken into four chapters: Spring, Summer, Autumn, and Winter. The photos are excellent, and the lens size, film type, shutter speed, etc., are all given so the studious reader-photographer can take note.

Park Ranger Guide to Rivers and Lakes

by Arthur P. Miller, Jr., and Marjorie L. Miller
(Mechanicsburg, PA: Stackpole Books, 1991)

In the first thirty pages the Millers give a general overview of riverine and lacustrine (lake) environments. They discuss flooding, erosion, the hydrologic cycle, vegetation, and a good deal more. Then they divide the United States into five regions and discuss, in very basic terms, things to look for in those regions. The regions are the Appalachians and Eastern Woodlands; Southern Mountains and Lowlands; Prairies and Plains; Desert Southwest; and Mountainous West. In the

SPEAKING WITH . . . .
ALEXANDRA AND GARRETT CONOVER

The Conovers bring to paddling a purity, a simplicity, and a spirit that often get sidetracked in this modern, crazy, no-time-for-anything world. They use traditional materials such as wood-and-canvas canoes, home-made wooden paddles, and natural fiber packbaskets. They run a classic wilderness guiding service called North Woods Ways and travel the lands and waters of Labrador, Quebec, and Maine. The boreal forests of Canada and the United States are their bailiwick. Their surroundings are important to them.

They share the traditional ways of travel (canoe in summer, snowshoe and toboggan in winter) with their clients. One does not go with the Conovers to be baby-sat. One goes to become "engaged with the habitat, to learn about it," as they say. A spirit of inquiry, a sharing of knowledge, and a land and water ethic are some of the stuff of a Conover guided trip.

In a sense, one becomes a part of the surroundings rather than a quickie visitor from the world of petrochemicals and metal alloys. Moreover, on a paddle with the Conovers, one learns the strengths and weaknesses of equipment as well as how to repair it when problems arise. These skills are what the Conovers call the "keys to autonomy" and they help one reduce dependencies on gimmickry.

What the Conovers represent goes against the grain of much of today's paddling. It goes strongly against the grain of virtually all messages we receive from ad agencies, equipment suppliers, and paddling magazines. Those folks will show you the latest plastic whatzit, the newest, lightest doodad, the field-tested, strongest, finest, ultra-fantastic gimmick that may well be broken, unrepairable, or in your town's landfill much sooner than you had anticipated.

If putting a historical or almost spiritual foundation under your paddling appeals to you, or the idea of traveling with informed, committed, traditional paddlers interests you, contact the Conovers and ask for their latest list of guided trips (207-997-3723). If going on a guided trip isn't your cup of tea but learning about these simple methods is, then get ahold of their books *Beyond the Paddle—A Canoeists' Guide to Expedition Skills: Poling, Lining, Portaging and Maneuvering Through Ice* (Gardiner, ME: Tilbury House, 1991) and *A Snow Walker's Companion* (Camden, ME: Ragged Mountain Press, 1995).

THE MACRO VIEW—THE MICRO VIEW

Some of your nature books will have you looking at the big picture. They'll be speaking of watersheds, regions, bioregions, large river basins, mountain areas, mountain chains, etc. Other books will be looking at the small stuff—things like a dot on a spider's abdomen, the dorsal fin of a fish, a weed's appearance in winter, or the subtle differences between the tracks of two animal species.

These might be thought of as the macro view and the micro view; the big picture and the small picture. William Blake (1757–1827) wrote of seeing "the world in a grain of sand." It's easy to focus one's attention on either the world or the grain, but it is far more interesting to be an observer of both the big and small pictures, the world in a grain of sand followed by a planet whizzing off through the universe. Nature guides help you move from the macro view to the micro view with more ease.

mountainous West, for example, one is encouraged to look for Canada geese, marmots, golden eagles, and mountain lions; in the southern mountains and lowlands, witch hazel, sumac, snapping turtles, kingfishers, and bats.

The Millers frequently encourage the river visitor to seek ranger assistance, saying things like "ranger guides can open up new vistas to the aquatic world around you" and "it is the rangers who will give you a close-up view of these surroundings." This book provides good groundwork for the beginning river naturalist.

The Pond

by Gerald Thompson and Jennifer Coldrey
(Cambridge, MA: MIT Press, 1984)

In a word, this book is superb. Care to find out just a bit about snails, algae, flatworms, or free-floating plants? Thompson and Coldrey will help you do it and with some lovely photos to boot. The book is a lot bigger than most field guides be-

cause it includes a lot of general material. *The Pond* is a representative sampling of the world of, well, the pond.

The Oceans: A Book of Questions and Answers

by Don Groves
(New York: John Wiley & Sons, 1989)

There is a whole genre of books out there that are essentially quiz books, testing you about all that stuff you were supposed to have learned in school. *The Oceans* would provide great entertainment on a sea kayaking voyage. Try these:

Q: How many kinds of tides are there?
A: Three—semidiurnal, diurnal, and mixed.
Q: Where do the whales often seen off California come from?
A: The Sea of Okhotsk.
Q: What is the highest open-ocean wave ever recorded?
A: 112 feet.

There are a few paragraphs explaining each answer, and both the questions and the answers are fairly basic and not terribly technical. Categories include the physical ocean, the chemical ocean, the biological ocean, the geological ocean, the meteorological ocean, the engineer's ocean, and finally the global ocean past, present, and future.

This book is bound to provoke discussion, friendly arguments, and other ocean trips.

Pond and Brook: A Guide to Nature in Freshwater Environments

by Michael J. Caduto
(Hanover, NH: University Press
of New England, 1990)

Caduto's book provides the curious paddler with an excellent introduction to the wet spots of the earth (excluding oceans). He divides freshwater environments into four parts. In the first he discusses water in the most general way—the water cycle, chemical and physical properties, surface water, groundwater, human influences, etc. In the second he writes about stillwater environments like lakes and ponds. In the third, he looks at flowing waters such as rivers and streams. And finally, in the fourth, he introduces wetlands, those long forgotten and abused places that are not quite land or water, but are surely greater than the sum of their parts. Unfortunately, only recently have we begun to appreciate their value ecologically

> "A mountain and a river are good neighbors."
> —17th-century proverb

because so many have been covered by parking lots and malls, housing developments, and suburbia.

Caduto's book will get you on the track of learning a few more things about your surroundings as you paddle along downstream or across the pond or through the wetland.

Many stream insects and other animals look virtually the same the world over. This is thought to be the result of highly successful dispersal mechanisms among some cosmopolitan species. Convergent evolution, the separate development of similar adaptations due to life in like environments, has also played a role that is especially obvious among the stream insects. Many North American species are hard to tell apart from those found in the Rhine of Western Europe, the Hwang Ho or Yellow River of northeastern China, and the Congo in Africa.

The Ecology of Running Waters

by H.B.N. Hynes
(Toronto: University of Toronto Press, 1970)

This book is something of a monument—comprehensive, broad in scope, yet detailed. Some would say it takes a small wheelbarrow to carry it around. It's really a textbook

Photo courtesy of the Library of Congress, Prints and Photographs Division, Washington, D.C.

126

on the biology of rivers and streams, probably best read by those who want to learn, in depth, about stream ecology.

There are chapters on water flow, physics and chemistry of running waters, higher plants, fish, invertebrates, and the effects on rivers and streams of those troublesome scoundrels known as humans. And that's only a sampler.

Both a classic book for the serious river rat and an unfailing doorstop.

Another book in the same general category (heavy sledding and detailed) is *Ecology of Fresh Waters* (Boston: Blackwell Scientific Publications, 1988) by Brian Moss.

Narrow-Bladed Paddles

If you plan on doing long-distance touring, or are prone to wrist or elbow stress, you might prefer a narrow-bladed sea kayak paddle, which takes less effort per stroke. If you want more power at the expense of more effort, you'll prefer a wider blade. Some paddlers buy one width for their primary paddle and another for the spare; they can then switch as conditions or moods dictate.

—JH & RH

The Natural History of Lakes

by Mary J. Burgis and Pat Morris
(Cambridge, UK:
Cambridge University Press, 1987)

For the paddler who would like an excellent overview of what lakes are all about—the water, the life in and around them, abuses of lakes, conservation, artificial lakes, and a lot more—this book provides all the background. Besides that, the illustrations and photos alone are worth the price of admission.

The authors look at lakes broadly—they take a global view of lakes and lake systems like the Great Lakes or the lakes that speckle the rift valleys of southeastern Africa. The authors write in the preface, "We hope that our book will be enjoyed by many who are interested in fishing, bird watching, sailing, geology, geography, and engineering, and who

READING WATER

People read books, they read music, and magazines, so why shouldn't they read water? What in the dickens is *reading* water anyway?

It's a long story, but the gist is this: water just doesn't like to stay put. It's always moving around—shifty stuff, water. When it moves, it behaves in all sorts of ways. Sometimes it jumps up, sometimes it rests. Sometimes it moves quickly, sometimes it ambles. Sometimes it leaps unpredictably, sometimes it seems to disappear. You just never know exactly what it's going to do, where it wants to go, and all that. The trick if you're a paddler trying to navigate via water is to learn some *patterns* so you can make educated guesses about what it *might* do. Then you make your boat do what you want according to what you've learned about those patterns.

So when you see whirlpools sucking down things the size of telephone poles, you learn to avoid them. Conversely, when you see bouncing waves, the sort that put some spice in your life, you head directly for them. Learning the behavior of all these water patterns is learning to *read* water.

want to know more about the lake ecosystems which support these activities, as well as by those who enjoy reading about familiar and far-away places." That's for sure. Read about polar lakes, mountain lakes, shallow lakes, deep lakes, saline lakes, or soda lakes.

THE MEANING OF RIVERS

by Verne C. Huser

Rivers drain the land, carve landscapes out of bedrock, make marshes where gradients lessen, and deposit deltas, alluvial fans, and terraces. They create lakes by filling natural depressions. Rivers serve as agents of erosion; they transport weathered materials from the mountains toward the distant oceans, in the process whittling gigantic lithic blocks into rounded boulders, polished pebbles, and grains of sand, cutting ever deeper into the face of the earth.

Water makes rivers flow, and without water rivers cease to exist. "Water plays a part in all physical and biological processes," points out Luna B. Leopold in *A View of the River* (Harvard University Press, 1994). In his conclusion to that important book he writes, "The river is the carpenter of its own edifice." Not only does it carve its way across the landscape, but it builds its banks and ultimately its grave.

In the natural scheme, rivers flood. Rain and melted snow flow downhill toward the seas. Water must have room or it will make its own way, engulfing the land. Before the evolution of civilized humankind, floods mattered not at all. They were simply part of the natural function of Earth, the only planet in our solar system blessed with a hydrologic cycle.

Floods watered the Nile Delta and Mesopotamia (literally, the land between the rivers), enriching them, enabling early agricultural peoples to grow food. People either built outside the flood plain or constructed their shelters to anticipate the annual floods. Over time, humans began to build artificial rivers—irrigation canals—to help them raise crops; eventually they created their own impoundments, permanently flooding vital riparian habitat in the name of flood control, expanded agriculture, water development, power production, and ultimately recreation.

Rivers serve as political boundaries, economic catalysts, and consolidating forces: they separate, divide, and unite. They led early explorers into the heart of the land; they provided power for early industry and sustenance for settlers. In wartime rivers have served as vital barriers and transportation corridors. How many battles of the Revolutionary War, Civil War, or World War II turned on control of a river, riverbank, or crossing?

Rivers provide water for manufacturing and municipal consumption as well as for farming and ranching. They offer habitat for fish, birds, and other wildlife; they provide opportunity for fishing, hunting, trapping, swimming, boating, camping, picnicking, sunbathing, wind-surfing—all kinds of outdoor recreation.

Furthermore, rivers decorate the lands they have carved and drained, offering reflecting pools for mountain vistas and bucolic scenes. Artists have painted riverscapes, photographers have enhanced their pictures with rivers, writers have used rivers as characters, setting, and scenery (example: Norman Maclean's *A River Runs Through It*). Some people value rivers' aesthetic qualities more than their utilitarian worth.

Bridged and dammed, diverted and polluted, rivers have been abused and destroyed in the name of progress. The floods of the mid-1990s were largely caused by a different abuse: as our towns and farms impinge on the rivers' natural courses, floods have nowhere to go—except over our towns and farms. Yet each year we produce more run-off (and higher floodwaters) with new roads and roofs, driveways, parking lots, and other paved surfaces. The damage that rivers do to human beings and their artifacts results primarily from our refusal to learn from nature.

The old adage about water, especially in the West, is "Use it or lose it"—it will flow somewhere else to be used by others downstream. But even such desert cities as Phoenix, which wastes more water than some states and cries for more, floods on rare occasions when the Salt River flashes. And the streets of Salt Lake City, capital of the second driest state, became rivers during a spring snow-melt run-off a couple of decades ago.

A Nez Perce Indian elder once

Wonder of Wildlife

✿

Wildlife of the Rivers

by William H. Amos
(New York: Abrams, 1981)

The theme of *Wildlife of the Rivers* is the flora and fauna that call the riverine environment home. Whether it's the ducks, beavers, or your favorite species of fish or something a little more off the wall like a barracuda, papyrus (an aquatic grass), or the Enot Dog, this book takes a look at the plant and animal life of the world's rivers.

REMINDER

Just about all of the books mentioned in this catalog can be obtained by: (a) patronizing a local bookstore; (b) contacting one of the many paddling suppliers listed in Chapter 3 (most have toll-free phone numbers); or (c) inquiring at a library. See also the section in Chapter 1 called "About This Book" for good sources of hard-to-find books.

Amos takes a broad, worldwide view of rivers. *Wildlife of the Rivers* will help you think globally; it will put your understanding of the rivers you know into a broader context. And it has great pictures and illustrations too!

The essence of a river is that it flows. Leonardo da Vinci wrote "When you put your hand in a flowing stream, you touch the last that has gone before and the first of what is still to come." It is almost as if river animals have read this statement and

taken heed. Every form of life associated with flowing water exists only because a streaming current brings food and oxygen, makes life difficult for all but the most specialized competitors and predators, carries wastes away, and provides an avenue to the farther penetration of the land.

The Audubon Society Pocket Guide to North American Birds of Lakes and Rivers

by Richard K. Walton
(New York: Alfred A. Knopf, 1994)

This fine book from the folks at Audubon is a very useful guide to the avian fauna most paddlers are likely to encounter. Audubon guides are easy to use and have excellent color photographs to aid even the most dense paddler in identifying birds.

You might also want to check out Audubon's nature guide series

on regions of North America. Published by Alfred A. Knopf under Chanticleer Press, these are slightly bigger than the pocket guides, and cover ecosystems more broadly. They include a little bit of everything—birds, plants, mammals, insects, fishes, and more. Paddlers would find the *Atlantic and Gulf Coasts, Pacific Coast,* and *Wetlands* most useful.

The Amateur Naturalist

by Gerald Malcolm Durrell
(New York: McKay, 1989)

If you've been wanting to expand your horizons both on the water and beyond the shore, this is a fine book to get you started. It includes chapters that introduce various ecosystems, like coastal wetlands, ponds and streams, marshlands, coniferous and deciduous woodlands, coastal wetlands, and more. The information is not only useful, but beautifully presented. Some of the items Durrell suggests that the naturalist carry are a pocket knife, clippers, a notebook and pen, field guides, a local map, binoculars, a camera, and more. The book is liberally illustrated with good graphics and pictures that will inspire you to greater study in natural history.

More Good Nature Guides

Pond Life: A Guide to Common Plants and Animals of North American Ponds and Lakes (New York: Golden Press, 1987). A nice little book intended for young adults but great for everyone. Truly will fit in a pocket.

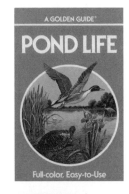

BRING YOUR SURROUNDINGS TO YOU— ## THROUGH BINOCULARS

Like humans, most wildlife likes water. This is good news for paddlers because lakes, rivers, and the ocean provide excellent habitat for viewing many different species, including moose, bears, fish, turtles, kingfishers, herons, beavers, deer (this list could go on forever . . .).

Get yourself a pair of simple binoculars and keep them in a dry bag when not in use. Or indulge in a pair of really good waterproof ones that you can keep around your neck. The return on the money invested will please you to no end. Binoculars come in a variety of magnifications, 7 x 35 being a good, general purpose one for paddlers (the 35 refers to magnification factor, the 7 refers to the 7mm diameter of the eye lens). If you get stronger ones, jiggling becomes a problem (boats don't sit still) and weaker ones just don't magnify enough.

The low end for decent binoculars is around $100 for a pair that will do the job—high end is $1,000. Go for a reputable brand. U.S. and Asian companies make good optics for less money; hardcore nature nerds will usually be found with something from Germany or Austria. Many outdoor suppliers carry binoculars. Birdwatchers (try your local Audubon Society, especially if they have a retail shop) are excellent sources of reliable information about binoculars and can direct you to good suppliers if they don't sell them.

Pacific Intertidal Life; Pacific Coast Fish; Pacific Coast Bird Finder; and *Life on Intertidal Rocks: A Guide to Marine Life on the Rocky North Atlantic Coast* (Berkeley, CA: Nature Study Guild; 800-954-2984). Even tinier than the Golden Guides, these are wonderful pamphlets that put some good information right at your fingertips.

Wonder of Weather

Weather for the Mariner

by William J. Kotsch
Rear Admiral, U.S. Navy (retired)
(Annapolis: Naval Institute Press, 1983)

Every boater, whether you are piloting an aircraft carrier or puttering around in a canoe, should know the basics of weather over the water. Even lakes can generate their own micro-weather.

This comprehensive book will take you from the basics of air flow and cloud formations, into an excellent treatment of barometers (and how to use them), and onward to advanced weather forecasting using that barometer (high- and low-pressure areas, etc.).

Because modern paddlers have access to all sorts of up-to-the-minute weather maps via the Internet, you really should also know what all those little greek symbols mean. *Weather for the Mariner* will teach you that (and then some). It's

"Look when the clouds are blowing
And all the winds are free:
In fury of their going
They fall upon the sea.
But though the blast is frantic,
And though the tempest raves,
The deep intense Atlantic
Is still beneath the waves."
—*Frederic William Henry Myers*
(1843–1901)

THE WEATHER RADIO

A very handy and inexpensive device for a paddler is a weather radio. From nearly four hundred places throughout the United States, the National Weather Service broadcasts continuous weather reports (roughly 90 percent of the U.S. population is within listening distance of a station). The reports are updated frequently and are broadcast twenty-four hours a day on seven frequencies, all at about 162 megahertz (FM). As is often the case, having up-to-date information at your disposal can be useful, even lifesaving under some circumstances. Weather radios are available from most general outdoor retailers and paddling or marine suppliers (see Chapter 3).

an excellent teaching tool, and it could even save your hide.

Weathering the Wilderness: The Sierra Club Guide to Practical Meteorology

by William E. Reifsnyder
(San Francisco: Sierra Club Books, 1980)

Don't get caught with your sprayskirt down. Get a feeling for the weather in your area and you will be much better prepared for whatever nature hands you.

This is an outdoorsperson's weather book. It explains things you need to know—about air masses and how and why they do what they do, frontal systems and storms, and more, though not so much more to overwhelm you. There is also a chapter on the climates for eight different regions of the United States, from the Sierra Nevada to the northern Appalachians.

Wonder of Winter

❄

A Guide to Nature in Winter

by Donald and Lillian Stokes
(Boston: Little, Brown and Company, 1979)

This guide offers sections on snow crystals, trees in winter, winter weeds, winter insects, birds, mushrooms, animal tracks, and more—all in their wintry environments. It's well illustrated, too.

This stuff we paddle on is a strange matter. Most often people refer to it as water, but it takes on different faces at different times. If you don't let a little season like winter get in the way of your appreciation of the wilds—the snow, the ice, the birds—then think about using this guide. You're sure to like nature's dormant season more.

⋎

Snow starts as a nucleus of dust or salt that attracts molecules of water from cloud droplets. As these water molecules accumulate on the nucleus, they form ice crystals, which become larger as more water molecules are added.

Rain starts as the microscopic droplets in the clouds are so concentrated that they join together into larger droplets. They soon become so heavy that they fall to the earth.

⋏

133

134

![book icon]

Life in the Cold:
An Introduction to Winter
Ecology

by Peter J. Marchand
(Hanover, NH: University Press
of New England, 1991)

Life in the Cold will provide excellent background reading on how
the plant and animal kingdoms live
through the darker months of the
year. Such topics as migration, hi-
bernation, and resistance are covered, as are snow's insulating values,
seeking wintertime food sources,
and keeping warm. Paddlers might
appreciate the chapter titled "Life
Under Ice," which focuses on lake
and stream life during the dead of
winter. While paddling under ice is
no fun at all, learning about what
goes on there will fascinate you.

More Good Books
on Winter

A Snow Walker's Companion by
Alexandra and Garrett Conover
(Camden, ME: Ragged Moun-
tain Press, 1995)
*The Essential Snowshoer: A Step-by-
Step Guide* by Marianne Zwosta
(Camden, ME: Ragged Moun-
tain Press, 1996)

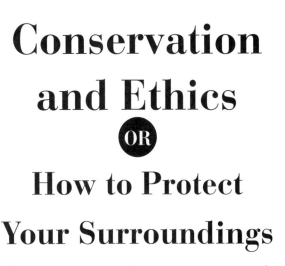

8

Conservation and Ethics

OR

How to Protect

Your Surroundings

"If we are to survive and prosper in an increasingly crowded world, where resources as basic as water become scarce, we shall need to re-learn some of the old skills and old attitudes to rivers and water."
—Fred Pearce in The Dammed: Rivers, Dams, and the Coming World Water Crisis
(London: The Bodley Head, 1992)

135

Leave
No Wake

≋

In addition to the rewards of relaxation and tranquillity, traveling by water in a paddle-powered craft also allows one to pass through a place and leave no trace of passage. It is a pure, natural mode of transportation.

But when paddlers pause to camp or explore, we can and do, however inadvertently, make an impact on those places. The following books provide some useful tips on how to minimize impact. Though most of us probably consider ourselves to be pretty conscientious campers, all of us can benefit from the information in these books.

Soft Paths: How to Enjoy the Wilderness Without Harming It

by Bruce Hampton and David Cole
(Mechanicsburg, PA: Stackpole Books, 1995)

Humans have taken to the outdoors, to the wilderness, to the rivers by the millions. If we want all those wild places to remain enjoyable, clean, beautiful, pristine, we need to take care of them—to think before we act. This book encourages that. Written by an instructor at the National Outdoor Leadership School and a U.S. Forest Service research biologist, it deals with issues like waste disposal in the wilds, campsite selection, and taking your conscience and ethics along on your trip. It has a chapter specifically on river and lake environments. It is well written and is a fast read.

Wild Country Companion

by Will Harmon
(Helena, MT:Falcon Press
Publishing Company, 1994)

Harmon offers some specific advice for paddlers in this general book on low-impact outdoor recreation. For example, he advises that if you want to chill beverages by hanging them overboard that you make sure they are in non-glass containers and are tied securely. He gives tips on preventing water contamination, and reminds paddlers that sounds travel far over water (low impact

> *"Water is the prophet's drink."*
> —*a Dutch proverb*

means sound, too). Harmon also covers all the usual leave-no-trace camping techniques.

Backwoods Ethics: Environmental Issues for Hikers and Campers

by Laura and Guy Waterman
(Woodstock, VT: Countryman Press, 1993)

Although this book is not specifically directed at paddlers, there is much about it to recommend. It is well written, by a couple who has thought a great deal about the impact of all those people "out there."

The Watermans discuss low-impact camping and cooking, values in the backcountry, noise pollution (jets, helicopters, etc.), and a good deal more. This is among the very best of a growing number of books on this topic.

Nailing Those Eddies

The best place to aim when entering an eddy is high and deep (in the center of the eddy's long axis nearest the obstacle forming the eddy). This spot contains exactly the type of currents you're looking for to bring your kayak to a screaming halt.

—*JB & TB*

MY WAY OR THE TIDY WAY

by Thomas A. Sebring

I'm mad about canoeing . . . not wacky, but ticked off. Why? Because so much of it is so damned crappy. The magazines publish trivial articles promoting overweight and clumsy canoes, and offer advice on how to travel with "baby on board." People hack away awkwardly with godawful plastic and aluminum clubs for paddles. Any whitewater river of note is populated with ghastly plastic bathtub toys called "sit-upons" (of all the nearly correct names!) and grown people in kayaks swirling about in holes like the tidy bowl man on a bad day.

The average paddler is irretrievably trapped in an eddy of mediocrity, with little hope of peeling out. Why? Part of it is what I call the Lowest Common Denominator (LCD) Syndrome. Manufacturers make the most money by appealing to the largest segment of the population—this means boats that are easy to afford, easy to "paddle," and last a long time regardless of mistreatment. Some manufacturers have even discontinued efficient hulls, fearing liability lawsuits over "tippy" boats! Hence the majority of boats for sale are poor excuses for canoes. Too wide, too heavy, too blunt, and not properly rigged. A fine canoe is like a good bicycle . . . it's not the easiest thing to ride the first time or two, but it rewards your learning.

Poor instruction is another reason for mediocrity. The national paddling organizations claim to teach paddling, but are populated by instructors who actually own and use the above-mentioned bathtubs and who lack understanding of the major elements of modern canoe technique. In this new world there are no intermediate paddlers. People are miraculously transformed—be it at summer camp, a weekend with the "Y," or an overnight with the Scouts—into "experts." By joining a national paddlers club and taking a weekend clinic they become anointed gurus! In most sports there is a logical progression. People employ golf or tennis "pros" to help them develop their skills. Not in canoeing.

What's the big deal? What are people missing? Here's what . . . *Efficiency*. The ability to move a well-designed canoe long distances with acceptable effort. *Maneuverability*. Knowledge of strokes and other techniques which can turn a drunkard's walk of progress down a meandering whitewater stream into a joyous carving of the river. *Style*. A sense of self-worth, pride, and confidence which makes the entire canoe experience transcendent. *Practicality*. The ability to confidently move through the wilderness, safely and quietly, the canoe replacing the water as it was, the traveler leaving no trace. *Safety*. Knowledge of the paddler's craft, which makes them and their companions more capable and keeps them from harm's way.
Elegance. The personal fulfillment realized from an art well practiced.

Sebring's rules for avoiding LCD Syndrome: Don't buy a canoe that weighs more than 60 pounds. Don't buy beavertail paddles or those made from aluminum and plastic. Don't buy a canoe made from ABS or polyethylene unless it's primarily for white-water use. Don't buy a paddle-craft that you sit on top of rather than in. Buy a quality canoe from an experienced dealer. Buy a canoe of fiberglass or, preferably, Kevlar, slight of form, efficient in design, and light upon the water. Use paddles that are light and efficient. Take several lessons from qualified instructors who can demonstrate and impart knowledge of the art. Practice your skills and refine your abilities.

When you easily unload your lightweight canoe from atop your car, board with grace, depart with elegant strokes that bespeak efficiency and control, you will be prepared to enjoy the transcendent canoe experience. Either that or you can wallow around with the tidy bowl people.

Thomas Sebring, who earns his living managing design and construction of large astronomical telescopes, has been Technical Editor of Canoe *Magazine and a Contributing Editor of* Canoesport Journal. *He and his wife Susan have long practiced many disciplines of paddling, from slalom and downriver racing to wilderness tripping and solo freestyle. In 1996 they finished sixth in their class at the USCA National Marathon Canoe Championships.*

Wilderness Ethics: Preserving the Spirit of Wildness

by Laura and Guy Waterman
(Woodstock, VT: The Countryman Press, 1993)

This book, also by the Watermans, is less a guide to low-impact camping than it is a look at how we perceive wild places and our role as travelers in them. The Watermans probe at what wilderness is and how the perception of it may vary from person to person. They encourage us to think about what being in wilderness means. For example, they talk about earlier times when our tents, clothing, and other outdoor equipment were made from natural colors—gentle beiges, soft greens, and other unobtrusive colors—making our camps barely visible to passing hikers or paddlers. Today our equipment is every color *but* earthtones. The Watermans ask, do we really need this?

Once we have "saved" the land, how do we preserve the spirit of wildness out there in the woods, up there on the heights? . . . Can we develop a higher respect for the innate character of wild land and of the wilderness experience? Can we protect both the quality of the human experience obtainable in wilderness and, more

basic, the integrity of the natural processes that define it as wilderness? Can we reverse the civilizing momentum and reclaim a touch of wildness even on land that appeared lost to the development or recreation mania? Is a concerned consensus possible that will leave islands of wildness left in a world overly dominated by humanity?

Photo courtesy of the Library of Congress, Prints and Photographs Division, Washington, D.C.

> "Wilderness is a place where we leave Earth alone; in the last analysis it is a gesture of planetary modesty."
> —Roderick Nash
> in his foreword to
> Wilderness Ethics: Preserving the Spirit of Wildness

How to Shit in the Woods: An Environmentally Sound Approach to a Lost Art

by Kathleen Meyer
(Berkeley: Ten Speed Press, 1994)

The author points out that we really don't have that big of a problem compared to dinosaurs, which must have contributed Cadillac-size droppings to their landscape.

The language alone makes this book amusing reading, and if you

138

don't like it the book would make good toilet paper (except the glossy covers). The chapter headings should give you an idea of whether your stomach can endure the ordure: Anatomy of a Crap; Digging the Hole; When You Can't Dig a Hole; Trekker's Trots; For Women Only: How Not to Pee in Your Boots; What? No T.P.? or Doing Without. Besides all that, at the hind end of this book is an appendix titled Definition of Shit that lists an appallingly extensive scatological vocabulary

of related, specialized terms.

The author recounts numerous ghastly tales, kindly protecting both innocent and guilty parties with anonymity. Despite (or because of) all that, this is a very worthwhile book that should be read by everyone who camps.

A Canoeist Manual for the Promotion of Environmental and Ethical Concerns

(Hyde Park, Ontario: Canadian Recreational Canoeing Association, 1983)
This manual is intended for use primarily by educators—a teacher's guide to promoting an environmental awareness. It covers minimum-impact camping, the stove vs. campfire debate, and much more.

Teacher's manuals don't often make for inspirational reading—this one included—but if your job is to teach paddling you also ought to be teaching something about an environmental awareness, river conservation, etc.

The New Wilderness Handbook

by Paul Petzoldt
(New York: W.W. Norton, 1984)
Petzoldt, a man of the wilderness for over seventy years, is one of the great lovers and protectors of our wild lands. This book, reviewed in Chapter Five, should be required reading for anyone who ventures into the wilderness to paddle, hike, or even just to sit.

Water Conservation and Management

None of us who paddles the wilds of the world can escape the truths we see: our streams, rivers, lakes, and oceans are suffering outrageous pollutions and destructions. It's a fact.

So what is the background of some of these problems? What really are the problems? What can you be thinking about, or better yet, in whose ear might you scream? And what else might you do to improve things?

This section contains resources on water conservation and management issues. The next section details resources that tell you how to do something about those issues. And the final section lists some

good organizations that are working on doing something, and could use the help of concerned paddlers.

World Wildlife Fund Atlas of the Environment

by Geoffrey Lean, Don Hinrichsen, and Adam Markham
(New York: Prentice Hall, 1990)
This is no regular atlas. It won't help you find East Gumshoe or the Paradise River. It's a *thematic* atlas and its theme is environmental issues.

Paddlers will probably find particularly interesting the chapters on Freshwater: Abundance and

Scarcity, Damaged Water-sheds, Freshwater Pollution, and Pollution of the Seas.

The maps, charts, and illustrations are all in color (nice) and the accompanying text provides brief, excellent summaries of the problem. The message isn't often pleasant (one map shows areas of persistent coastal pollution, including nearly all of Europe's coastline, ditto Japan, China, India, and virtually all coastline between Newfoundland and the Yucatan peninsula in Mexico).

A California firm called agAccess produces a leaflet listing books on environmental restoration, drinking water, water quality, water policy, rivers issues, irrigation, and more. For a copy of their latest issue of the free *Water Books Catalog*, contact

agAccess
P.O. Box 2008
Davis, CA 95617
(916) 756-7177
FAX (916) 756-7188

The American Rivers Outstanding Rivers List, Second Edition

compiled and edited by
Matthew H. Huntington and John D. Echeverria
(Washington, D.C.: American Rivers, 1991)
This is a state-by-state directory of significant rivers, or sections of

rivers, that either have or deserve some form of protection. The rivers included have been identified in a variety of sources, including studies by the National Park Service, state agencies, conservation groups, etc. An intention of this directory is to help river lovers *prioritize* their protection strategies. Let's face it, with about 68,000 dams already in place in the United States, the battle against developers of dams has been no smashing success. A list or directory like this one may help us at least choose our battles.

The Dammed: Rivers, Dams, and the Coming World Water Crisis

by Fred Pearce
(London: The Bodley Head, 1992)
If you are interested in some background on, and a world view of, a variety of water projects and their consequences, then *The Dammed* is for you. But don't expect to be entertained. The tale is a grim one the world over. Anyone familiar with the vocabulary of dams and damming recognizes the words Aswan (Egypt), James Bay (Quebec), Colorado River (United States), Yangtze (China), Ganges (India), Parana (Brazil/Paraguay border), and World Bank. The list could go on and on. Fred Pearce speaks of modern river basin mismanagement as well as the problems associated with the short-term and narrow vision of most modern engineers. Sadly, your children may pay the price of rectifying the problems that some of these dams have created. The author tells us,

GREEN PADDLER'S TO DO LIST

- Go paddling, not only for paddling's sake, but to really take a look at your surroundings. Is the water clean or fouled? If fouled, try to find out what caused it and who's working on fixing it.
- Join a conservation organization. There may be local, state, provincial, or national organizations that share your viewpoints and are engaged in improving the lot of some waters that mean a great deal to you (see the list at the end of this chapter).
- Speak up! Bend someone's ear for a while about "your/our/their" waters. Whether it's a friend, relative, neighbor, or especially one of those antediluvian-thinking politicians, let 'em have it. You (who have actually been on the water) will be doing them the service of education.

"If we are to survive and prosper in an increasingly crowded world, where resources as basic as water become scarce, we shall need to re-learn some of the old skills and old attitudes to rivers and water."

Two books that show us what happens when a dam is built are Eliot Porter's *The Place No One Knew* (San Francisco: Sierra Club Books, 1963) and *The Colorado River Through Glen Canyon Before Lake Powell* edited by Eleanor Inskip (Moab, UT: Inskip Ink, 1995). Both are marvelous, bitter-sweet collections of photos of the vanished Glen Canyon, submerged under Lake Powell behind the Glen Canyon Dam on the Colorado River. Inskip applied the particu-larly effective method of citing the current Lake Powell navigational buoy marker associated with the now-vanished place in each photograph. Be prepared to (a) get depressed and (b) go out and persuade a civil engineer to become an artist.

The Wild and Scenic Rivers of America

by Tim Palmer
(Washington, D.C.: Island Press, 1993)
An excellent book on the Wild and Scenic Rivers system, in-cluding portions devoted to the background of the federal legislation that created the sys-tem, the future of these rivers, other rivers that should be in-cluded in this system, and a good deal more.

Palmer gives the reader a short blurb on each river in-cluded in the system. For each river he gives its location, which

REMINDER

Just about all of the books mentioned in this catalog can be obtained by: (a) patronizing a local bookstore; (b) contacting one of the many paddling suppli-ers listed in Chapter 3 (most have toll-free phone numbers); or (c) inquiring at a library. See also the section in Chapter 1 called "About This Book" for good sources of hard-to-find books.

agency administers it, maps recom-mended if visiting a particular river, degree of paddling difficulty, as well as sources of more detailed infor-mation for each river.

If you want to get up to speed on the "Wild and Scenic Story," Tim Palmer's book would make a superb starting place. This book ought to be required reading for anyone aspiring to political office at any level. And those political aspi-rants who haven't read it should have their heads dunked for an hour or so . . .

The national rivers system may be the natural areas program of the fu-ture, the pioneer in coping with the difficult conflicts between existing de-velopment and the protection of what is left. Since the early 1900s when leg-islation was passed to dam, channel-ize, and promote building along rivers, hundreds of laws have speeded development. In 1968 the Wild and Scenic Rivers Act was passed to favor the rivers for their natural qualities. A promise of balanced use of water has become a central aspect of conservation and the environmental move-ment, but balance has not yet been achieved.

Through reformed thinking and progressive action that saves rivers while recognizing the com-plexities of life and the needs of people, the national rivers can stand boldly for a new steward-ship of the earth.

Tim Palmer's book *Lifelines: The Case for River Conservation* (Washington, D.C.: Island Press, 1994) is highly recom-mended reading as well.

141

Down by the River: The Impact of Federal Water Projects and Policies on Biological Diversity

by Constance Elizabeth Hunt
(Washington, D.C.: Island Press, 1988)

You'll curse the government yet again if you put your nose into this book. Hunt tells us that riparian habitats are among the world's richest habitats, yet have been abused and neglected by the American culture—its citizens, its policy makers, its developers. The federally funded damming, channelization, development of flood-prone land, the deepening and the straightening—all have contributed to the deterioration of the land immediately surrounding rivers. Sadly, one needn't look far to see evidence of such activity. And, even more sadly, *it continues.*

The author's suggestions for change are many, but include (a) saving what remains through regulation, acquisition, etc.; (b) attempting to reverse existing trends; (c) restoration of riparian ecosystems; and (d) legislation (the creation of an Endangered Ecosystems Act).

> *"The longing to be primitive is a disease of culture."*
> —George Santayana, Spanish-American philosopher/poet (1863–1952)

This book describes the impacts of federal water projects and policies on riparian habitats. Using various river basins as examples of specific types of impacts, I have attempted to illustrate weaknesses in the water resources planning system. This system results in many rivers being controlled as if they were garden hoses. The hands turning the spigot too often make decisions based on impulse and political circumstance rather than on comprehensive planning. Catastrophe results for many living things, including mammals, fish, birds, reptiles, amphibians, and taxpayers.

Endangered Rivers and the Conservation Movement

by Tim Palmer
(Berkeley: University of California Press, 1986)

In the preface, Tim Palmer writes, "People have worked to protect the rivers—to leave some of them the way they are—and this book is the story of those efforts."

Endangered Rivers is an excellent look at the history and the politics surrounding the movement to protect the rivers of the United States. Palmer hits on all the key players (heroes and culprits) over the years, from the Sierra Club to

> *"The word river is so symbolic that it is used in the titles of scores of novels having nothing to do with water flowing toward the sea."*
>
> —Tim Palmer in
> Endangered Rivers and the
> Conservation Movement
> *(University of California Press, 1986)*

the Bureau of Reclamation, from Teddy Roosevelt to Richard Nixon, from the Hohokam Indians who dug irrigation canals around 300 B.C. to the U.S. Army Corps of Engineers.

Palmer has included about forty color photos showing some of the towering successes of river conservationists as well as a few of the colossal failures. Some of his shots are of places you will never see—they've been submerged by recently constructed dams. If seeing these photos doesn't rile the river conservationist in you, then nothing is likely to.

Reservoirs have flooded the oldest known settlement in North America,

the second-deepest canyon, the second most popular whitewater, the habitat of endangered species, one of the first national parks, tens of thousands of homes, rich farmland, desert canyons, and virgin forests. In building dams we have blocked the best runs of salmon and broken the oldest Indian treaty—one that George Washington signed.

The American Whitewater Affiliation Nationwide Whitewater Inventory

edited by Pope Barrow
(Washington, D.C.: American
Whitewater Affiliation, 1990)

This book will have you traveling all over the United States in search

of whitewater, at least in your mind. The trick is to get your body and boat to follow.

Actually, this inventory of sections of whitewater throughout the United States was compiled by Barrow and the AWA because dams and other developments continue to erode what little is left of the original whitewater on the North American continent. In the preface, Barrow writes, "The absence of adequate data on whitewater resources leaves a troubling gap in the information base used by the Federal Energy Regulatory Commission, the U.S. Army Corps of Engineers, the Pacific Northwest Power Planning Council, the National Park Service, the National Forest Service, the Bureau of Land Management, the Tennessee Valley Authority, the President's Commission on American Outdoors, and by other federal, state, and regional agencies. These agencies do resource planning, river management, and—most importantly—some of them build, or authorize the building of, hydroelectric power projects, dams, diversions, and other water resource projects. Partly because of the absence of information about white-

143

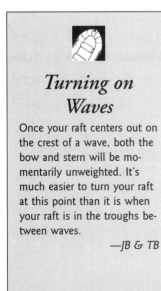

Turning on Waves

Once your raft centers out on the crest of a wave, both the bow and stern will be momentarily unweighted. It's much easier to turn your raft at this point than it is when your raft is in the troughs between waves.

—JB & TB

CONSERVATION AND ETHICS

water recreation, these planning and development activities have proceeded without consideration of their effect on whitewater recreation opportunities."

This inventory lists about 2,200 river segments that include some 36,000 miles of whitewater. Sound impressive? Don't be fooled. That's a meager one percent of the river miles in the country. Barrow estimates that roughly 500,000 river miles have been submerged beneath waters impounded by dams. Think of it this way: what value do we place on the desire to open a can with an electric can opener powered by lost whitewater?

The inventory is arranged alphabetically by state; for each river, the whitewater segments are listed as are the number of miles of each segment, the class (degree of difficulty), and the counties.

The compilation of this inventory was a big job. Kudos to the many volunteer members of the AWA for this work and to Barrow

for pulling it all together. Let's hope the work invested in this inventory will pay off in terms of future river protection.

> *"Engineering art is now defying nature everywhere, and daring feats of bridge-building are daily accomplished; but the old routes and passes still remain the most practicable, and in the long run pay best. In spite of the fact that tunnels can go wherever money dictates, and bridges can be swung across the most baffling chasms, at the same time the fiercest struggles for rights of way (outside the cities) are being waged today for the portage paths first trod by the Indian."*
>
> —*from* Portage Paths: The Keys of the Continent *by Archer Butler Hulbert (AMS Press, reprinted 1971 from 1902 original)*

> *"If you can't see the bottom, don't try to cross the river."*
> —*an Italian proverb*

Gaia: An Atlas of Planet Management

edited by Dr. Norman Myers
(New York: Anchor Books, 1993)

This atlas will get you thinking big. It's not a collection of maps, but an atlas of *issues* such as population control, resource use, and land and water husbandry. Its message is not one of doom and gloom, but one of thinking in ways that will help us solve some of these monstrous problems that we face.

Paddlers can find plenty of interest in *Gaia;* there is plenty on water supplies and uses, as well as water pollution, for example. But a rafter, kayaker, or canoeist will also see how the water on which we paddle is integrated with everything else on this planetary spaceship we're zooming around on. For informed zooming, pick up a copy of *Gaia.*

More Good Books on Water Conservation and Management

The Social and Environmental Effects of Large Dams by E. Goldsmith and N. Hildyard (San Francisco: Sierra Club Books, 1986)

Imperiled Planet: Restoring Our Endangered Ecosystems by Edward Goldsmith et al. (Cambridge, MA: MIT Press, 1990)

How to Affect Water Policy and Legislation

![envelope icon]

**The American Rivers Guide
to Wild and Scenic Rivers
Designation:
A Primer on National
River Conservation**

by Kevin J. Coyle
(Washington, D.C., American Rivers, 1988)

The glorified, candied views of the history of the United States that one so often gets in history lessons do not, lamentably, pertain to its rivers. If you think you'd like to argue that point, first consider a few points Kevin Coyle makes in this very useful compilation:

- 60,000 miles of U.S. rivers qualify for inclusion in the Wild and Scenic Rivers System. Of those, just over 9,000 miles are protected. That is roughly one fourth of one percent of all U.S. river miles.
- 600,000 miles of what used to be free-running rivers have been drowned by the impounded waters of 60,000 dams (for every mile of river preserved, 65 miles have been destroyed).
- "The Wild and Scenic Rivers System appears . . . to be the least-fulfilled of what Congress has identified as the nation's five great protection programs—

forests, parks, wilderness, wildlife refuges, and rivers."

This is actually a sixty-page loose-leaf notebook that includes sections on the planning process, how citizens can participate in the process of designation as a system river, the impact designation has, and more. In the chapter titled "Why Protect Rivers?" Coyle elaborates on each of these points:

- Conserved rivers are key to preserving nature.
- River conservation improves water quality.
- River conservation can save taxpayers money.
- River conservation helps strengthen and diversify state and local economies.
- River conservation planning can give localities more control over their own land use futures.

The book includes several appendices on such useful stuff as the text of the Wild and Scenic Rivers Act, a table of rivers in the system with numbers of miles included, and a list of those rivers authorized for study. One of the nicest things is that the whole kit and caboodle is all in a slim notebook. You won't have to slog through some hefty tome looking for the proverbial needle in a haystack. Copies are available from American Rivers, Washington, D.C., (202) 547-6900; (http://www.amrivers.org/amrivers/).

145

Source unknown.

> *"Local residents who want their river to remain 'as is' often make the mistake of thinking that change can be averted by doing nothing. Pro-active planning is a necessity for river protection."*
>
> —*from* Grassroots River Protection *(American Rivers, 1992) by Christopher Curtis*

Flowing Free: A Citizen's Guide for Protecting Wild and Scenic Rivers

(Washington, D.C.: The River Conservation Fund, 1977)

While plenty of the information in this little (seventy-six pages) paperback is dated, plenty of the principles it touts are not. Those timeless strategies—communicating well, developing plans, having goals, forming committees to get work done, getting the word out (publicity)—are the stuff of grassroots river protection. If you are thinking about protecting your river under the Wild and Scenic Rivers Act, then this booklet could get you thinking in the right direction.

Rivers at Risk: The Concerned Citizen's Guide to Hydropower

by John D. Echeverria, Pope Barrow, and Richard Roos-Collins

(Washington, D.C.: Island Press, 1989)

Rivers at Risk is a "how-to-save-your-local-river" book. The authors review, in straightforward language, how to formulate a strategy for preserving a river. They give an overview of the regulatory process and give an idea of who's who or what's what in the government that needs to be reckoned with during the process of dam licensing. If you want to protest, intervene, or do anything else except join a "monkey wrench gang," the authors explain how it should be done.

If the developers are eyeing your river, you will want to be eyeing this book. Better to pull the plug on their idea than to have it pulled on your river.

> *"A great many of our best rivers have long ago been ruined by dams; and the latest types of power dams have created larger and uglier backwaters than the old mill-dams. Let us hope that the development of hydroelectric power has nearly run its course. It has ruined fishing as well as canoeing."*
>
> —*John C. Phillips and Thomas D. Cabot in* Quick-Water and Smooth *(1935)*

The book aims to help you (1) intervene in hydropower proceedings; (2) direct hydro development away from rivers deserving preservation; (3) deal efficiently with the Federal Energy Regulatory Commission (FERC); and (4) use hydro licensing and relicensing procedures to guarantee adequate fish passage, sufficient water releases, and better public access to rivers.

Riverwork Book

(Philadelphia: U.S. Department of the Interior, National Park Service, 1988)

If you are at the very beginning stages of a strategy to protect a river, this could be a useful booklet. You will learn how to gather pertinent information, how to identify and prioritize important issues, how to get the public involved and supportive of your efforts, and plenty more. There are checklists scattered throughout the text to guide you and to ensure that you're thorough. There are notes on writ-

146

CUYAHOGA: A GOOD WORD TURNED DIRTY

The Cuyahoga River drains a small part of northeastern Ohio, discharging its waters into Lake Erie at Cleveland. The word *Cuyahoga* is said to be of Mohawk Indian origin meaning "crooked river." And crooked it is, as it meanders through many oxbows in downtown Cleveland just before entering the lake.

John D. Rockefeller's oil empire was built, in part, on the banks of the Cuyahoga. The steel, rubber, chemical, oil, and other industries all contributed their part to its demise. The river was dumped into, trashed, afflicted, saturated, and demeaned. By June 22, 1969, the Cuyahoga River was so extraordinarily sick, so covered with oil and contaminants from the steel and other mills, that it caught on fire.

Dante's *Inferno* visits Cleveland.

Any paddler could tell any steel magnate that a low-flow river that has little current can't take much abuse (the portion of the winding river in the vicinity of the fire is still known as "The Flats"). But things are changing at the Flats these days. Although it's conceivable (but unlikely) that your great great great great great great grandchildren might drink from the Cuyahoga, there is some recreational boating traffic there now and people are beginning to look at the Cuyahoga and appreciate it. Paddlers should consider making pilgrimages there to ponder both its history and its future. And to make *sure* that its history and your neighborhood river's history share nothing more in common than, say, a name with an Indian derivation.

ing press releases, on setting goals, and on securing funding. Think of it as "River Conservation 101."

This Land is Your Land: A Guide to North America's Endangered Ecosystems

by Jon Naar and Alex J. Naar
(New York: HarperPerennial, 1993)

The authors have selected problems of several types, and for each they provide background followed by a "what you can do" section. Several of the categories are: rivers, lakes, oceans, grasslands, chaparral, forests, and deserts. In the chapter on rivers they list a few of the North American continent's most deeply troubled rivers—due to pollution, dam threats, etc. For each they give a synopsis of the problem and then list several things the concerned citizen can do. The lists typically include things like clubs and organizations to join, government agencies to which you can let off steam, publications to read, etc.

Grassroots River Protection: Saving Rivers Under the National Wild and Scenic Rivers Act through Community-Based River Protection Strategies and State Actions

by Christopher Curtis
(Washington, D.C.: American Rivers, 1992)

This is one of the best, most up-to-date manuals for river lovers and protectors. Read this before you get your feet wet in the public policy arena.

Our culture is tough on rivers. Witness, as stated in *Grassroots*:

CONSERVATION AND ETHICS

- 30% of the native freshwater fish species in North America are threatened, endangered, or of special concern
- 10% of all North American freshwater mussels have become extinct in this century and many of those remaining are rare or imperiled
- 106 seasonal runs of Pacific salmon, steelhead and sea-run cutthroats on specific rivers are extinct, 102 face extinction, 58 are at moderate risk, and 54 are of concern
- 10 species of freshwater fish became extinct in the decade 1979–1989
- 66% of North America's crayfish are now rare or imperiled

. . . The purpose of this book is to tell the story of the Allagash, the Little Miami, the Westfield and other rivers protected through grassroots efforts, which resulted in state-initiated National Wild and Scenic River designation. It is hoped that these successful efforts will inspire others to work to achieve protection for the many beautiful and as-yet unspoiled rivers across the country.

More Good Books on How to Affect Policy and Legislation

A Citizen's Guide to River Conservation by Rolf Diamant, J. Glenn Eugster, and Christopher J. Duerksen (Washington, D.C.: The Conservation Foundation, 1984). Highly recommended—five stars.

The Stream Conservation Handbook edited by J. Michael Migel (New York: Crown, 1974). Directed at a fishing audience, but has excellent information, especially how-to's on saving a stream.

Natural Rivers and the Public Trust by W. Kent Olson (Washington, D.C.: American Rivers, 1988)

How to Save a River: A Handbook for Citizen Action by David M. Bolling (Washington, D.C.: Island Press, 1994)

Entering the Watershed: A New Approach to Save America's River Ecosystems by Bob Doppelt, et al., and the Pacific Rivers Council (Washington, D.C.: Island Press, 1993)

MAGNETS FOR MONEY

"*Time after time the [World] Bank turned to large dams as the vehicle for establishing a relationship with a new borrowing country. The first loan by the Bank to a developing country, only its fifth loan overall, was to Chile for construction of three large hydro-electric schemes. Large dam projects accounted for the Bank's first loans to Brazil ('49), El Salvador ('49), Mexico ('49), Iraq ('50), Iceland ('51), Austria ('54), Lebanon ('55), the Philippines ('57), Malasia ('58), Ghana ('61), Uganda ('61), Portugal ('63), Swaziland ('63), Bolivia ('64), Syria ('74), Vietnam ('78), and Lesotho ('86).*

With many of its key borrowers, the World Bank based its early relationship primarily on large dam lending. For example, between 1949 and 1971, more than 63 percent of Brazil's borrowing was for construction of 16 large dams. Half of Colombia's first 24 loans, over a 15 year period, were for large dams. Mexico's first three loans were for hydroelectric dams, and by 1962 funds for construction of 18 dams accounted for more than two-thirds of that country's debt to the World Bank."

—*from* World Rivers Review, *journal of the International Rivers Network, Berkeley*

SPEAKING WITH . . .
POPE BARROW

Pope Barrow has paddled internationally and lives in the Washington, D.C., area. He writes frequently for *American Whitewater*, the journal of the American Whitewater Affiliation (AWA), and has been active with the AWA for some time.

He is interested in numerous paddler's issues, perhaps foremost among them rights of passage on navigable and non-navigable waterways. For paddlers, he says, this is an issue of terrific importance because our access to countless rivers (and some ocean areas) is dependent on the good graces of private property owners. With ever-increasing numbers of paddlers looking for put-ins and take-outs, we are encountering resistance in some places to access to the riverbanks or beaches. Given both population projections and the explosive growth in recreational paddling, these pressures aren't likely to subside.

So, what to do?

Pope Barrow recommends keeping a low profile and not intentionally antagonizing landowners. Additionally, he says, paddlers would be well advised to work on changing state laws so the laws are better adapted to a "recreational test of navigability." If we don't change these laws, we run the risk in some places of being arrested for trespassing or damaging property.

In addition to modifying your behavior as well as state laws, things you might consider include (a) joining paddling associations and conservation groups that keep up on these issues; (b) letting your legislators know these issues are important; and (c) infecting someone else with your enthusiasm for your favorite river or bay.

The Restoration of Rivers and Streams: Theories and Experience edited by James A. Gore (Boston: Butterworth, 1985)

Clean Water in Your Watershed: A Citizen Guide to Watershed Protection by Susan V. Alexander (Washington, D.C.: Terrene Institute, 1993)

Water Conservation Resources

Amidst all the gloom and doom, it will give you hope to know there are hundreds and hundreds of groups out there working to clean up, free up, and preserve the world's rivers, lakes, and oceans. Following are some resources to contact (and remember, they can't do their work without the support of paid memberships).

Organizations

American Rivers

American Rivers, Washington, D.C., (202) 547-6900; (http://www.amrivers.org/amrivers/)

Centre for Marine Environmental Initiatives, Fisheries and Marine Institute of Memorial University of Newfoundland, St. Johns, Newfoundland, (709) 778-0648; cmerits@gill.ifmt.nf.ca

Cousteau Society, Chesapeake, VA, (804) 523-9335; (http://www.sky.net/~emily/cousteau.soc/)

International Rivers Network, Berkeley, CA, (510) 848-1155; irn@igc.apc.org (http://www.irn.org/irn/index.html). The IRN is a non-profit organization dedicated to preserving the world's rivers and watersheds, no small task.

National Audubon Society, New York, (212) 979-3000; join@audubon.org (http://www.igc.apc.org/audubon/). Audubon is very active in wetland, river, and ocean conservation. They operate numerous hotlines, including the Activist Network (212-979-3158) and Government Affairs Hotline (800-659-2622).

River Network, Portland, OR, (503) 241-3506; (http://www.teleport.com/~rivernet/)

Sea Shepherd Conservation Society, Marina del Rey, CA, (310) 301-7325; nvoth@igc.apc.org (http://www.envirolink.org/

THE ANNUAL LIST OF ENDANGERED WATERWAYS

Each year, generally in April, American Rivers in Washington, D.C., produces a list of seriously endangered or threatened rivers. And each year this list will frighten you because you are sure to find one river you love on that list. Portions of the following have appeared on recent annual lists due to proposed dams, development, oil spills, wildly fluctuating water flows, and a host of other troublesome reasons: the Mississippi, the Colorado, the Columbia, the Everglades, the Gunnison, the Susquehanna, and the Rio Grande.

For the current list, contact (and join) American Rivers, Washington, D.C., (202) 547-6900; (http://www.amrivers.org/amrivers/).

orgs/seashep/)

Surfrider Foundation, San Clemente, CA, (800) 743-SURF, (714) 492-8170; (http://www.sdsc.edu). Works toward international protection of waves and beaches.

There are also hundreds of small, regional conservation groups that are working to preserve rivers and lakes and oceans. To find out about them, start by contacting your local Sierra Club or National Audubon Society chapters, which are usually active in local conservation and are well networked with other groups. Most of the organizations listed above are also excellent clearinghouses of regional information.

Finding Out Who's Doing What . . .

The following directories will help you find even more people working on the issues that concern you.

Riverworks: A Directory of NGO's, Activists and Experts Working on River and Watershed Issues Around the World by the International Rivers Network (IRN) in Berkeley (contact information above). This list is printed on demand (about $15) from a database at IRN.

1990 River Conservation Directory (Washington, D.C.: National Park Service and the National Association for State River Conservation Programs, 1990). Though out of date, this directory lists about a thousand federal agencies, national organizations, multi-state and state groups, watershed associations, canoe clubs, advisory councils, natural resource districts, etc., that all have some aspect of river conservation at heart. It includes both public and non-profit organizations.

Protecting Plastic Kayaks

Plastic sea kayaks have a reputation for toughness. As a result, many owners drag them over rocks with scant regard for long-term consequences. But such treatment rapidly frays the hull, which slows the boat through the water. Better to carry the boat when you can, and let the plastic's resiliency protect it when you can't. Burrs from scrapes can be sanded off to help restore the smoothness of the hull. Be especially careful when transporting or storing plastic sea kayaks. Their long hulls can deform if not supported properly, or if cinched down too tightly on a rack. This can greatly affect handling and tracking.

—JH & RH

Conservation Directory (Washington, D.C.: National Wildlife Federation). Published every spring, this guide is very helpful when used with resources like the River Conservation Directory, which is outdated.

Green Links on the Internet

The Internet is one of the best places to get and share the most current conservation information. If you want a head start on navigation, try these great books:

EcoLinking: Everyone's Guide to On-line Environmental Information by Don Rittner (Berkeley, CA: Peachpit Press, 1992), which is an excellent guide that is not overly technical,

and

Environment Online: The Greening of Databases (Wilton, CT: Eight Bit Books, 1992), which is good and fairly technical.

More tips

One of the most odious aspects of activism, though among the more important, is keeping your legislators informed of your views. The magic of e-mail can make this a much easier task (you can also maintain a "hot" list of fellow paddler-activists to whom you can e-mail alerts about water conservation issues; they can then e-mail their legislators, and their friends and their legislators, and so on, like ripples on a lake that someday may become big waves).

A frequently updated list of e-mail addresses for all our federal elected officials is available on the University of Michigan's Library Gopher. You can gopher to the University of Michigan Library Gopher or telnet to: una.hh.lib.umich.edu (tip: login as gopher) Path: Social Sciences/Government/U.S. Government: Legislative Branch/E-Mail Addresses

Keep up on water-related issues on the Internet by regularly visiting web sites of the conservation organizations listed above, and the paddlers' associations listed in Chapter 2 (see also the Internet information in Chapter 2).

151

AMERICA'S WHITEWATER RAFTING OUTFITTERS—WHAT GOOD ARE THEY?

by John Connelly

It's a hot summer weekend on one of America's more popular whitewater rivers. The casual passerby might think the congested and chaotic scene at the put-in resembles an amusement park. The staging area on these days can indeed boggle the mind, and appears to be a contradiction to why people came to the river in the first place: rafting guests with colorful paddling gear, guides barking orders, rafts being hauled by their crew to the put-ins, outfitting companies sporting their team colors and logos, vehicles and equipment being shuffled about—it all appears to be anything but a wilderness experience.

This activity leaves some people with the impression that this is all just a commercial enterprise orchestrated by a few rafting operators as a "get-rich-quick" scheme. Some people even think that outfitters have conspired to create these businesses and have maneuvered themselves into the position of taking advantage of their unsuspecting rafting guests. I heard someone suggest that outfitters all but turn their guests upside down and shake the money from their pockets before sending them home.

I think this is largely a misconception. What most people don't realize is that, in addition to running trips and taking money, whitewater rafting outfitters advocate for public interest in river recreation and play a key role in shaping the landscape of river running in this country. The future of their businesses depends on providing the type of experience the public seeks, and outfitters support policy and management that benefit the public at large.

Rafting outfitters are entrepreneurs who take on a substantial business risk and who have chosen to be public service providers. Their customer is the American public. Generally, people who use outfitters possess neither the specialized equipment nor the skills to participate in river recreation on their own.

In fact, and in law, these are the people who actually own America's rivers. Rivers are a publicly owned resource. Rafting outfitters play an important role in facilitating the American public's use and enjoyment of these precious and valuable national resources. What outfitters have discovered is that to best serve the public and to protect their businesses, they must be involved in the politics of river use. The issues of water flows from dams, river access, carrying capacity limits, support facilities, and user fees, are issues outfitters are forced to be involved with.

The role of the rafting outfitter has changed over the years. Now, outfitters play a vital role in exposing people to whitewater recreation resources. Outfitters help their clients understand and appreciate the value of these rivers, and so create an awareness that these are resources worth protecting. These people become a constituency that can be called upon to help influence river conservation and recreation management policy even on stretches of river they have not paddled.

The politics of river running is complex, difficult, and delves deeply into the often contentious issues of river access with landowners; river-use issues with federal, state, and local regulatory and management agencies; water flow issues with hydropower developers, who may be public utilities or private industrial producers; and the issues of providing adequate and appropriate facilities to manage riverside impacts and sanitation.

Outfitters also deal with the issue of licensing and user fees charged to the river running public through the outfitting companies by management and regulatory entities. The concern of outfitters is that the combination of these fees threatens to put whitewater recreation out of financial reach for a great many Americans.

The National Park Service and other land and river management agencies recognize that public use of river resources through commercial outfitting businesses results in fewer river emergencies that involve outside help, and a cleaner river environment because outfitters patrol the river and pick up everyone's debris, including anything that floats down from above the sections of river they run.

Outfitters play an important role in river conservation. Because of their vested interest in the preservation and management of the river resource for recreation, no group is more willing to catalyze and fund these efforts when the need arises.

Alliances have been formed between outfitters and other user groups to successfully save rivers from inappropriate and damaging development. These alliances have affected management along a number of rivers, furthering enhancement and protection of river recreation opportunities for outfitters, for the general public they serve, and for the private users of the resource. Examples are Maine's West Branch of the Penobscot, West Virginia's Gauley, and the Ocoee in Tennessee.

The Federal Energy Regulatory Commission periodically evaluates competing uses of rivers below dams and attempts to balance these needs through an operating plan. Outfitters have used their influence to ensure that whitewater recreation is included. A successful effort results in securing access for outfitters while providing guarantees that the public will be able to enjoy the resource for decades to come.

Outfitters operating on rivers used by private boaters, campers, families, and fishermen train their river staff to be both sensitive and respectful of everyone's right to use the river. Although inappropriate behavior can surface with any user group, there is a very conscious effort by outfitters to create harmony on the river.

So who are the people in those rafts anyway? Are they simply a bunch of mindless yahoos from the city looking for a way to bring the city to the woods and ruin it for those seeking serenity, those more deserving to be here? Well, some elitists perceive it that way, but that's not how it really is at all.

The people in those rafts are your children's teachers and school principals, your clergy and your politicians, your dentist and your waitress from your favorite restaurant. They are seeking the opportunity to enjoy the river, too. And they have a right to be there. But they don't have the equipment or the skills to paddle it on their own.

Not everyone may like what they see on the river on those really busy days. But those days are busy for a reason and it's not a bad thing. Rafting outfitters have been working hard to serve the general public's interest in river running and they have been doing a really good job.

Just as rafters who prefer a less crowded experience plan their trips on low-use days, so should boaters who want uninterrupted wave- and hole-surfing. Paddling on low-use days assures you of fewer boats coming down the river, and fewer impatient fellow boaters cueing up for your favorite play spot.

Many times, we private boaters grudgingly relinquish our surfing waves or holes to flotillas of laughing and screaming rafters. We need to keep in mind that it's their river, too, and there are more of them than there are of us. A little tolerance and an appreciation of what they are experiencing—and even a smile—can go a long way toward making everyone's day that much better. And if you see an outfitter, smile and wave!

—John Connelly resides in Falmouth, Maine, and has been in the river outfitting business for nineteen years. He has been active in river conservation, hydropower relicensing, and resource management consulting. He sold his company, paddles creeks and rivers regularly, and provides risk management and liability coverage for the commercial recreation industry.

153

9

Water Arts

OR

How to Express and Explore Your Paddlemania

". . . above the roar of the falls came a strange murmur in the forest—not the hoot of an owl, nor the howl of a wolf, but the sound of men singing in concert, which quickly increased until it became a veritable roar. Then over the trees came a great canoe full of men paddling for dear life . . . the great canoe flew through the air like a flock of wild geese bound for some distant shore."

—*from* The Flying Canoe *(La Chasse-Galerie), a short story by J. E. LeRossignol (Toronto: McClelland and Stewart, 1929)*

154

Waterlore:
In Praise of Museums

❖

One could spend a pleasant lifetime bopping from museum to museum, just looking at old boats. From the relics, remnants, gems, and masterpieces of the past we can learn a great deal about and greatly enhance our passion—paddling.

Take as just one example—the Haida Ceremonial Canoe on display at the American Museum of Natural History in New York City. It is magnificent. The Haida Indians of British Columbia's Queen Charlotte Islands are known for their textiles, masks, and totem poles, but this v-e-r-y long canoe (which was brought to New York in 1884) would probably have been used in association with an Indian potlatch (ceremonial festival). If you ever find yourself in the Big Apple, you are guaranteed not to regret a visit to the Haida Ceremonial Canoe.

On your future travels look for

the following museums, all of which have fine examples of kayaks, canoes, or small craft from earlier times. (Another traveler's tip: historical societies and associations may have boats of interest they will show you—so never hesitate to ask. For example, sea kayakers may want to contact the Baidarka Historical Society in Port Moody, British Columbia or canoeists the Wooden Canoe Heritage Association in Blue Mountain Lake New York.)

- The Peabody Essex Museum, Salem, Massachusetts
- Mystic Seaport, Mystic, Connecticut
- Chesapeake Bay Maritime Museum, St. Michaels, Maryland
- The Smithsonian Institution, Washington, D.C.
- The Adirondack Museum, Blue Mountain Lake, New York
- The Antique Boat Museum, Clayton, New York
- The Center for Wooden Boats, Seattle, Washington
- John Wesley Powell River History Museum, Green River, Utah
- The Anchorage Museum of History and Art, Anchorage, Alaska
- University of British Columbia Museum, Vancouver, British Columbia
- The Voyageur Heritage Center, Mattawa, Ontario
- The Marine Museum of Upper Canada, Toronto, Ontario
- The Canadian Canoe Museum, Peterborough, Ontario
- The Canadian Museum of Civilization, Hull, Quebec (near Ottawa)
- Maine Watercraft Museum, Thomaston, Maine

For further listings, try this great little book:

North America's Maritime Museums: An Annotated Guide by Hartley Edward Howe (New York: Facts on File, 1987)

or

The Official Museum Directory (New Providence, NJ: R.R. Bowker, published annually). Lists hundreds if not thousands of museums and tells a wee bit about what each does.

155

Waterwords:
Literature, Poetry, and Plays

Paddlers know intimately the rewards and trials of travel on the world's waterways. A crimson sunrise over jagged rock islands in Baja. Mist enshrouding the secrets of a forest-capped Maine island. The primal fear of a whitewater rapid. The soothing sluice of tide waves on a sandy shore. The trip from hell. Camps you never want to leave, tucked away on some secret shore known only to you, the night-herons, and the stars.

Below are some of the hundreds of books that were inspired by those images and emotions we all know.

Literature

Canexus: The Canoe in Canadian Culture

edited by James Raffan and Bert Horwood (Toronto: Betelgeuse Books, 1988)
Back in the fall of 1987, a conference on "The Canoe in Canadian Culture" was held at Queen's University, Ontario. This book is a collection of the presentations; it consists of fifteen chapters with titles such as "Symbols and Myths:

Images of Canoe and North"; "Canoeing and Gender Roles"; and "Probing Canoe Trips for Persistent Meaning."

The writings in this book demonstrate that the canoe is a very important symbol in northern culture. For the serious reader, this is interesting stuff, though it is not fluffy or peppered with pictures. After reading this collection, one begins to understand why for more than fifty years a canoe appeared on one side of the Canadian dollar.

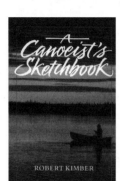

A Canoeist's Sketchbook

by Robert Kimber
(Post Mills, VT: Chelsea
Green Publishing Co., 1991)
A collection of essays on many aspects of paddling and camping. Delightful winter reading.

'Roughing it' has always struck me as a dumb phrase. It suggests that there is some kind of virtue in discomfort and inconvenience. Just get wet, cold, hungry, and exhausted enough, it says, and you will experience the true essence of the outdoors.

Untrue. The only thing you'll experience is wet, cold, hunger, and exhaustion. You won't have any energy or attention left over to appreciate the flight of the kingfisher or the damp touch of the morning mist on your face or the raccoon tracks in the mud or any of the other little million things there are to attend to.

Marked by the Wild: An Anthology of Literature Shaped by the Canadian Wilderness

edited by Bruce Littejohn and John Pearce
(Toronto: McClelland and Stewart, 1973)
Editors Littejohn and Pearce write, "If there is one distinguishing element that sets Canadian literature apart from most other national literatures, it is the influence of the wild." In *Marked by the Wild,* Littejohn and Pearce have pulled together many of the writings that capture that spirit, that essence of what Canada is, including very well-known writers Sig Olson, Farley Mowat, Robert Service, and Jack London. But you will also find many other excellent selections from the likes of Emily Carr, Hugh MacLennan, and Margaret Atwood. This anthology is a sampler of what Canada is all about.

On the River: A Variety of Canoe & Small Boat Voyages

edited by Walter Magnes Teller
(Dobbs Ferry, NY: Sheridan House, reprinted 1988)
Many paddlers simply know of this book as Teller's *On the River.* It enjoys the status of the Bible among many. And, indeed, it is one of the nicest companions any paddler might own. *On the River* is an anthology of some of the best writings over the years about boating, mostly canoeing, including works by Thoreau (from his *Journal*), Nathaniel Bishop (from *Voyage of the Paper Canoe*), Isobel Knowles (*Two Girls in a Canoe*), and Anna Kalland (*It Can't Be Done*). Teller introduces each of the writers and explains how each piece fits in the context of paddling literature.

The canoe is the American boat of the past and of the future. It suits the American mind: it is light, swift, safe, graceful, easily moved; and the occupant looks in the direction he is going, instead of behind, as in the stupid old tubs that have held the world up to this time. . . . Boats are for work; canoes are for pleasure. Boats are artificial; canoes are natural. In a boat

157

WATER ARTS

you are always an oar's length and a gunwale's height away from Nature. In a canoe you can steal up to her bower and peep into her very bosom.
—John Boyle O'Reilly, in Teller's On the River

Roll On, River: Rivers in the Lives of the American People

edited by Peter C. Mancall
(Washington, D.C.: National Council on the Aging, 1990)

Peter Mancall has pulled together a fine selection of writings on America's love for and abuse of its rivers. He divides the book into eight chapters: "Imagining Rivers"; "The Promise of Prosperity"; "Exploration"; "Travel"; "A Spiritual Voyage"; "Working on the River"; "Floods"; and "The Costs of Development". Each chapter contains several selections, including the expected, such as a portion of *The Adventures of Huckleberry Finn* and Annie Dillard's *Pilgrim at Tinker Creek,* but also some less frequently found items, such as a poem by Langston Hughes, "The Negro Speaks of Rivers," and Willis F. Johnson's *History of the Johnstown Flood.*

The selections in this anthology should transport the reader to the edge of his or her favorite river. Yet as we gaze over these watercourses, and perhaps lull ourselves into believing that we are looking upon a river that has always flowed just as it flows today, we need to be aware that rivers remain precious but precarious resources. At the present time Americans continue to wage war on rivers. . . . Unless Americans take

GET THEE TO A BOAT

Every paddler's library should include Shakespeare.

Huh? Shakespeare mentioned in a book about paddling? Why?

Well, for starters, he was about 400 years ahead of his time with his comment, "No more dams" (Caliban says it in *The Tempest*).

It's true what they say about how incredible the man was. And if you are one of those people who despised reading Shakespeare in eighth, tenth, or twelfth grade, try it again. Your English teacher had a way of stripping it of its life, of making it powerfully dull, of bringing on sleep in even the most alert teenager.

Now that you've got some life experience under your belt, let the paddler in you ponder how the Bard speaks of rivers, streams, water, boats and more. While he doesn't specifically mention whitewater rafting, the Mississippi, or the Mackenzie River, he speaks of all kinds of things that are of interest to paddlers—things like astronomy and astrology, the vastness of the ocean, flowers on the riverbank, the benefits of traveling. See, for example, the following:

"To shallow rivers, to whose falls
Melodious birds sing madrigals."
　　　　　　　　—The Merry Wives of Windsor

"Smooth runs the water where the brook is deep."
　　　　　　　　—Henry VI, Part 2

"A little water clears us of this deed."
　　　　　　　　—Macbeth

Don't miss the boat. There are a lot of goodies the paddler can sift from the pages of Shakespeare.

action to halt the continued spillage of oil and other chemical pollutants into our waterways, future generations may grow up in a country where the odes to fishing written by Norman Maclean and Ernest Hemingway are artifacts of a world gone by. Unlike other changes over time, however, we will not have simply lost the world of the past; we will have destroyed it through our careless and selfish pursuit of gain.

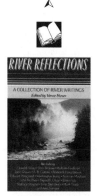

River Reflections: An Anthology

edited by Verne Huser

(Charlotte, NC: East Woods Press, 1984)

Here is another anthology, this one a paddler's collection of writings if

The "Low" High Brace

The key to making your high braces quick and effective is to keep them low. By keeping your hands in front of you and below chin level, your blades will reach the water faster and your shoulders will be protected from exposure to dislocations.

—JB & TB

SPEAKING WITH . . .
VERNE HUSER

One need only speak with someone like Verne Huser, who has been paddling since 1957, to get a sense of perspective on what is important about paddling. His career has included a wide range of activities— professor of English, mediator, writer, and river guide, just to name a few. Now in his mid-sixties, Huser spends much of his "water time" in a canoe, but in earlier days he guided raft trips on the Snake and other western rivers. It all began in the 1950s when he was working in Grand Teton National Park. He had mornings off, and one day a boatman who worked mornings quit; Huser filled in for him. Perhaps his life hasn't been the same since the day that boatman quit. But besides taking over (and then some) where that boatman left off, Huser has shared his enthusiasm for rivers, and

for the environment generally, through his continuation, even today, as a guide on the Snake.

There is a strong vein of Henry David Thoreau in Huser—he is an advocate of the simple life. He is concerned about the overuse of rivers, but believes that as long as users are minimum-impact campers, their floating on rivers is not harmful to those rivers. He is a strong advocate of *planning* prior to getting on the water. Thoughtful planning, he believes, is a way to minimize impact, through less generation of waste, less habitat destruction, etc.

In addition to editing *River Reflections*, Huser is the author of *Snake River Guide, River Camping*, and articles such as "River Classics: The Literature of Flowing Water," which appeared in *River Runner* Magazine, July 1987. He is soft-spoken, committed to simplicity, informed, and experienced on the water. One could do far worse than live a life like his . . .

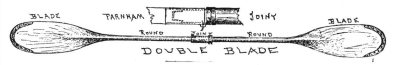

there ever was one. Verne Huser is a paddler who has done us all a favor by pulling together selections from about two centuries and roughly fifty writers on—what else—rivers! To whet your appetite: selections from Sigurd Olson's *The Lonely Land*, Raymond Patterson's *Dangerous River*, John Malo's *Love Affair with a River*, Roderick Haig-Brown's *A River Never Sleeps*, Tom Brokaw's *That River Swallows People*, Michael Frome's *Must This Be*

Lost to the Sight of Man?, Ann Zwinger's *Run, River, Run*, Edward Abbey's *Down the River*, and Huser's own *Alive But Not Well*.

The Seaside Reader

edited by Dery Bennett

(New York: Lyons & Burford, 1992)

Editor Bennett reminds us that about three-quarters of all Americans live within fifty miles of a

An Environmental Chronology, 1626–1989

1626 .... Plymouth Colony passes ordinances regulating the cutting and sale of timber on colony lands.

1634 .... Plymouth prohibits the setting of forest fires.

1639 .... Newport, Rhode Island, prohibits deer hunting for six months.

1681 .... William Penn, proprietor of Pennsylvania, decrees that for every five acres of land cleared, one must be left forested.

1691 .... British colonial policy provides for reserving large trees, suitable for masts, in New England by marking them with a "broad arrow."

1710 .... Massachusetts protects waterfowl in coastal regions.

1711 .... The White Pine Act of Parliament extends protection of trees suitable for masts.

1718 .... Massachusetts prohibits deer hunting for four years.

1739 .... Connecticut creates an annual closed season for deer.

1772 .... New York creates a closed season on quail and partridge.

1804–06 .... Meriwether Lewis and William Clark lead the first American transcontinental exploration.

1828–31 .... First experiment in federal forest management with live oaks on Santa Rosa Peninsula, Florida.

1832 .... George Catlin proposes a national park.

1849 .... U.S. Department of the Interior established.

1858 .... Mount Vernon purchased as a historical site.

1864 .... Yosemite Valley, California, reserved as a state park.

1864 .... George Perkins Marsh publishes *Man and Nature*.

1869 .... John Wesley Powell descends the Colorado River through the Grand Canyon.

1871 .... U.S. Fish Commission created.

1872 .... Arbor Day designated as April 10 as a result of the efforts of J. Sterling Morton; currently celebrated last Friday in April.

1872 .... Yellowstone National Park established.

1875 .... American Forestry Association organized.

1876 .... Appalachian Mountain Club organized.

1878 .... John Wesley Powell publishes *Report on the Lands of the Arid Region of the United States*.

1879 .... U.S. Geological Survey established.

1881 .... Division of Forestry created in the Department of Agriculture as a fact-finding agency.

1882 .... American Forestry Congress organized.

1885 .... New York, in cooperation with Ontario, creates the Niagara Reservation, protecting the Falls.

Continued on page 161

coast. And when actually at the coast looking to sea, one only sees out about five miles (on a good day) to the horizon. Those five miles are the primary interest of this collection of writings.

You will find selections from Rachel Carson, Henry Beston, John Steinbeck, Jacques Cousteau, Peter Matthiessen, Izaac Walton, and others. Included are selections on several themes, among them: beaches, watery habitats, going underwater, fishing, creatures, and vessels. Several selections deal with the consequences of humans and their developments along seasides.

The format of this anthology is a good, simple one. Each piece is introduced by the editor with just a short paragraph or two, putting it in context or giving the reader a quick backgrounder on its author.

American Environmentalism: Readings in Conservation History, Third Edition

edited by Roderick Frazier Nash
(New York: McGraw-Hill, 1990)

Roderick Nash has pulled together an anthology of many significant writings in environmental history. Among others, this book includes Thoreau, John Muir, Aldo Leopold, Rachel Carson, Edward Abbey, Wendell Berry, William O. Douglas, Gifford Pinchot, Black Elk, and John Wesley Powell.

A useful addition is a handy American Environmental Chronology, a timeline of the major events in U.S. conservation history that occurred between 1626 ("Plymouth Colony passed ordinances regulating the cutting and sale of timber on colony lands") and 1989 ("massive oil spill in Prince William Sound, Alaska, arouses national indignation").

Nash is retired professor of history and environmental studies at the University of California at Santa Barbara, and author of many other books and articles, among them *The Big Drops: Ten Legendary Rapids of the American West* (Boulder, CO: Johnson Books, 1989).

Rivermen: A Romantic Iconography of the River and the Source

by Frederic S. Colwell
(Montreal: McGill-Queen's University Press, 1989)

This book offers a fascinating look at river lore over time. Wordsworthian rivers, nymphs, the Nile, Shelley, the River Meander, the Charon, and other real and mythological streams and rivers all flow on and off the pages of Colwell's book. Highly recommended river reading.

An Environmental Chronology, Continued

1885 ....New York establishes the Adirondack Forest Preserve (later Adirondack State Park).

1885 ....Predecessor of the U.S. Biological Survey created in the Department of Agriculture as the Division of Economic Ornithology and Mammalogy.

1885 ....Boone and Crockett Club founded.

1886 ....New York Audubon Society organized.

1886 ....Bernhard E. Fernow assumes direction of an expanded Division of Forestry.

1890 .......U.S. Census announces the end of the frontier as a definable line.

1891 ....Forest Reserve Act permits the president to establish forest reserves (later national forests) on the public domain.

1891 ....Yosemite National Park established.

1891 ....National Irrigation Congress organized.

1892 ....Sierra Club founded.

1895 ....American Scenic and Historic Preservation Society founded.

1897 ....Forest Management Act defines purpose of the forest reserves.

1898 ....First college-level work in forestry offered at Cornell.

1898 ....Gifford Pinchot named head of the Division of Forestry.

1899 ....River and Harbor Act establishes the first legal basis for banning pollution of navigable waterways.

1900 ....Society of American Foresters founded.

1900 ....Lacey Act makes interstate shipment of game killed in violation of state laws a federal offense.

1902 ....Reclamation (Newlands) Act establishes Bureau of Reclamation in the Department of the Interior and launches a federal reclamation program.

1905 ....National Audubon Society formed.

1905 ....Forest reserves transferred from the Department of the Interior to the Forest Service within Department of Agriculture.

1906 ....Antiquities Act permits reservation of areas of scientific or historical interest on federal land as national monuments.

1907 ....Inland Waterways Commission established.

1908 ....Grand Canyon of the Colorado made a national monument.

Continued on page 162

161

An Environmental Chronology, Continued

1908 ....Theodore Roosevelt hosts a conference of governors at the White House on the subject of conservation.

1908 ....National Conservation Commission appointed to inventory resources.

1909 ....North American Conservation Conference held in Washington.

1909 ....National Conservation Association organized as a private group to replace the National Conservation Commission.

1910 ....The Forest Products Laboratory established by the Forest Service in Madison, Wisconsin.

1910 ....The Ballinger-Pinchot controversy disrupts the conservation movement.

1911 ....American Game Protective and Propagation Association founded.

1911 ....Weeks Act, permitting purchase of forested land at headwaters of navigable streams for inclusion in the national forest system, makes possible the establishment of national forests in the East.

1913 ....Hetch Hetchy Valley in Yosemite National Park granted to San Francisco for a reservoir after prolonged controversy.

1916 ....National Park Service Act.

1918 ....Migratory Bird Treaty Act implements 1916 treaty with Canada to restrict hunting of migratory species.

1918 ....Save-the-Redwoods-League founded.

1920 ....Mineral Leasing Act regulates mining on federal lands.

1920 ....Federal Water Power Act gives the Federal Power Commission authority to issue licenses for hydropower development.

1922 ....Izaak Walton League organized.

1924 ....Oil Pollution Control Act.

1924 ....Teapot Dome scandal.

1924 ....The Forest Service designates first extensive wilderness area in the Gila National Forest, New Mexico.

1924 ....The first National Conference on Outdoor Recreation held in Washington, D.C.

Continued on page 164

Photo courtesy of the Library of Congress, Prints and Photographs Division, Washington, D.C.

More Good Books

River Days: Travels On Western Rivers: A Collection of Essays edited by Jeff Rennicke (Golden, CO: Fulcrum, 1988)

The Norton Book of Nature Writing edited by Robert Finch and John Elder (New York: W.W. Norton & Co., 1990). Includes all the heavy hitters.

The Ragged Mountain Portable Wilderness Anthology edited by Jan Adkins (Camden, ME: Ragged Mountain Press, 1993)

The Wilderness Reader edited by Frank Bergon (Reno, NV: University of Nevada Press, 1994)

Words for the Wild: The Sierra Club Trailside Reader edited by Ann Ronald (San Francisco: Sierra Club Books, 1987)

RAMBLINGS ABOUT THE
LANGUAGE OF PADDLERS

Paddlers talk funny.

Brace, broach, peel-out, ferry, j-stroke, portage, rock garden, keelson, stem, ABS, PFD, laminate, wet out, blind drop, cfs, eddy line, endo, haystacks, sprayskirt, pitch, dam controlled, boulder field, hole hydraulic, standing wave, ribs, trim, tumblehome, head, tailrace, Class III. What does it all mean?

Human beings, being social creatures generally, like to communicate with one another about a wide variety of things. Sometimes they talk about water, sometimes trees, sometimes the sky, sometimes boats, rarely about work, frequently about sex, and so on. For those times when they get around water with their boats, they have developed a unique dialect in which to converse. Just as a plumber speaks of elbows, pipe cutters, and PVC, a paddler might speak of Hypalon, rooster tails, or a shuttle; just as an investor might speak of a financial pyramid, a futures option, or the beta, a paddler might mention a souse hole, a keeper, or a deadwater. We all do it to share a common experience.

In some cases a dictionary would be useful; in others words are in use only in a particular region (for example, the South or the West). The *Random House Dictionary of the English Language* tells us, for example, that the word:

- **Souse** dates back to about 1350, is Germanic in origin, and had to do with pickling or immersing in

a brine. Ponder that next time you or your boat is stuck in a souse hole.

- **Ferry** dates to before 1150 A.D. and can be traced to the Old English word *ferian*, which meant "to carry."

- **Hypothermia** means "subnormal body temperature," and use of the word dates back to about 1885. *Hypo* is Greek for "under" or "below" and *therm* is Greek for heat. So . . . *underheated*. Remember that next time your raft flips while running one of the rapids in the cold waters of the Grand Canyon.

- **Squirt**—the meaning is obvious, the derivation is not. It comes from the Middle English word *sqwyrt* which pertains to, of all things, diarrhea. It is not recommended that you raise this issue when speaking with squirt boaters.

- **River** hardly needs a definition. English use of the word can be traced to about 1250 A.D. The French use the closely related word *riviere*, while the Romans used the Latin word *riparia*, from which both the French and English are derived.

- An **eddy** is something every boater sees once in a while. The word dates back to about 1425 and is from the Old English *ed* plus *ea* ("turning" plus "water"). So, *turning water*.

You might not have good luck looking up charc, endo, boof, Pawlata Roll, highside, or chicken route. These are the words and phrases we use in conversing with each other. The cashier at the drug store and the short order cook won't have a clue what you're talking about if you use these words (unless, of course, they're paddlers). But we often can understand each other because of the all-important context.

The upshot is this, then: when paddlers use a word you're not familiar with, ask them what it means. Odds are good that you're not alone in not understanding.

For anyone more interested in terminology used on the riverbank today, there are glossaries in the back of countless books on paddling. There is also a little pamphlet by David W. Zimmerly called *An Illustrated Glossary of Kayak Terminology* (Ottawa: Canadian Museums Association, 1970s, exact date unknown) that lists those terms most often associated with the construction and use of an Eskimo kayak.

163

An Environmental Chronology, Continued

1924 ......Clarke-McNary Act extends federal ability to buy lands for inclusion in the National Forest system and provides for private, state, and federal cooperation in forest management.

1926 ......Restoration of Williamsburg, Virginia, begun.

1928 ......Boulder Canyon Project (Hoover Dam) authorized.

1928 ......McSweeney-McNary Act authorizes a broad program of federal forestry research.

1933 ......Civilian Conservation Corps established.

1933 ......Tennessee Valley Authority created.

1933 ......Franklin D. Roosevelt creates the Soil Erosion Service as an emergency measure.

1934 ......Taylor Grazing Act provides for retention and federal regulation of use of unreserved public domain.

1935 ......Soil Conservation Act extends federal involvement in erosion control and establishes the Soil Conservation Service in the Department of Agriculture.

1935 ......Wilderness Society founded.

1936 ......National Wildlife Federation, with 4.6 million members by the 1980s, founded.

1936 ......Omnibus Flood Control Act establishes a national flood prevention policy under the U.S. Army Corps of Engineers and the Department of Agriculture.

1937 ......Federal Aid in Wildlife Restoration (Pittman-Robertson) Act makes federal funds available to states for wildlife protection and propagation.

1939 ......Forest Service "U" regulations extend the policy of wilderness preservation in the national forests.

1940 ......The creation of the U.S. Fish and Wildlife Service consolidates federal protection and propagation activities.

1944 ......Soil Conservation Society of America founded.

1946 ......U.S. Bureau of Land Management established to consolidate the administration of the public domain.

1948 ......Federal Water Pollution Control Law enacted to regulate waste disposal.

1948 ......Donora, Pennsylvania, experiences severe air pollution; twenty die and 14,000 become ill.

Continued on page 165

Poetry

GATHERED WATERS

An Anthology of River Poems Selected by Cort Conley

Gathered Waters: An Anthology of River Poems

selected by Cort Conley
(Cambridge, ID: Backeddy Books, 1985)

All paddlers benefit greatly from Cort Conley's *Gathered Waters*. He has pulled together about sixty poems, all with the river as their primary literary theme. Here are a few you can expect to find in this inspiring book:

"River" by Ted Hughes
"Voyageurs" by Edwin Godsey
"The River Voyagers"

Photo courtesy of the Library of Congress, Prints and Photographs Division, Washington, D.C.

by Wendell Berry
"Currents" by Stephen Pett
"The Negro Speaks of Rivers"
    by Langston Hughes
"Rivers" by Henry David Thoreau
"The Canoer" by Diane Wakoski
"Inside the River" by James Dickey
"West-Running Brook"
    by Robert Frost
"Canoeing at Night"
    by Brad Leithauser

This is one of those gems that any paddler with a literary or poetic bent should be sure to read—in fact, it ranks right up there with actually being on the water.

> *"Snaggle-Tooth, Maytag,*
>   *Taylor Falls—*
> *long before we measured with*
>   *our eyes*
> *the true size of each monstrosity*
> *its name, downriver, was famous*
>   *to us."*
>
> —*by Jonathan Holden, this is taken from the title poem of* The Names of the Rapids *(Amherst, MA: University of Massachusetts Press, 1985)*

An Environmental Chronology, Continued

1949 ....The first Sierra Club Biennial Wilderness Conference held.

1949 ....Congress charters the National Trust for Historic Preservation.

1949 ....Aldo Leopold's *A Sand County Almanac* published posthumously.

1952 ....London's "Killer Smog" leaves 4,000 dead in a weekend and leads to effective air pollution regulations.

1956 ....Mission 66 launched as a ten-year improvement program for the national parks.

1956 ....Echo Park Dam, scheduled for construction in Dinosaur National Monument, deleted from the Upper Colorado River Storage Project, marking a major victory for wilderness preservation and the National Park system.

1956 ....Water Pollution Control Act provides federal grants for water treatment plants.

1958 ....Congress appoints the Outdoor Recreation Resources Review Commission to study and report on the nation's future needs.

1960 ....The Multiple Use–Sustained Yield Act defines the purpose of the national forests to admit nonmaterial benefits.

1962 ....President John F. Kennedy and Secretary of the Interior Stewart Udall host a White House Conference on Conservation.

1962 ....Rachel Carson publishes *Silent Spring*.

1963 ....Clean Air Act authorizes federal hearings and legal actions.

1963 ....The Bureau of Outdoor Recreation established within the Department of the Interior to coordinate federal efforts.

1964 ....Wilderness Act establishes the National Wilderness Preservation System.

1964 ....Canyonlands National Park established.

1965 ....Land and Water Conservation Fund Act makes money available for local, state, and federal acquisition and development of park land and open space.

1965 ....Storm King (Scenic Hudson) case admits scenic and recreational criteria in legal actions.

1965 ....Lyndon B. Johnson hosts a White House Conference on Natural Beauty.

Continued on page 166

Photo courtesy of the Library of Congress, Prints and Photographs Division, Washington, D.C.

165

An Environmental Chronology, Continued

1966 ....National Historic Preservation Act passed.

1966 ....Endangered Species Act begins federal involvement in habitat protection and rare species identification.

1967 ....Environmental Defense Fund established.

1968 ....Paul Ehrlich publishes *The Population Bomb*.

1968 ....National Wild and Scenic Rivers Act and National Trails System Act passed.

1968 ....Grand Canyon Dams defeated.

1968 ....First manned flight to circle the moon produces dramatic photographs of "spaceship earth."

1968 ....Redwoods National Park established.

1969 ....Santa Barbara, California, oil spill dramatizes the problem of pollution.

1969 ....Friends of the Earth founded by David R. Brower after his ouster from the Sierra Club.

1969 ....Greenpeace organized.

1970 ....National Environmental Policy Act signed January 1.

1970 ....Natural Resources Defense Council founded.

1970 ....Zero Population Growth founded by Paul Ehrlich and others.

1970 ....Resource Recovery Act (Solid Waste Disposal Act).

1970 ....Clean Air Act amends and strengthens 1963 measure.

1970 ....First "Earth Day" celebrated April 22.

1970 ....National Oceanic and Atmospheric Administration created October 3.

1970 ....Environmental Protection Agency (EPA) created December 2.

1970 ....Environmental Education Act endeavors to promote environmental awareness in the schools.

1971 ....Calvert Cliffs Decision by U.S. Court of Appeals mandates environmental impact decisions for federal projects affecting the ecosystem.

1971 ....Barry Commoner publishes *The Closing Circle*.

1971 ....Congress abandons support of the supersonic transport aircraft.

1971 ....Alaska Native Claims Settlement Act authorizes federal nomination of "national interest lands" for permanent protection.

1972 ....League of Conservation Voters organized.

1972 ....Federal Water Pollution Control Act (Clean Water Act).

1972 ....Federal Environmental Pesticide Control Act.

1972 ....Ocean Dumping Act.

1972 ....Coastal Zone Management Act empowers states to lead in planning and regulation.

Continued on page 167

Canoe Country Poems

by Marianne Ranson Giangreco
(New York: Vantage Press, 1974)

While inspiration for these thirty or so poems came from the Boundary Waters region of northern

"They made her a grave,
too cold and damp

For a soul so warm and true;

And she's gone to the Lake
of the Dismal Swamp,

Where, all night long,
by a fire-fly lamp,

She paddles her white canoe.

And her fire-fly lamp I soon
shall see,

And her paddle I soon shall
hear;

Long and loving our life shall
be,

And I'll hide the maid
in a cypress tree,

When the footstep of death
is near."

—from the poem
"The Lake of the Dismal
Swamp" in The Poetical Works
of Thomas Moore *(New York:*
Hurst & Co., 1880)

Minnesota, the themes are broad. For example, titles of a few of the poems are: "The Loon;" "Rain;" "Mosquitos;" "Northern Lights;" "Busy Beavers;" and "Starlight." If you and your chums enjoy reading something together around a campfire, or if you simply head for the water for solitude and rejuvenation, take along this small book of poems.

Poetry for the Earth

edited by Sara Dunn and Alan Scholefield
(New York: Fawcett Columbine, 1991)

This book is described by the editors as "a collection of poems from around the world that celebrates nature." It includes themes such as celebration, observation, contemplation, and more. Variety is what you'll find here, from Elizabeth Weston's "Concerning the Flooding of Prague after Constant

An Environmental Chronology, Continued

1972 ....United Nations Conference on the Human Environment held in Stockholm.

1972 ....The Club of Rome's publication of *The Limits of Growth* triggers worldwide debate.

1973 ....E. F. Schumacher publishes *Small IS Beautiful*.

1973 ....Walt Disney Enterprises abandons plans for a ski resort in Mineral King Valley, California, after a 1972 Supreme Court decision affirms the legal standing of the Sierra Club in the case.

1973 ....Endangered Species Act expands federal involvement in resisting species extinction.

1973 ....Congress authorizes construction of an 800-mile oil pipeline across Alaska to Prudhoe Bay.

1974 ....Safe Drinking Water Act.

1976 ....Federal Land Policy and Management Act formalizes multiple-use administration of public lands under control of Bureau of Land Management.

1976 ....Resource Conservation and Recovery Act promotes recycling of solid wastes.

1976 ....Toxic Substances Control Act.

1977 ....Clean Air Act amendments.

1977 ....Federal Water Pollution Control Act amendments.

1977 ....Surface Mining Control and Reclamation Act.

1978 ....National Energy Act.

1978 ....Love Canal near the Niagara River, New York, revealed to be the site of buried chemical wastes endangering the health of local residents.

1979 ....Three Mile Island (Pennsylvania) nuclear generating plant narrowly avoids meltdown and widespread radioactive pollution.

1980 ....Comprehensive Environmental Response, Compensation and Liability Act establishes the "superfund" for toxic waste abatement.

1980 ....Alaska National Interest Lands Conservation Act protects 104 million acres including 56 million acres in the National Wilderness Preservation System.

1980 ....*Global 2000 Report to the President* released.

1980 ....Fish and Wildlife Conservation Act protects nongame species.

1981 ....Earth First! organized; lists 12,000 members by 1988.

1981 ....Anne Gorsuch resigns as head of the Environmental Protection Administration after revelations of mismanagement.

1983 ....Sierra Club lists 350,000 members.

Continued on page 168

167

An Environmental Chronology, Continued

1983 ....James G. Watt resigns as Secretary of the Interior under mounting public criticism for antienvironmental policies.

1986 ....The Chernobyl (Russia) disaster pollutes large areas of northern Europe and further damages the reputation of the nuclear power industry in the United States.

1986 ....Superfund reauthorized (see 1980).

1986 ....Federal water pollution control programs reauthorized.

1987 ....The United States joins other industrialized nations in signing a protocol designed to protect the ultraviolet-shielding ozone layer.

1988 ....Drought conditions attributed to the "greenhouse effect" alarm Americans about global climate change.

1989 ....Massive oil spill in Prince William Sound, Alaska, arouses national indignation.

Reprinted with permission from American Environmentalism: Readings in Conservation History, *Third Edition by Roderick Frazier Nash (New York: McGraw-Hill Publishing Company, 1990)*

SINGLE BLADE

Rains" to Elizabeth Coatsworth's "Whale at Twilight," from Robert Bly's "Driving Toward the Lac Qui Parle River" to Thoreau's "Low-Anchored Cloud."

Plenty of this poetry isn't just for the earth; it's for the waters, too. If you are not a reader of poetry, think again. A book like this one could change your mind.

Legend of the White Canoe

by William Trumbull
(New York: G.P. Putnam's Sons, 1894)

If you ever want to torment your fellow paddlers, a reading from this poem would surely do it.

"How can we know the dancer from the dance?"
—from the poem "Among School Children" by William Butler Yeats
(And with apologies to Yeats, How can we know the paddler from the paddle?)

THE PLEASURES OF PLACE NAMES

One has to wonder what circumstances caused Satan's Falls to get its name. Or the Jaws of Death, Bloody Falls, the Kicking Horse River, Garvin's Chute, the Dangerous River, and hundreds of others. The rivers of North America are littered with colorful names, some of which are easily traced, others not. It's always fun finding out just what lurks behind a place-name, and it helps you appreciate your surroundings, adding another dimension to your trip.

There are several ways to find out a thing or two about place-names on any river. The first and easiest is to get a reputable guidebook for the area you are in. Often some history of the area is given, including tidbits on place-names. If you can't find a guidebook, look in old issues of *National Geographic* magazine. It has been published for more than one hundred years, and it is surprising how many of the articles are about rivers, lakes, or other bodies of water. Tip: there is an index to the hundred years of articles.

If this doesn't work, ask around, talk with old-timers in the area. The older they are, the more of the history they've actually lived. And if that doesn't work, inquire at a local historical society or library. You'll never find out if you don't ask!

Definitely worth reading for its ghastliness.

Long before the solitudes of western New York were disturbed by the advent of the white man, it was the custom of the Indian tribes to assemble occasionally at Niagara, and offer sacrifice to the Spirit of the Falls. This sacrifice consisted of a white birch bark canoe, which was sent over the terrible cliff, filled with ripe fruits and blooming flowers, and bearing the fairest girl in the tribe who had just attained the age of womanhood.

"Mid the rush of mighty waters, in the thundering cataract's roar,
Where Niagara's streaming rapids down in headlong torrent pour;
Where the serried waves like chargers madly leaping to the fray,
Fling aloft their snowy crests and toss their manes of flying spray,
Rearing, plunging, onward urging—Nature's glorious cavalry!"

Watermusic:
Songbooks and Recordings

If you would like to learn a few (or a few more) of the great tunes that musicians and composers have left in their wake, try a few of these songbooks. In them you will find everything from "The Water is Wide" to "The Rivers of Babylon," from "Red River Valley" to "One More River," from "Roll On, Columbia" . . .

Photo courtesy of the Library of Congress, Prints and Photographs Division, Washington, D.C.

Mason Williams' Water Songs

A portion of Mason Williams' *Master List of River/Water Songs and Music.* Reprinted with permission of Mason Williams. To request the complete list, contact Mason Williams via his website, at http://www.efn.org/~masonwms.

Across the Rio Grande, ©1916, ***Composer:*** Harris & Lee
Across the River, ***Artist:*** Witmark
Across the Wide Missouri, ***Lyrics by:*** Traditional
Adelina, The Boola Girl, ***Written:*** 1903, ***Publisher:*** Atwater, G.L.
Alice of Old Vincennes (I Love You), ***Written:*** 1914, ***Lyrics :*** Keithley & Thompson
All Along the River, ***Artist:*** Chappell
All My Children of the Son, ***Written:*** 1969, ***Composer:*** Pete Seeger
All Quiet Along the Potomac Tonight, ***Written:*** 1864, ***Composer:*** Hewitt, John Hill
Along the Mississippi, ***Composer:*** Pride, Charlie
Along the Mississippi Shore, ©1915, ***Composer:*** Donaldson, W.
And Still the Volga Flows, ***Publisher:*** Witmark
Annie O' the Banks O' Dee, ©1868, ***Composer:*** Glover, S.
As the Wild River Rises, ***Publisher:*** Tree
At the River Front, ***Publisher:*** Witmark

Continued on page 170

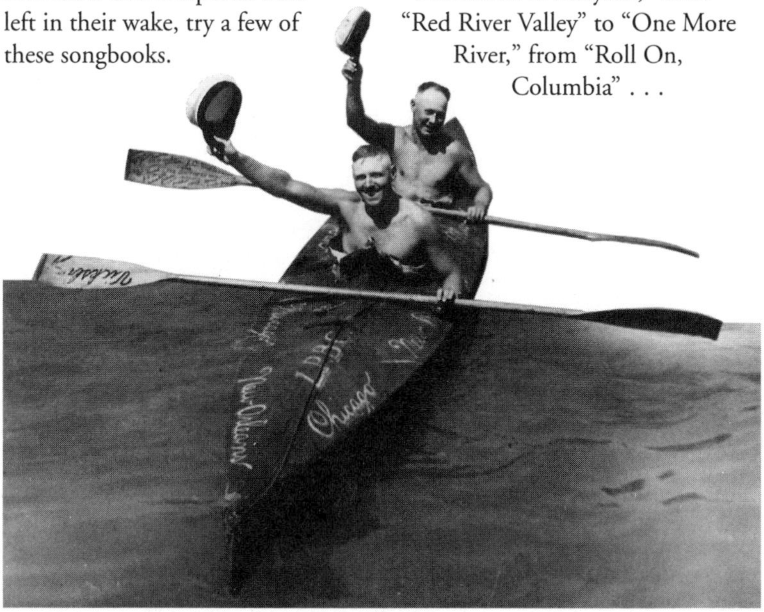

Mason Williams'
Water Songs, Continued

Banks of the Blue Mosell,
  Written: ND,
  Composer: Rodwell, G.H.
Banks of the Dee (The),
  Written: 1787, **Lyrics:** Tait,
  John
Banks of the Little Eau Plaine
  (The)
Banks of the Ohio (The)
Banks of the Old Rio Grande
  (The), ©1930
Bayou Pompon, ©1977,
  Composer: Traditional, **Lyrics:**
  Dole, Gerard, **Album:** "Tradi-
  tional Cajun Accordion,"
  Label: Folkways,
  Source: Jim Bartz
Bear Creek Hop, **Composer:** Tradi-
  tional, **Label:** Byron Berline
Beautiful Blue Danube, ©1874,
  Composer: Strauss, J.
Beautiful Blue Danube Waltzes
  (Piano Solo), **Written:** ND,
  Composer: Strauss, J.
Beautiful Ohio (The), **Written:**
  1918, **Composer:** Earl, Mary
Beautiful Swanee River Hornpipe,
  Label: Hollis Taylor
Belle of the Silvery Nile, ©1904,
  Composer: Hoffmann, M.
Bend of the River,
  Publisher: Leeds
Beside a Babbling Brook, **Written:**
  1923, **Publisher:** Remick
Beside the Rio Grande,
  Written: 1930
Big Muddy
Big River, **Composer:** Cash, John
Big River, **Written:** 1880,
  Label: Byron Berline
Big Sandy River, **Composer:** Tradi-
  tional, **Artist:** Monroe, Bill,
  Source: Hollis Taylor

Continued on page 171

170

Songbooks

Songs of the Rivers
of America

edited by Carl Carmer
(New York: Farrar & Rinehart, 1942)

Oh, what a fun one this is. This songbook has about two hundred pages of songs about rivers all over the United States. It is divided into sections on the East, South, and West. The book includes songs from four broad categories: (1) nostalgic yearning for the old days—e.g. "The Banks of the Genesee;" (2) songs of historical content—e.g. "All Quiet Along the Potomac;" (3) folk songs, those inspired by jobs—e.g. "The Ogallaly Song" or those inspired by crimes committed by the river's side—e.g. "The Unconstant Lover;" and finally (4) minstrel songs—e.g. "Poor Juna."

Both the music and words are included. The music is arranged for the piano. This songbook is out of print, so you'll have to get a copy from your library or used bookstore. Then learn a tune and sing it on your next outing. Better yet, let's all tell anyone we know in the publishing field to reprint either this book or something else like it. Some of the tunes in this book deserve to be remembered, revived, and carried on . . . never forgotten.

Folksong in the
Classroom Magazine

(Volume 7, no. 2, Winter 1987 and Spring 1987)
Back in 1987, two issues of a magazine called *Folksong in the Class-*

DID YOU
KNOW
THAT . . . ?

- Randy Newman composed the song "Burn On" about the infamous burning of the Cuyahoga River in 1969.
- Al Jolson and many others have sung "Ol' Man River."
- The name *Bach* means "brook."
- Haydn's oratorio, *Creation*, includes a bass aria titled "Rolling in Foaming Billows."
- Dvorak's *Der Wasserman* is about a Water Sprite.

Lean toward the Danger

If you can't avoid hitting a hole, pillow, or boulder sideways, lean into it. You'll not only set yourself up for an effective brace, you'll keep your upstream edge high and prevent your kayak from broaching.

—JB & TB

room featured many fine river songs. In fact, the editors devoted these issues exclusively to river themes in folk music, in parts one and two in the Winter and Spring issues, respectively.

It's no secret that the rivers of the United States contributed to the country's growth. One can easily get a feeling for that by looking at these issues of *Folksong in the Classroom*. The first discusses transportation, history, geography, political science, and economics, and repro-

- Shostakovich's Opus 95 is called "Song of the Great Rivers."
- Roy Orbison and Linda Ronstadt both sang versions of "Blue Bayou."
- Neil Young sang "Down By the River."
- Kenny Rogers and Dolly Parton sang "Islands in the Stream."
- Joe Cocker sang "Cry Me A River."

duces about ten songs. Among those are "One More River," "Hudson River Steamboat," "Banks of the Sacramento," "Red River Valley," "All Quiet on the Potomac," and "No More Cane on the Brazos."

The second issue hits on ecology, natural resources, wildlife, literature, folklore, the arts, aesthetics, recreation, tragedy, and includes, among others, "My Bark Canoe," "Lovely Ohio," "Down by the Riverside," "Roll On, Columbia," and "My Dirty Stream."

These can be located in the ERIC collection of educational materials (ED344784) found in some libraries, or by contacting the magazine directly: *Folksong in the Classroom*, 433 Leadmine Road, Fiskdale, MA 01518.

New World Ballads

by John Murray Gibbon
(Toronto: Ryerson Press, 1939)

This is a marvelous songbook, generally containing songs on Canadian themes. The chapter Ballads of the Canoe offers a half-dozen tunes: "Shadowy Footpath," "The Ghost Canoe," "Canoe Song," "River Song," "Qu'Appelle (Who is Calling?)" and the "Canoe Cradle Song." Both words and music are given for each song. Someone ought to take these tunes and others on the

Mason Williams' Water Songs, Continued

Big Wide River, *Composer:* Summers, W., *Publisher:* Cooper

Bitter Creek, *Composer:* Traditional, *Label:* Hollis Taylor

Black Water, *Artist:* Doobie Brothers, *Label:* Warner B, *Source:* BB Publications

Blue Bayou, *Artist:* Ronstadt, Linda, *Label:* Asylum, *Source:* BB Publications

Blue Danube (The), ©1867, *Composer:* Straus, J.

Blue Danube Waltz, ©1935, *Composer:* Strauss, J.

Blue Juniata (The), *Written:* 1844, *Composer:* Sullivan, Marion Dix

Blue Nile, *Publisher:* Morris

Blue River, *Composer:* Young-Washington, *Publisher:* Crawford

Blue River, *Composer:* Meyer-Bryan, *Publisher:* Remick

Blue River Train, *Publisher:* SB

Blue Water Hornpipe, *Composer:* Traditional, *Artist:* Eyerki, Ed, *Source:* Byron Berline

BO-LA-BO, ©1919, *Composer:* Fairman, G.

Boatin Up Sandy, *Label:* Hollis Taylor

Boatmen's Dance, ©1843, *Composer:* Emmett, D.D.

Bonaparte Crossing the Rhine, *Label:* Hollis Taylor

Bonny Eloise, ©1858, *Composer:* Thomas, J.R.

Bonny Eloise, The Belle of Mohawk Vale, ©1858, *Composer:* Thomas, J.R.

Continued on page 172

171

Mason Williams'
Water Songs, Continued

Bords Du Hudson, ©1846,
  Composer: Grobe, C.
Bords Du Mississippi, ©1858,
  Composer: Grobe, C.
Bords Du Mohawk,
  Composer: Marsh, J.B.
Bords Du Rhin,
  Composer: Huenten, F.
Brazos River Waltz, **Composer:**
  Ferguson, Dave, **Source:** Byron
  Berline
Broad Tennessee, ©1907,
  Composer: Madden Music Co.
Brooklet, **Publisher:** RJ
Brooklet (The), **Written:** 1820,
  Composer: Schubert, F.
Brooklet Came from the
  Mountain, **Publisher:** GS
Bulldog on the Bank
By a Quiet Stream,
  Publisher: Presser
By a Rippling Stream Waiting For
  You, **Publisher:** Whitman
By a Waterfall, **Written:** 1933,
  Composer: Fain, Sammy,
  Lyrics by: Kahal, Irving
By an Old Southern River,
  Publisher: Leeds
By the Banks of Old Willamette,
  ©1909, **Composer:** Wilson,
  I.M.
By the Bend of the River, We Shall
  Meet **Publisher:** Forester
By the Brook, **Publisher:** GS
By the Brooklet, **Publisher:** CF
By the Ganges, **Composer:** Popy,
  Publisher: GS
By the Ganges, **Composer:**
  Stoughton, **Publisher:** Morris
By the Rio Grande, ©1913,
  Composer: Friedland, A. &
  Schmid, J.C.

Continued on page 173

paddling theme and pull them all together into one good modern songbook for paddlers. In the meantime, find a copy of this songbook through your local library.

"There's a lake of stew and of gingerale too,

And you can paddle all around it in a big canoe,

On the Big Rock Candy Mountain."

—from *"The Big Rock Candy Mountain,"* a well-known ballad about hobo life

Carry It On! A History in Song and Picture of the Working Men and Women of America

by Pete Seeger and Bob Reiser
(New York: Simon and Schuster, 1985)

Ever heard of the "Seneca Canoe Song?" (" . . . Kayowajineh, yo ho hey yo ho Kayowajineh . . . ") or "Somos el Barco/We Are the Boat?" (" . . . We are the boat, we are the sea, I sail in you, You sail in me . . . ")? These two songs focus on paddling/water themes and other songs will likely sound familiar. *Carry It On!* is a songbook containing words, music, and often background notes telling you a bit about each tune.

Roll On Columbia: The Columbia River Collection, Songs by Woodie Guthrie

collected and edited by Bill Murlin
(Bethlehem, PA: Sing Out Publications, 1991)

In 1941 the Bonneville Power Administration (BPA) was trying to muster support for its efforts to dam the Columbia River and produce electricity for much of the Pacific Northwest. These were the times of Roosevelt's New Deal.

The BPA's strategy included contracting Woodie Guthrie, the roving folk songwriter, for just one month to write a few songs in support of the development. Guthrie was a strong supporter of workers' rights and, with several young mouths to feed, needed the money. According to Murlin, "He saw the majestic Grand Coulee Dam as the creation of the common man to harness the river for the common good—work for the jobless, power to ease household tasks, power to strengthen Uncle Sam in his fight against world fascism."

The musical legacy Guthrie left is an astonishing one; the merits or evils of the Columbia River basin's development, and the consequent drastic alteration of the river, will be debated for many years to come.

This is a songbook of the roughly two dozen tunes and lyrics Guthrie composed during May of 1941. The lives and struggles of working people are chronicled in now-familiar tunes like "Roll On, Columbia, Roll On," "Ballad of the Great Grand Coulee," "Jackhammer Blues," and "Columbia Waters."

There is also a companion recording by the same title, distributed under the Rounder recording label.

Mason Williams' Water Songs, Continued

By the River, **Composer:** Morse, **Publisher:** CF

By the River, **Composer:** Young, **Publisher:** Famous

By the River of Roses, **Publisher:** SB

By the River Saint Marie, **Written:** 1931, **Composer:** Warren, Harry, **Lyrics by:** Leslie, Edgar, **Publisher:** Robbins, **Artist:** Smith, Kate (made famous)

By the River Saint Marie, ©1931, **Composer:** Warren, H.

By the River Seine, **Publisher:** Craw

By the Rivers of Babylon, **Publisher:** GS

By the Saskatchewan, ©1910, **Composer:** Caryll, I.

By the Silver Rio Grande, **Written:** 1918

By the Stream, **Composer:** Axt, Rappes, **Publisher:** Robbins

By the Stream, **Composer:** Phillips, **Publisher:** Chappell

By the Susquehanna Shore, ©1914, **Composer:** Silvers, L.

By the Waters of Minnetonka, **Publisher:** Presser

Can I Canoe You up the River, **Publisher:** Leeds

Caney Creek, **Composer:** Alxendes, J., **Source:** Byron Berline

Canoe the Wabash and You

Cash River Waltz, **Publisher:** 4-Star

Chant of the Amazon, **Publisher:** BVC

Christians Creek, **Source:** Hollis Taylor

Cimmaron, Roll On

Come Back to the Mississippi Shore, ©1922, **Composer:** Bernie, D. & Bibo, I.

Continued on page 174

173

Continued on page 175

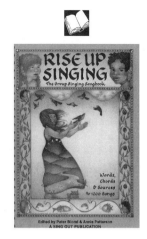

Rise Up Singing: The Group Singing Songbook

edited by Peter Blood and Annie Patterson
(Bethlehem, PA: Sing Out Publications, 1992)
This is a particularly good songbook for several reasons. First, it gives the words, chords, and sources of some 1,200 songs on a variety of themes (ecology, funny songs, sea songs, traveling, outdoors, mountain voices, and good times). Second, for the paddler who wants to learn a few new tunes, the publisher has produced a series of tapes—they don't reproduce the entire song, just enough for you to learn it.

You'll find lots of goodies in *Rise Up Singing,* like "River" by Bill Staines ("River, take me along in your sunshine, sing me your song . . . "), the "Canoe Round" by Margaret Embers McGee ("My paddle's keen and bright, flashing like silver, follow the wild goose flight . . . "), the "Black Fly Song,"

and the "Swimming Song."

The Sing Out Corporation can be reached at Box 5253, Bethlehem, PA 18015; (215) 865-5366.

"The Hopkins Book of Canoe Songs"

(*The Beaver* Magazine, vol. 302, no. 2, Autumn 1971)
From their garden at Lachine, Quebec, Frances and Edward Hopkins could hear the Voyageurs singing as they headed east or west in their great freight canoes on the St. Lawrence River. Frances, who died in 1919, sketched and painted numerous works on Voyageur themes,

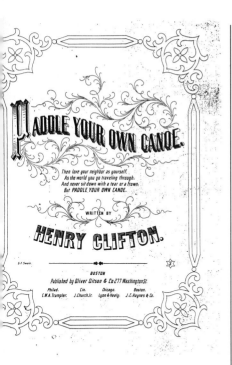

and Edward, who died in 1893, kept a sketch book of canoe songs he heard these Voyageurs singing. This article details his sketch book and its background. A couple of the songs are reproduced in the article.

Backpacker's Songbook

compiled by Ron Middlebrook
(Fullerton, CA:
Centerstream Publications, 1982)

This hundred-page songbook contains the words and chords for more than two hundred familiar favorites. If your thing is to sing, don't let the title word "Backpacker's" throw you; it would work as well for a paddler.

Here you will find "Banks of the Ohio," "Cripple Creek," "Michael, Row the Boat Ashore," "On the Banks of the Wabash," "Red River Valley," as well as other tunes on non-paddling themes that might yet have some relevance on your trip, including "Nobody Knows the Trouble I've Seen," "Hard, Ain't it Hard," "Good Night Ladies," "Bile Them Cabbage Down," and "The Blue-Tail Fly."

The peculiar thing about this songbook is that it contains instructions on how to perform CPR, how to deal with insect bites, and other first aid measures. Probably not too many people would think to go looking in their songbook for first aid remedies, but never mind. There are some things in this world that there simply aren't answers for . . .

"Living on the river was nice and easy;

People on the river just take their time . . ."

—*from the song "Living on the River" by Jerry Rasmussen*

More Good Songbooks

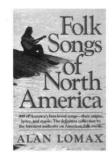

Folk Songs of North America by Alan Lomax (New York: Doubleday, 1960). Includes "The River in the Pines," "The Wild Rippling Water," etc.

175

Mason Williams' Water Songs, Continued

Down the River of Memories
Down Where the Congo Flows,
  ©1903, **Composer:** Cooke, S.G.
Down Where the Silv'ry Mohawk
  Flows, ©1905, **Composer:**
  Heinzman, J. & Heinzman, O.
Down Where the Swanee River
  Flows, ©1903, **Composer:**
  Von Tilzer, A.
Down Where the Swannee River
  Flows, **Publisher:** Broadway
Down Where the Wurzberger
  Flows, ©1910, **Publisher:** VT
Dream River, **Publisher:** SB
Dreaming on the Silv'ry Rio
  Grande, ©1906, **Composer:**
  Avril, C.
Dreamy Rio Grande,
  Publisher: B. Miller
Dreamy River,
  Publisher: Plymouth
Drifting Along, ©1916, **Com-**
  poser: Smith, W.
Drifting Down the Dreamy Ol'
  Ohio, **Publisher:** Morris
Drifting Down the River of
  Dreams, **Publisher:** Whitmark
Drifting Down to Dixie, ©1921,
  Composer: Carey, J.B.
Dry Creek Reel, **Composer:** Tradi-
  tional, **Label:** Byron Berline
Ducks on the Millpond, ©1981,
  Composer: Traditional,
  Artist: Cotten, Beverly,
  Album: "Clogging Lesson,"
  Label: Flying Fist,
  Source: Hollis Taylor
Ducks on the Pond,
  Source: Hollis Taylor
E-RI-E Canal (The), ©1825

Continued on page 177

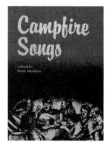

The American Songbag by Carl
Sandburg (New York: Harcourt
Brace Jovanovich, 1990). In-
cludes "The Wide Mizzoura,"
"Flat River Girl," "Red River
Valley," etc.

Campfire Songs edited by Irene
Maddox (Old Saybrook, CT:
The Globe Pequot Press, 1994).
Includes "Erie Canal," "Loch
Lomond," "Michael, Row the
Boat Ashore," "One More
River," "Over the River and
through the Wood," "Song of
the Volga Boatmen," etc.

SPEAKING WITH . . . MASON WILLIAMS

Mason Williams has much to say
about music, water, and the relationship between the two. Here
are a few of those thoughts:

*"Songs . . . reflect the nature of
our on-going relationship with 'the
river.' The songs of a river tell a
story, they speak of our long-term
relationship. We sing of it, and in
doing so, reflect ourselves. Rivers
have been the routes of exploration,
the boundaries of territories, the
highways of commerce; they have
sustained us with water, food,
recreation, beauty and inspiration.
Some of the more recent songs, unfortunately, speak of the degrada-
tion the rivers have experienced in
modern times. They literally 'take
out the garbage' on their way out.*

*The image of 'the river' runs
deeply through all levels of our
culture, and the cumulative effect
of this would perhaps draw attention to the multicultural expres-
sion of this universal experience,
showing that it not only flows
through the land, but through our
hearts and minds as well. The
wide variety of types of music
would give a cohesive*

176

sense of America's rich and varied cultural history. We would see how people with different backgrounds have expressed 'the river's' impact on their lives, past and present. The body of work to draw from is enormous, including the works of some of the greatest composers and songwriters in history. An English teacher once remarked to me that he thought the three great themes in life, as reflected in art, literature and music are 'birth, death, and the river.'

The development of new technologies throughout history, such as the player piano, the phonograph player, the radio, the recording industry, the jukebox era, the music business explosion of the '40s and '50s, the advent of the LP, the cassette, the video, the CD and now, the CD-ROM have all had a tremendous impact on the 'song of the river.' It has wound its way through all of these changes, and having gone from songs about natural splendor and adventure to metaphorical songs about the flow of time, and the forces of life, the 'song of the river' has itself changed and grown in the process. By giving 'the river' a voice, a chance to speak to us through the music it has inspired, songs remind us of what we mean to each other."

Recordings

Of Time and Rivers Flowing

by Mason Williams
(Oakridge, OR: Skookum Records, 1984)
Everyone knows Mason Williams for his instrumental tune "Classical Gas," but he is a river lover, too, and says, "This collection of songs and music is taken from a concert that some friends and I put together during the summer of 1982. The concept was to present, in chronological order, songs about rivers and water that have been popular throughout history. The intention was to show our longstanding relationship with rivers; that they run not only through the land, but through our hearts and minds as well."

Here are just a few of the tunes included:

"Shenandoah" (Traditional), ca. 1830
"De Boatmen's Dance" (Daniel Emmett), ca. 1843
"Deep River" (Traditional), ca. early 1800s
"The Beautiful Blue Danube" (Johann Strauss), ca. 1867
"Cripple Creek" (Traditional), ca. late 1800s

This recording is available from Williams at P.O. Box 5105, Eugene, OR 97405.

Mason Williams' Water Songs, Continued

Echoes of Time and the River, **Written:** 1967, **Composer:** Crumb, George
Erie Canal (The), ©1840
Fair Lotus Flower, ©1915, **Composer:** Lynes, F.
Fall Creek, **Composer:** Berline, Byron, **Source:** Byron Berline
Fishin Creek, **Composer:** Traditional, **Source:** Byron Berline
Floating Down a Moonlight Stream, **Publisher:** SB
Floating Down the Mississippi River **Composer:** Tilzel, A.
Floating Down the Nile, ©1906, **Composer:** Johnson, J.R.
Floating Down the Ohio, **Publisher:** Lang Worth
Floating Down the River, **Publisher:** Vogal
Flood (The), ©1965
Flow Along River Tennessee, ©1913, **Composer:** Gumble, A. & Wells, J.
Flow Gently Sweet Afton, ©1838, **Composer:** Hume, Alexander, **Lyrics by:** Burns, Robert
Flow On Thou Shining River, **Written:** ND, **Composer:** Stevenson, J. Arr.
Flower of the Nile, ©1907, **Composer:** Losey, F.H.
Flowing River
Flowing Thru My Veins
Foggy River, **Composer:** Monroe, Bill, **Source:** Byron Berline
Four Rivers (The), **Publisher:** Mills
Franz Schubert Songs, ©1815
From the Land of Sky Blue Waters, **Composer:** Melrose

Continued on page 178

177

Hap-py to-geth-er 'in all kinds of weather, Just we two._____ And it's

just   we   two, _____ In our frail   can - oe

Mason Williams' Water Songs, Continued

Goin' to the River, **Written:** 1957, **Composer:** Domino, Fats

Going Down the River, **Source:** Hollis Taylor

Golden River, **Publisher:** Cole

Good-by Betty Brown, ©1910, **Composer:** Morse, T.

Grand Coulee Dam, **Written:** 1941, **Composer:** Gutherie, Woodie

Green River, **Composer:** Fogerty, J.C.

Green River, **Written:** 1969, **Artist:** Creedence Clearwater Revival, **Album:** Fantasy, **Source:** BB Publications

Green River, **Artist:** Alabama, **Source:** Cort Connely

Handel's Water Music, **Source:** Cort Connely

Harlem River Dance, **Publisher:** Leeds

Hermit on the Mississippi Shore, ©1907, **Composer:** Vogel, V.

High Water, **Publishser:** Crawford

Hindu River Chant, ©1921, **Composer:** Mowrey, D.

Home of The Girl I Love, ©1899, **Composer:** Graham, H. & Rosenfeld, M.H.

Hoosier Sweetheart, ©1927, **Composer:** Goodwin, J., Ash, P. & Baskette, B.

Horse Creek, **Composer:** Wise, Jay, **Source:** Byron Berline

Hot Water, **Publisher:** AAM

Housatonic at Stockbridge, **Composer:** Ives, Charles

How High's the Water, Mamma?

I Am The Bayadere, ©1849, **Composer:** Bochsa, N.C.

I Can't Get Mississippi Off My Mind, **Publisher:** Witmark

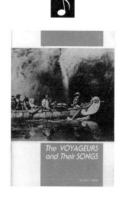

12 Voyageur Songs

sung by the all-male choir of the University of Moncton, New Brunswick (St. Paul, MN: Minnesota Historical Society, 1966)

This collection of songs, which are sung in French, is accompanied by a booklet titled "The Voyageurs and Their Songs" by Theodore C. Blegen; the words are included, too.

The booklet explains that "the Voyageurs were the French-Canadian canoe men of the North American fur trade. They sang as they paddled birch-bark canoes over the rivers and lakes of the continent from Montreal to the Pacific in the 17th, 18th, and early 19th centuries. Their songs were adapted to accompany the motion of paddles dipped in unison, and they also contributed to the morale of the paddlers."

The recording is available from the Minnesota Historical Society, St. Paul, MN 55102.

Music River: Original White-water Songs & River Ballads

by Brant N. Miller and Tom Joy (Nashville, TN: Music River, Inc., 1993) Including such tunes as "Riverlove," "Rafting Rhapsody," "There's So Much You Can Do in a Canoe," "Whitewater Woman," and others. Available from Music River, Inc., Box 53545, Knoxville, TN 37950.

River Songs

by Abbie Endicott (Bethesda, MD: EOP Records, 1989) Abbie Endicott sings and plays guitar for songs such as "Rio Bravo," "Chile Song," "Slalomia (Rioni)," "Ode to the 1989 U.S. Whitewater Team," "Merci, Paris!" and "Life Is a River." Available from EOP Records at P.O. Box 30682, Bethesda, MD 20814.

Al-ways to - gether we're sweethearts for - ev - er It's just we two.

Waterscapes:
Images by Brush and Lens

Some would say that paddling is a fine art. Not just a few artists have taken their brushes in hand to prove the point. The likes of Wyeth, Homer, Remington, John Singer Sargent, and dozens of other well-known and not-so-well-known artists have chosen paddlers in rafts, kayaks, and canoes, rivers, rapids, and more as their themes. And innumerable photographers, and even computer artists, also have applied their skills to the world of the paddler. Following is a sampling of the high art of paddling.

The Paddler by Paint

- *The Blue Boat*, watercolor, 1892, by Winslow Homer (Museum of Fine Arts, Boston)
- *Paul Helleu Sketching with His Wife*, oil on canvas, 1889, by John Singer Sargent (Brooklyn Museum, New York)
- *Young Ducks*, watercolor, 1897, by Winslow Homer (Portland Museum of Art, Portland, ME)
- *Picture Rock at Crooked Lake* (also known as *Return of the Voyageurs*), oil, 1947, by Francis

Lee Jaques (Minnesota Historical Society, Saint Paul)
- *Ojibway Indians, Lake Superior*, oil on canvas, 1899, by Freder-ick Arthur Verner (National Gallery of Canada, Ottawa)
- *Canoe Shooting a Rapid*, oil on canvas, 1876, by Valentine Walter Bromley (Department of External Affairs, Ottawa)
- *Canoe Running a Rapid*, water-color, 1872, by John B. Wilkinson (National Archives of Canada, Ottawa)
- *Canoe in Rapids*, 1897, water-color, by Winslow Homer (Fogg Art Museum, Cambridge, MA)
- *Fur Traders Descending the Missouri*, oil on canvas, 1845, by George Caleb Bingham (Metropolitan Museum of Art, New York)
- *The Trappers Return*, oil on

THE AUTHOR'S SANCTUM.

canvas, 1851, by George Caleb Bingham (Detroit Institute of Arts)

- *Raftsmen Playing Cards*, oil on canvas, 1847, by George Caleb Bingham (St. Louis Art Museum)
- *Woodboatmen on a River*, oil on canvas, 1854, by George Caleb Bingham (Museum of Fine Arts, Boston)
- *Ouananiche Fishing*, watercolor, 1897, by Winslow Homer (Museum of Fine Arts, Boston)
- *Trappers Resting*, watercolor, 1874, by Winslow Homer (Portland Museum of Art, Portland, ME)
- *Sioux Boat Race*, tempera, 1955, by Oscar Howe (Joslyn Art Museum, Omaha, Nebraska)
- *An Adirondack Lake*, oil on canvas, 1870, by Winslow Homer (University of Washington, Seattle)

- *Playing Him, or The North Woods*, watercolor, 1894, by Winslow Homer (Currier Gallery of Art, Manchester, NH)
- *News from Home*, oil on canvas, 1916, by N. C. Wyeth (Minnesota Historical Society)
- *Paddling at Dusk*, watercolor on paper, 1892, by Winslow Homer (Memorial Art Gallery of the University of Rochester, NY)
- *A Good Time Coming*, oil on canvas, 1862, Arthur Fitzwilliam Tate (Adirondack Museum, Blue Mountain Lake, NY)
- *Radisson and Grosseiliers*, oil on canvas, undated, by Frederic Remington (Buffalo Bill Historical Center, Cody, WY)
- *White Mud Portage, Winnipeg River*, oil on canvas, 1850s, by Paul Kane (National Gallery of Canada, Ottawa)
- *Canoeists at Chatou*, oil, 1879, by Piere-Auguste Renoir (National Gallery of Art, Washington, D.C.)
- *Wolfe's Cove*, 1895, watercolor, by Winslow Homer (Bowdoin College Museum of Art, Brunswick, ME)
- *Canoe of Indians*, oil on canvas, 1857, by Eastman Johnson (St. Louis County Historical

Society, Duluth, MN)

- *Voyage of Life: Manhood*, oil on canvas, 1842, by Thomas Cole (National Gallery of Art, Washington, D.C.). Cole produced a series of four canvases on this allegorical theme; they are subtitled: *Childhood, Youth, Manhood,* and *Old Age,* and all are in the National Gallery of Art.
- *Indian Voyageurs Returning from the Hunt*, watercolor, 1820, anonymous (Beaverbrook Art Gallery, Fredericton, New Brunswick)
- *The Franklin Expedition Crossing Lake Prosperous, Northwest Territories*, watercolor, 1820, by Robert Hood (National Archives of Canada, Ottawa)
- *A View Near Point Levy Opposite Quebec with an Indian Encampment*, 1788, by Thomas Davies (National Gallery of Canada, Ottawa)
- *The Crossing of the Stygian Lagoon*, oil on panel, after 1521, by Joachim Patinir (Prado Museum, Madrid). Shows a naked paddler crossing the lagoon and headed straight for hell.
- *Micmac Indians*, oil, ca. 1820–30, anonymous (National

Photo courtesy of the Library of Congress, Prints and Photographs Division, Washington, D.C.

Gallery of Canada, Ottawa)
- *Indian Encampment on Lake Huron*, oil, undated, by Paul Kane (Art Gallery of Toronto)
- *Mending the Canoe*, watercolor, undated, by Thomas Fripp (McCord Museum, McGill University, Montreal)
- *Indian War Canoe*, oil, 1912, by Emily Carr (Montreal Museum of Fine Arts)
- *The Howl of the Weather*, 1906, by Frederic Remington (Frederic Remington Art Museum, Ogdensburg, NY)
- *The Trapper*, by Winslow Homer (Colby College Museum of Art, Waterville, ME)
- *Two Men in a Canoe*, watercolor, 1895, by Winslow Homer (Portland Museum of Art, Portland, ME)
- *A Boating Party*, oil on canvas, 1889, by John Singer Sargent (Museum of Art, Rhode Island School of Design, Providence)
- *The Old Hunting Grounds*, oil on canvas, 1864, by Thomas Worthington Whittredge (Reynolda House, Winston-Salem, NC)
- *Deer Hunting by Torch Light in Bark Canoes*, ca. 1830s, by George Catlin (National Collection of Fine Arts, Smithsonian Institution, Washington, D.C.)
- *Deer Driving*, 1857, by Arthur F. Tait (Kennedy Galleries, New York)
- *The Guide and the Goose Shooter*, 1915, by Robert Wesley Amick (Remington Arms Collection of Game Art, Bridgeport, CT)
- *Moose Hunters in Canoe*, 1920, by Carl Rungius (Glenbow-Alberta Institute, Calgary, Alberta)
- *Shooting the Rapids*, watercolor, 1902, by Winslow Homer (Brooklyn Museum, NY)
- *A Good Pool, Saguenay River*, watercolor, 1895, by Winslow Homer (Sterling and Francine Clark Art Institute, Williamstown, MA)

There are many more sketches, engravings, and other renderings in books such as:

- *The Canoe: A History of the Craft from Panama to the Arctic* (Camden, ME: International Marine Publishing Company, 1983)
- *Paul Kane's Frontier: Including Wanderings of an Artist Among the Indians of North America* (Fort Worth, TX: Amon Carter Museum, 1971)
- *Francis Lee Jaques, Artist-Naturalist* (Minneapolis: University of Minnesota Press, 1982
- *Francis Lee Jaques: Artist of the Wilderness World* (Garden City, NY: Doubleday, 1973)

Also, from 1984 to present, *Sea Kayaker* Magazine in Seattle has featured an original work of art on each issue's cover (since they went to bi-monthly, they have been using photographs more often as well). Many were stunningly rendered in oils, watercolor, acrylic, and other media. Back issues are available (206-789-9536).

181

Spare Paddles

Don't be tempted to economize on your spare sea kayak paddle. If you lose the primary paddle, it's likely to be in bad conditions—not the time to rely on cheap equipment.

—JH & RH

Frances Anne Hopkins, 1838–1919: Canadian Scenery

by Janet E. Clark and Robert Stacey
(Thunder Bay, Ontario:
Thunder Bay Art Gallery, 1990)

The name Frances Anne Hopkins should ring familiar to many paddlers. Her well-known paintings of the fur trading Voyageurs chronicled the end of an era. Travel by canoe to the Canadian interior was winding down at the end of the nineteenth century when Frances Hopkins was painting her Voyageurs. At that time, she and her husband Edward were living near Montreal on the banks of the St. Lawrence River, so she had ready access to her subject matter. In addition to observing the river traffic, Edward Hopkins was an officer in the Hudson's Bay Company, so both he and Frances traveled up and down the river into the heart of Canada.

Frances Hopkins came from an artistic English family. She never lost her interest in art, and paddlers are the better for it today. A number of her works are owned by the Public Archives of Canada, but have been reproduced as fine art prints by the Minnesota Historical Society (St. Paul, MN 55102).

Frances Anne Hopkins, 1838–1919: Canadian Scenery is without a doubt the best book yet written about her. It gives an overview of her life, her art, and her times. Many of her works are reproduced in it. For the paddler with any sort of artistic bent, this is a fine book that comes highly recommended.

Paddlers by Celluloid: Videos and Films

Video production is a thriving industry, so if you want to see a video about some aspect of sea kayaking, freestyle canoeing, racing, water rodeos, places to paddle, or learning to paddle, you can probably find a video that will help you along.

The best sources for videos are paddling outfitters. Try some of the ones listed in Chapter Two, or look on the Internet (see also Chapter Two). The American Canoe Association used to maintain their film library pretty well, but lately it is a feeble and dying creature. Films and videos are not being added to it. You might also try a reference book called *Wilderness Waterways: The Whole Reference for Paddlers* by Ronald Ziegler (Canoe America Associates, 1991) which lists videos, among many other resources.

Here are some known videos of interest to paddlers:

- *Five Easy Paddles Video Series* including *California 1, California 2, Florida, Hawaii, Boundary Waters West,* and *Along the Lewis & Clark Trail* (Placid Videos, Simi Valley CA; 800-549-0046). Trip accounts of places to paddle that are especially well suited for beginners or families.
- *Sea Kayaking: Getting Started* (Larry Holman, Corte Madera, CA; 415-927-3786)
- *Surf Kayaking Fundamentals* (John Lull, P.O. Box 564, El Granada, CA, 94018)

- *Performance Sea Kayaking: The Basics . . . and Beyond* (Performance Video and Instruction, Inc., Durango, CO; 970-259-1361)
- *Ultralight Boatbuilding.* Offers viewers a start-to-finish, step-by-step guide to building a unique, lightweight, small wooden boat. (Brookfield Craft Center, Brookfield, CT)
- *In Pursuit of the Ultimate Run.* Features an Olympic paddling team and coach discussing a five-step program for managing a team and achieving excellence. (United Training Media, Niles, IL)
- *The Kayaker's Edge* (Whitewater Instruction, Durango, CO)

- *Solo Playboating.* Demonstrates stroke techniques for intermediate whitewater solo paddlers to reach the advanced level. (Whitewater Instruction, Durango, CO)
- *Fast and Clean* (Nichols Productions, Annapolis, MD)
- *Kayaking Basics: Paddling With Olympic Champion Greg Barton* (Vernal Productions)
- *Wildwater Champions.* Whitewater kayaking for pleasure and competition, set against the breathtaking scenery of the

183

Alps. (Teleculture Inc., New York, NY)

- *Waterwalker* (National Film Board of Canada, Ottawa)
- *Solo Canoeing, Whitewater Bound.* Explains the technical concepts and fundamental skills required for whitewater playboating and demonstrates paddling techniques and maneuvers. (Outdoor Centre of New England, Millers Falls, MA)
- *Ric Taylor's Solo Canoe* (Space Canoe Research Institute, Los Angeles, CA)
- *White Water Rafting* (Stoney-Wolf Productions, Lolo, MT)
- *Wet Shorts* (Don Briggs Films & Video, San Francisco, CA)
- *White Water, Grey Hair.* Records a group of senior citizens enjoying their descent through the Grand Canyon on a raft trip. (Sterling Educational Films, New York, NY)

Filmography: A List of Canoe, Kayak, Raft and River Conservation Films (Including Where to Obtain Them)

by Bruce E. Stafford

(Lorton, VA: American Canoe Association, 1983) Bruce Stafford put together this list of about 250 films and videos of interest to paddlers. Categories include Black & White, Canoeing, Colorado, Conservation, Dories, Flatwater, Historical, Instructional, International, Kayaking, Ocean, Other Than 16 mm, Racing, Rafting, Safety, and Whitewater.

Stafford did an admirable job of compiling this sixty-ish-page booklet, but by now it is pretty out of date. Getting your hands on some of these films (and the equipment to run them) could be quite a challenge—perhaps that winter project you've been looking for—so good luck and pop a lot of popcorn.

184

Index

186

189

190

192

193

INDEX TO USEFUL SIDEBARS